IMAGES
of America

THOMAS TOWNSHIP
MICHIGAN

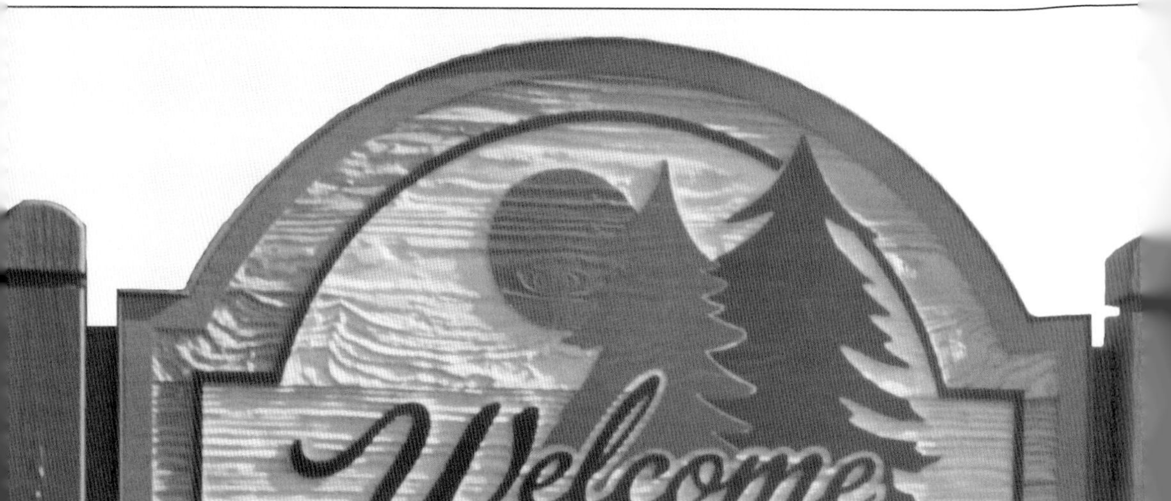

On the cover: Geddes School children display a 46-star flag in the early 1900s.

IMAGES
of America

THOMAS TOWNSHIP MICHIGAN

Roselynn Ederer and Ronald F. Picardi
for the Thomas Township Historical Society

ARCADIA
PUBLISHING

ISBN 978-0-7385-0724-8

Published by Arcadia Publishing
Charleston, South Carolina

Printed in the United States of America

Library of Congress Catalog Card Number: Applied for

For all general information contact Arcadia Publishing at:
Telephone 843-853-2070
Fax 843-853-0044
E-mail sales@arcadiapublishing.com
For customer service and orders:
Toll-Free 1-888-313-2665

Visit us on the Internet at www.arcadiapublishing.com

Contents

ACKNOWLEDGMENTS

The Thomas Township Historical Society would like to extend its appreciation and thanks to the many former and present Thomas Township residents who have offered their moral support, memories, and photographs of the township. This book has developed because of the combined efforts of many people.

The information for this publication has come from *History of Thomas Township, 1855 to 1976*, published by Thomas Township on July 30, 1976; memories as told by many residents; and the many photographs collected by the society.

Special thanks go to Marcia Strong for initiating and helping to organize the historical society and inspiring the members to do this publication; Shirley Oatten for her dedicated efforts in contacting businesses, churches, and individuals; Gerald Kluck for sharing three generations of his family's photographs; Ronald F. Picardi for sharing many family and community photographs and scanning all the photos submitted; Ralph K. Roberts for his 1800's river boat photographs; Robert Day for his 1800's and early 1900's township photographs; Mary Lou Ederer for photographing current scenes; and a grant from the Ederer Family Fund administered by the Saginaw Community Foundation.

For the past three years, members of the Thomas Township Historical Society have met monthly to discuss township history, share memories, and gather photographs. Through a united effort, this beautiful pictorial history of Thomas Township from the 1850's to the present was made possible. We know there are still many more memories and stories yet to tell. The committee members are as follows:

Richard Borm
Carl Russell
Marcia Strong

Shirley Oatten
Mark Gilson
Michael Slasinski
Roselynn Ederer
Linda Gilson
Harvey Leuenberger
Ronald F. Picardi
Nina Fischer

INTRODUCTION

The Chippewa Indians found the Saugenah Wilderness a beautiful, peaceful country for centuries. They established their villages along the Saginaw and Tittabawassee Rivers, including seventeen which were located in Thomastown. The rich soil on the river bottoms was ideal for raising corn while the river provided abundant fish. The Chippewa gathered nuts—black walnut, butternut, hickory—from the dense forest and wild plums, berries, and a cranberry bog provided excellent fruits. Remnants and artifacts from their burial mounds and villages have been found in later years along the banks of the Tittabawassee River and on farm land throughout the township.

In the 1830s, settlers from the East started settling along the banks of the Saginaw and Tittabawassee Rivers, where they also found the fertile banks ideal for growing corn and vegetables. They lived in log cabins with crude fireplaces, traveling by foot through the forest or by canoe along the many tributaries of both rivers.

The boundaries of Thomastown Township have changed frequently. In 1835, Saginaw Township governed the entire county, including the Thomastown area. When Thomastown was the third township to be organized in 1855, its boundaries included Richland Township, Jimtown, and six sections east of the Tittabawassee River. However, these six sections soon became part of Saginaw Township in 1857 as the river made the six sections difficult to reach. By 1871, two more townships had been organized: Richland Township in 1862 and Jimtown Township (now James Township) in 1871. Thomastown Township retained its name until 1958 when it was shortened to Thomas Township.

Thomas Township's 1877 population of 618 was more than triple its population only two decades before. Settlers from Ohio and New York were making their way into the township. The Great Potato Famine which affected Bavaria, Germany and Ireland in the 1840s to the 1860s brought settlers from both of those countries into the township. Immigrants from Prussia, England, Ireland, Scotland, and Canada settled in the northern sections of the township while those from Bavaria settled in the southern sections of the township.

The lumber industry played an important role in Thomastown. The Tittabawassee Boom Company was organized in 1864 and became the largest Michigan boom company for 30 years. Each spring, when millions of logs floated down the Tittabawassee River from the many streams in central Michigan, they were held back at Bryant's Trip located on the river in Thomastown. John Bryant tended this natural bend in the river to regulate the flow of logs to be released for processing. All along the river to its mouth were pockets in which the logs were sorted, pinned, and rafted to be towed by tug boats to the Saginaw River sawmills. The Boom Company built two of its nine boarding houses in Thomastown.

Agriculture prospered and timber grew abundantly. The rich soil was drained by the Tittabawassee on the eastern boundaries and by Swan Creek throughout the township. Settlers dug their own drainage ditches allowing for 24 flowing wells and springs. Wheat, corn, and orchards flourished abundantly and horses, oxen, milk cows, swine, and sheep were raised. Descendants of many early settlers continued to farm in the township for decades. Several of those original farms have become centennial farms having been owned by the same family for more than one hundred years.

Transportation was a problem. Crossing the Tittabawassee River was first done by ferry, then by the State Road Bridge in 1870. Although this toll bridge was later replaced, it brought people from western villages into Saginaw City. The difficult trip to Saginaw would take another day. Shields Corner with a hotel, blacksmith, post office, and general store emerged. Similar corners were established at Frost and Dice for isolated farm families.

These early settlers built and maintained their own roads along survey lines from their homesteads to existing roads or trails. Roads and schools were named after these early settlers, such as the Liskow School, organized in 1856 as the first school of the township. The Liskow School was joined by the Wiltse, Geddes, Graham, Dice, and Grove schools until overcrowding necessitated additional schools to be built.

The township retained its rural society until the mid-1950s when a new Gratiot Road bridge, new four-lane Gratiot Road, and city water began the township's rapid expansion. Soon to follow were subdivisions, a sanitary sewer system, a school consolidation with James and Swan Creek Townships, parks, churches, a library, and fire and police departments. Dow Corning Corporation built its semi-conductor plant and medical products plant in the 1960s. Meijer's was soon added. Many businesses along the Gratiot Corridor changed ownership and new ones were built as some of the long-established businesses and all the residential neighborhoods disappeared.

Thomas Township has grown to 12,500 in population. It is a society where industry, commercial businesses, subdivisions, and agriculture exist. The Tittabawassee River still drains the land, floods it annually, and provides recreational uses to its residents. New construction, subdivisions, bridges, roads, and water and sewer lines are being built each year. But as it has throughout the past century, Thomas Township has retained its friendly, hometown atmosphere. Its residents continue to live here for several generations. Thousands of visitors and customers from several miles away travel daily to the Shields commercial hub. Residents continue to work together and volunteer their time and talents to make the entire township a better place to live, work, and do business.

One

Life on the Tittabawassee

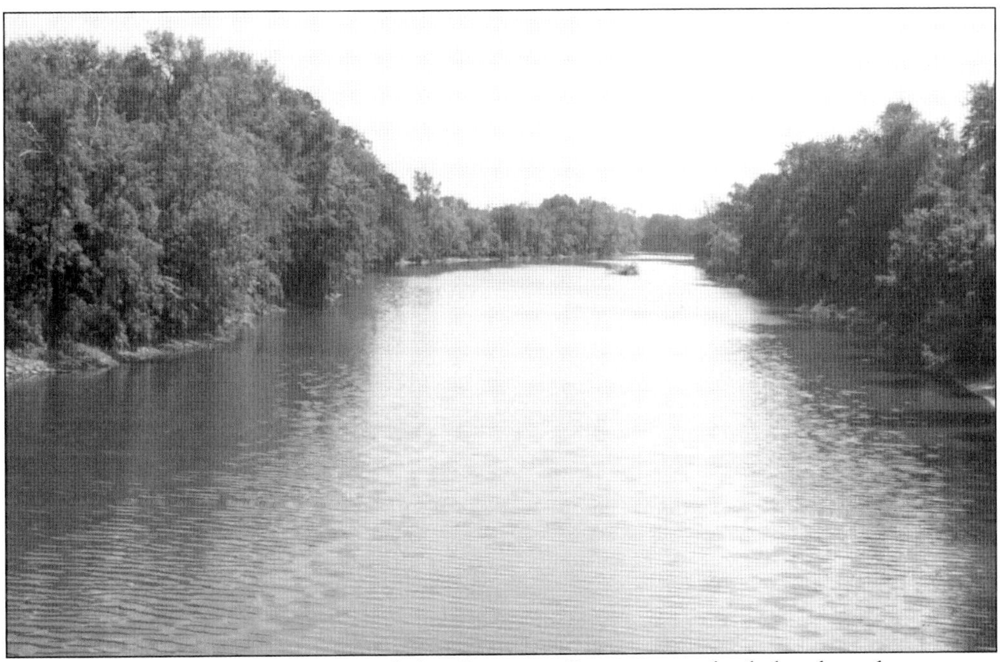

The Tittabawassee River, part of the Saginaw River watershed, borders the eastern sections of Thomas and James Townships. In the past few centuries, it has played an important role in commerce for the Chippewa Indians, used for lumbering and farming. Today the Tittabawassee is a recreational river. This beautiful river flows uninterrupted for miles during its quiet periods. Its annual spring floods renew the fertility of the bottom lands but can also create destruction and havoc at other times.

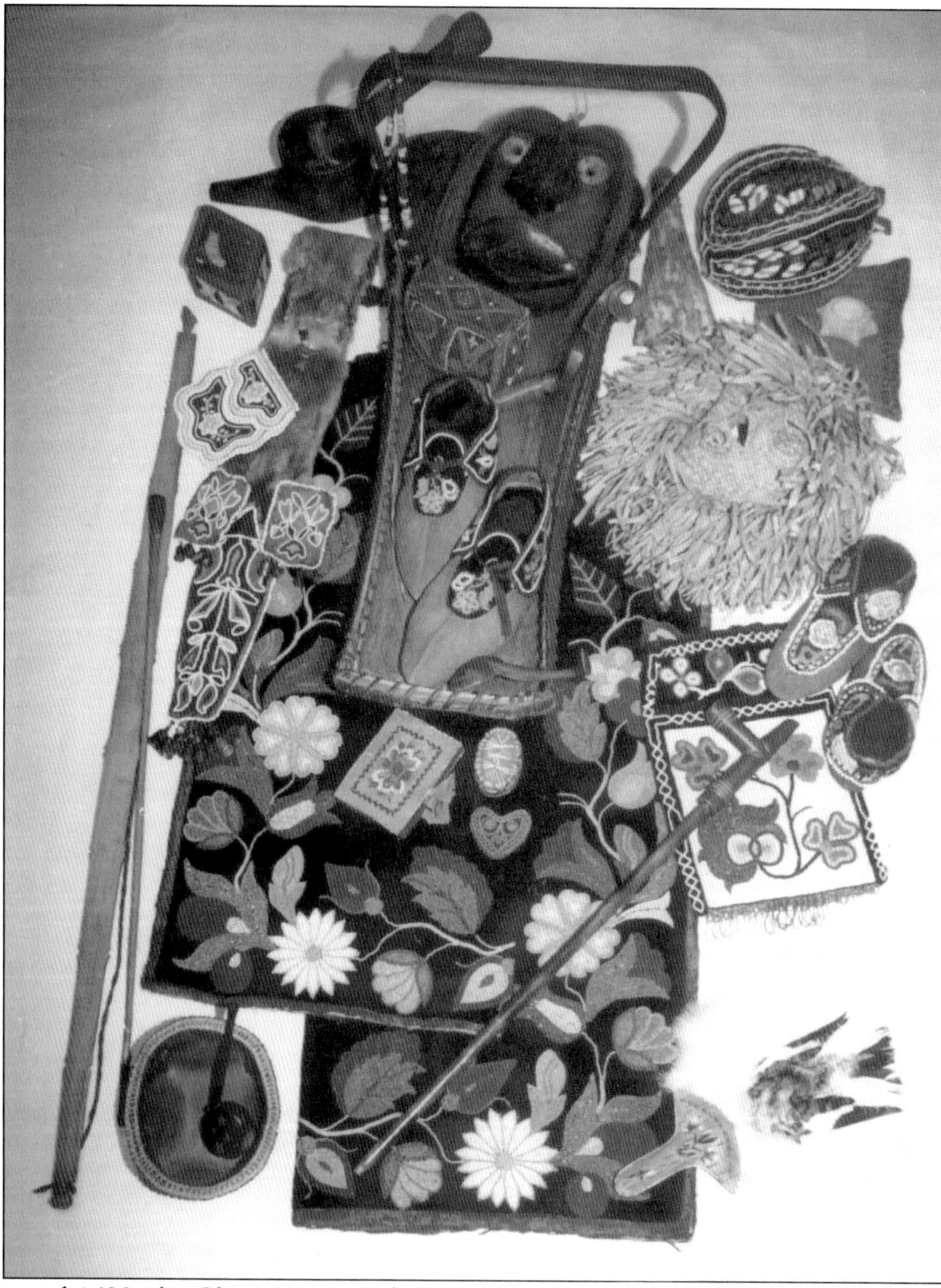

Around 1620, the Chippewa or Ojibwa Indians lived in the Saugenah Wilderness in villages along the Saginaw and Tittabawassee Rivers, including the aforementioned 17 in Thomas Township. Branch Flats was near the present State Road Bridge, another village was by Bryant's Trip, Frazer Village was located near Shields Elementary School, and Sand Ridge was located in Section 31, in the southwest part of the township. The Native Americans traveled by canoe on the rivers, fishing and farming along the river banks. Their villages were located on high knolls in the summer or along the river banks in the winter. The artifacts shown above were some of the important articles they used in their everyday life.

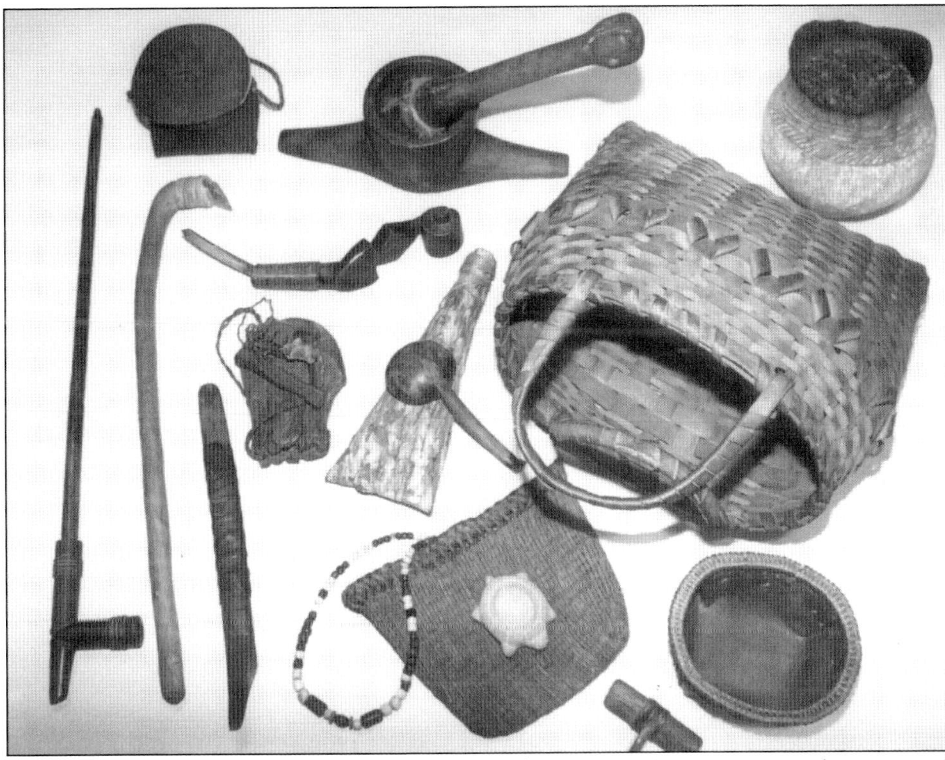

Some tools, implements, and containers used by Native Americans in their everyday life are shown here.

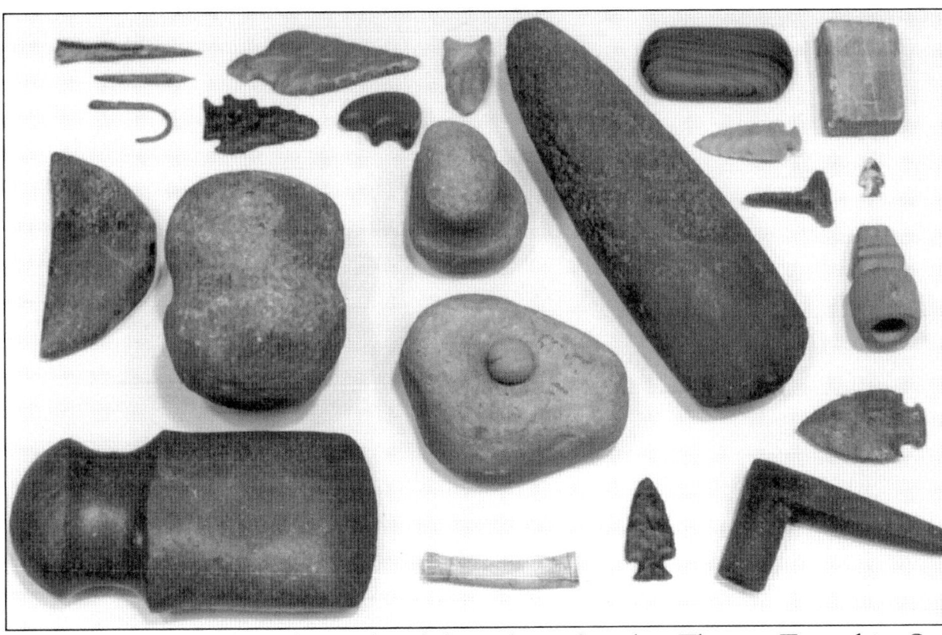

Native American tools and arrowheads have been found in Thomas Township. Some of the artifacts pictured here are made of stone, copper, bone, and clay, and were found along the banks of the Tittabawassee River.

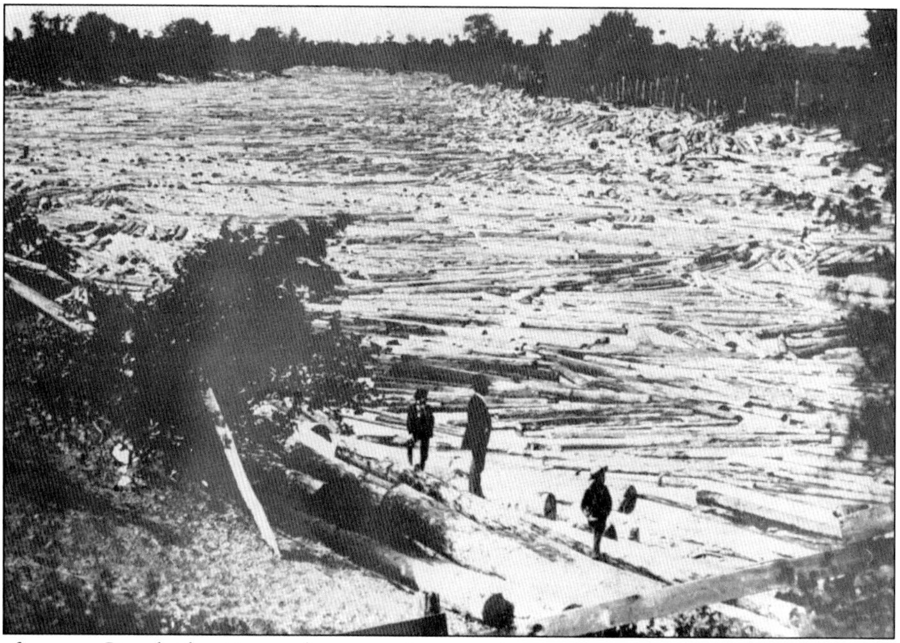

This famous Goodridge Bros. photograph was taken at Bryant's Trip along North River Road in the spring of 1873. Logs were floated down all the streams in central Michigan into the Tittabawassee to be sawed into lumber in the Saginaw River sawmills. The logs that year created an unusual log jam, from the Gratiot Road bridge to 130 miles upstream, some two to five logs deep. Men could walk across the river on the logs.

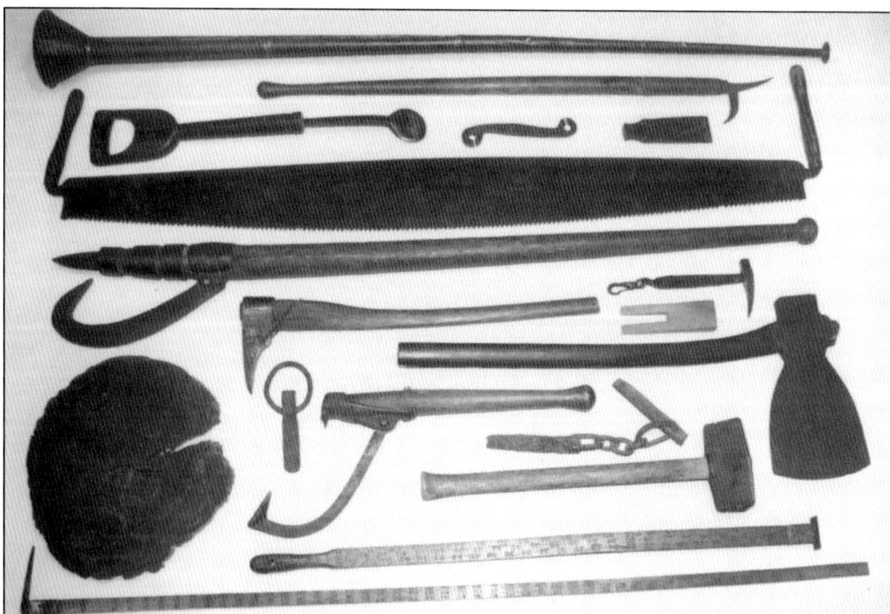

Lumbering during the 19th century was a labor intensive business. Some of the tools used in the lumber industry are shown here: peavey, crosscut saw, wooden rafting pins, pike pole, log mark, ax, measuring stick, gaberial horn, bark spud, saw sets, and snow knocker hammer.

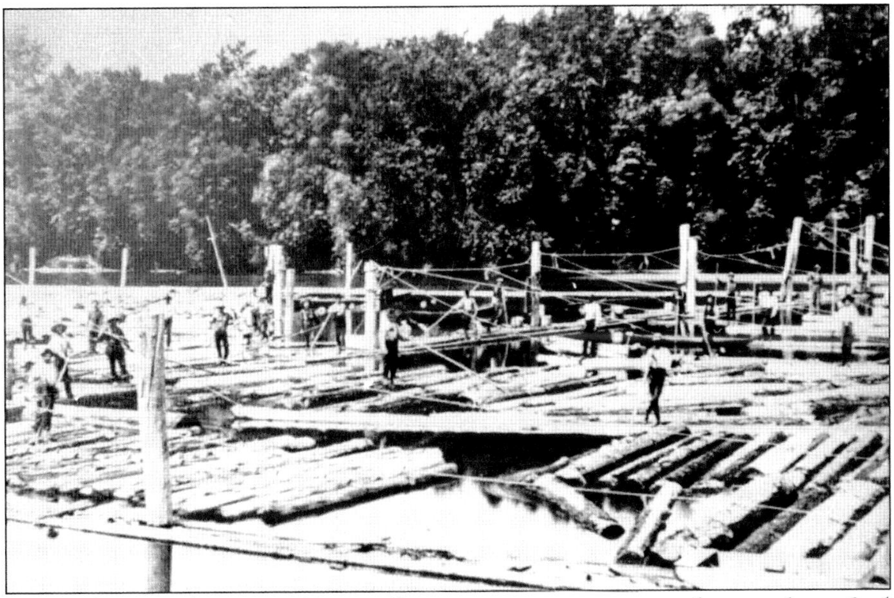

Men from the Tittabawassee Boom Company are sorting out logs to be rafted and towed by tug boats to the Saginaw River sawmills. The Tittabawassee Boom Co., which was incorporated on February 4, 1864, became a giant in the booming industry, rafting 11,848,549,293 board feet during its 30 years of existence. Scenes such as this occurred along the River from Bryant's Trip down to Merrill Bridge, which is now Center Road Bridge.

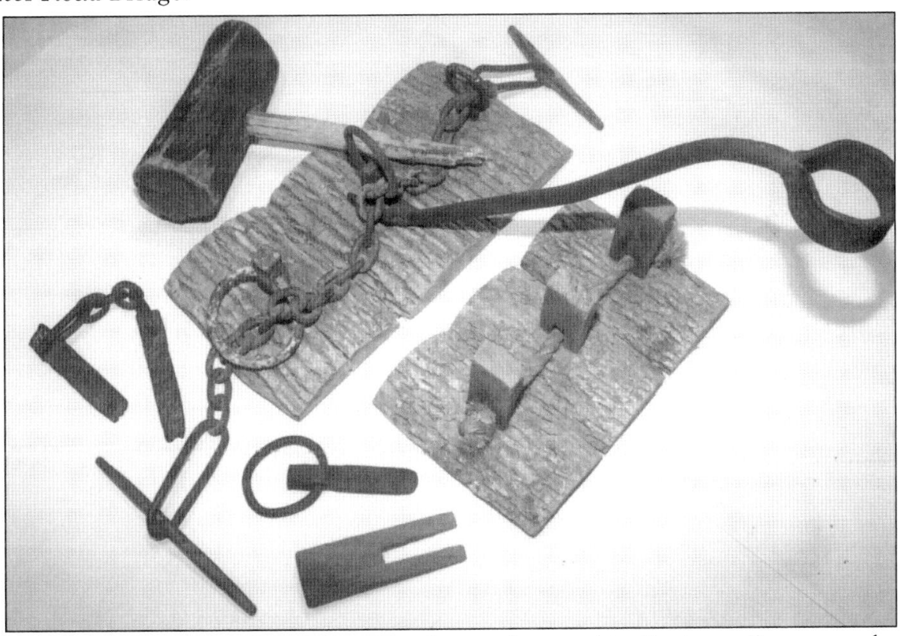

The wooden rafting pin was invented and manufactured in Saginaw. Rope was thrown across several logs and secured with wooden pins hammered into the logs to create long rafts for towing to the sawmills. Ropes were worn out after two years of use. Chains were occasionally used to raft logs. This illustration gives examples of raft construction using chain and rope, and the maul used to drive in the metal and wooden rafting pins.

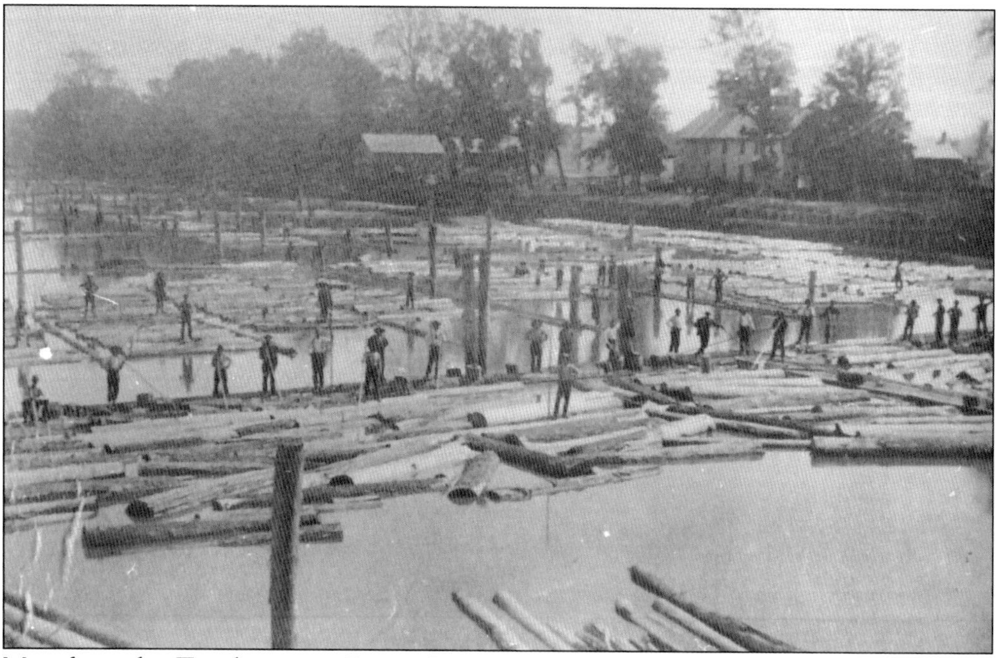

Men from the Tittabawassee Boom Co. are sorting logs into their respective booms. Logs were marked with the owner's log marks at the lumber camp before they made their journey down the rivers. When the sawmill owner needed more logs, the Boom Co. would tow a raft of his logs downstream to the mill. Men walked on the logs over the river.

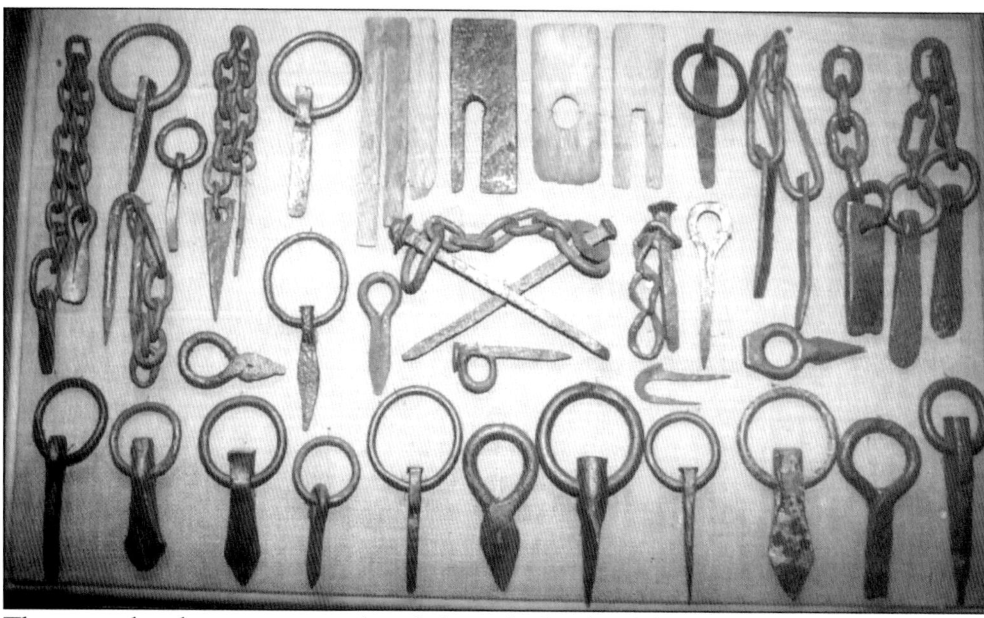

These wood and iron pins were found along the banks of the Tittabawassee River. They are just a sample of the many types of pins used for rafting logs. Hundred-year-old pine logs and the artifacts remaining on them are still washing up on the river banks after a major flood.

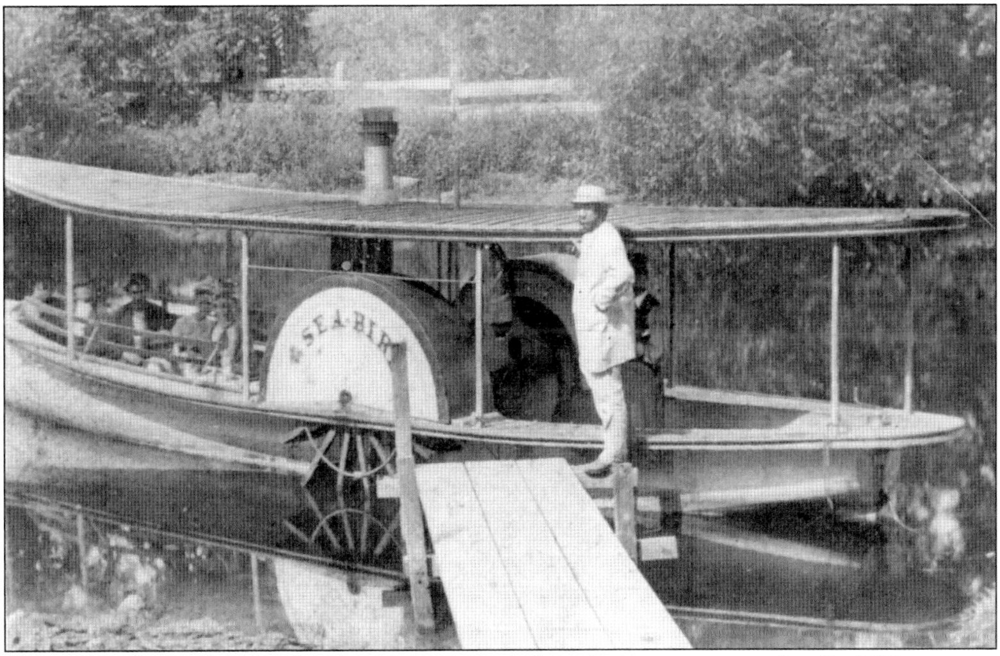

The *Seabird*, a side wheel steamer, is pictured making a stop on the Bad River near St. Charles. It carried passengers and cargo along the navigable tributaries of the Saginaw and Tittabawassee Rivers in the 1880s and made frequent stops in Thomastown on its way upstream to Midland.

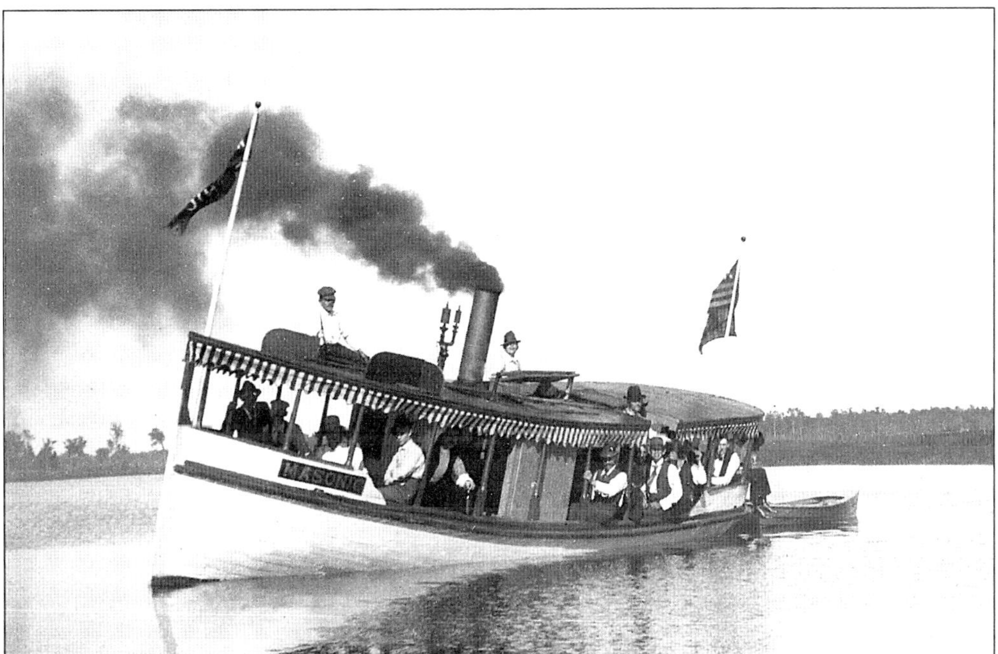

This photo of the steam yacht *Masonic* was taken in the flats on the Shiawassee River around 1890. She would pick up passengers in Thomastown and take them out into the Saginaw Bay as far as Tawas.

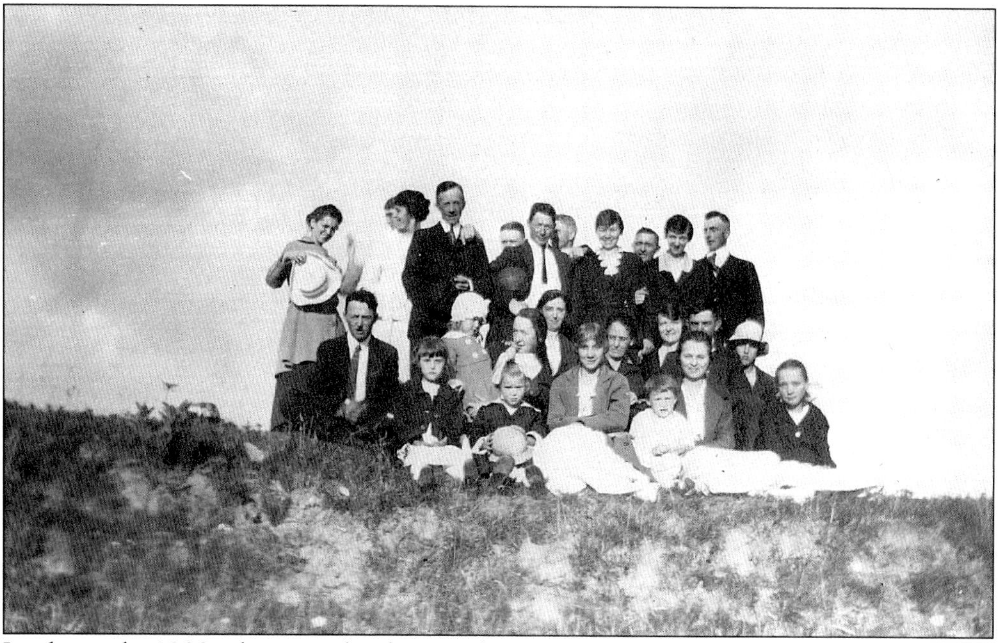

In the early 1900s the river bank served as a park for pleasurable family activities. Family and friends of Walter and Frieda (Zorn) Kluck have gathered for a picnic on the banks of the Tittabawassee River on July 20, 1920. They are celebrating the Klucks' forthcoming marriage with a shower.

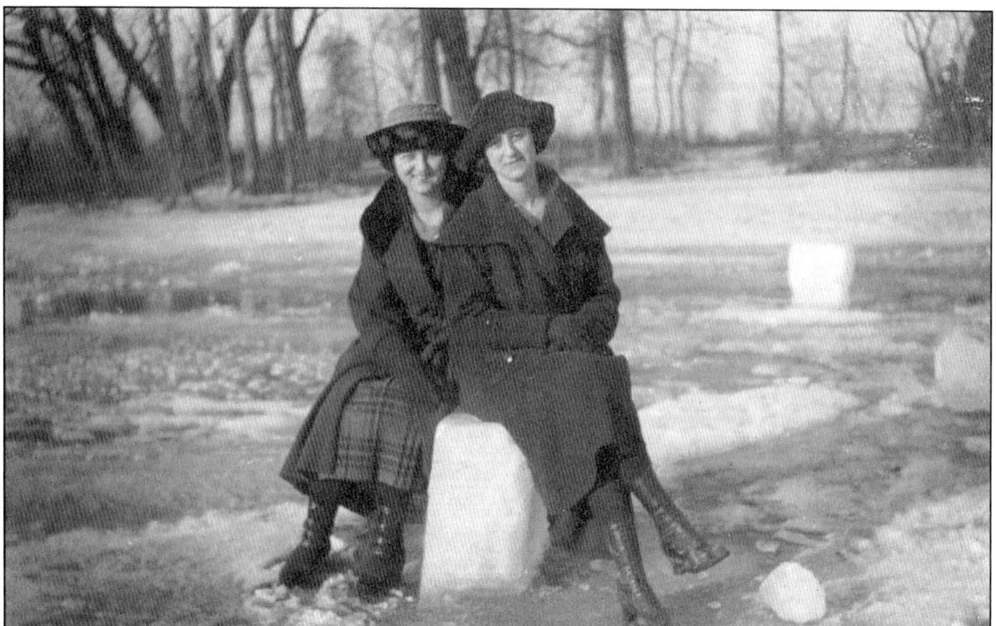

The Tittabawassee River became a source of recreation in the 1900s. It was the perfect place for winter activities. Here, Vera Zorn Buckel on the left with an unidentified friend, are relaxing on an ice chunk on the River in 1922.

These two sisters have found fishing very plentiful on the Tittabawassee River in 1922. On the left is Vera Zorn Buckel and on the right is Nora Zorn Ledtke.

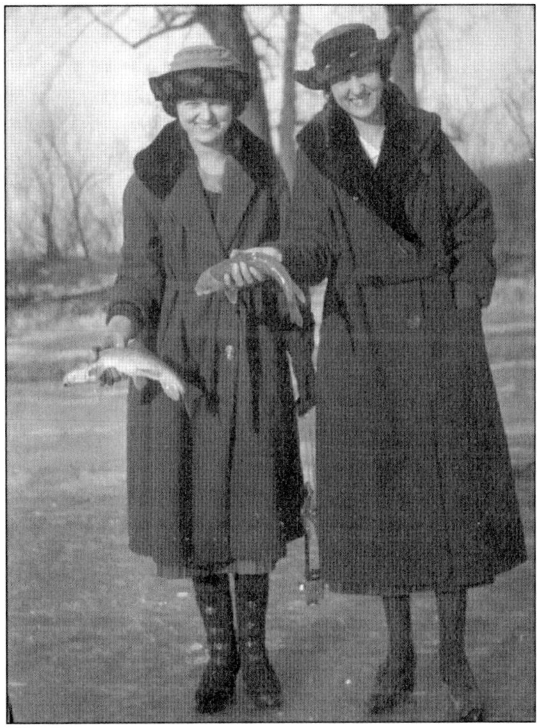

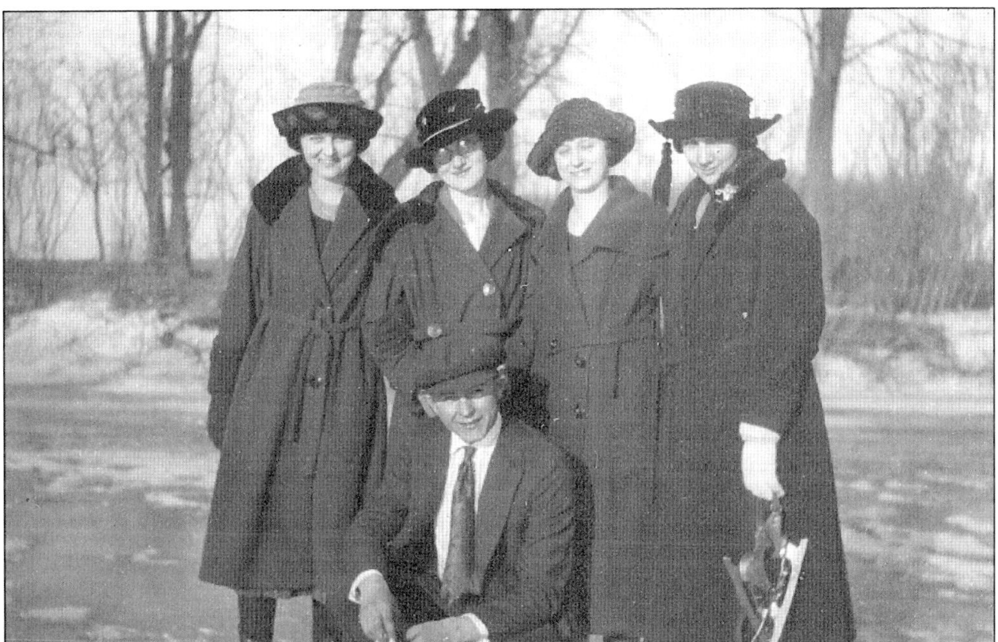

A pleasurable Sunday afternoon could be spent both skating and fishing on the Tittabawassee River. These friends are enjoying themselves and have paused just long enough for a photo in 1922. Vera Zorn Buckel is on the left; Martin Zorn is kneeling. The others are unidentified.

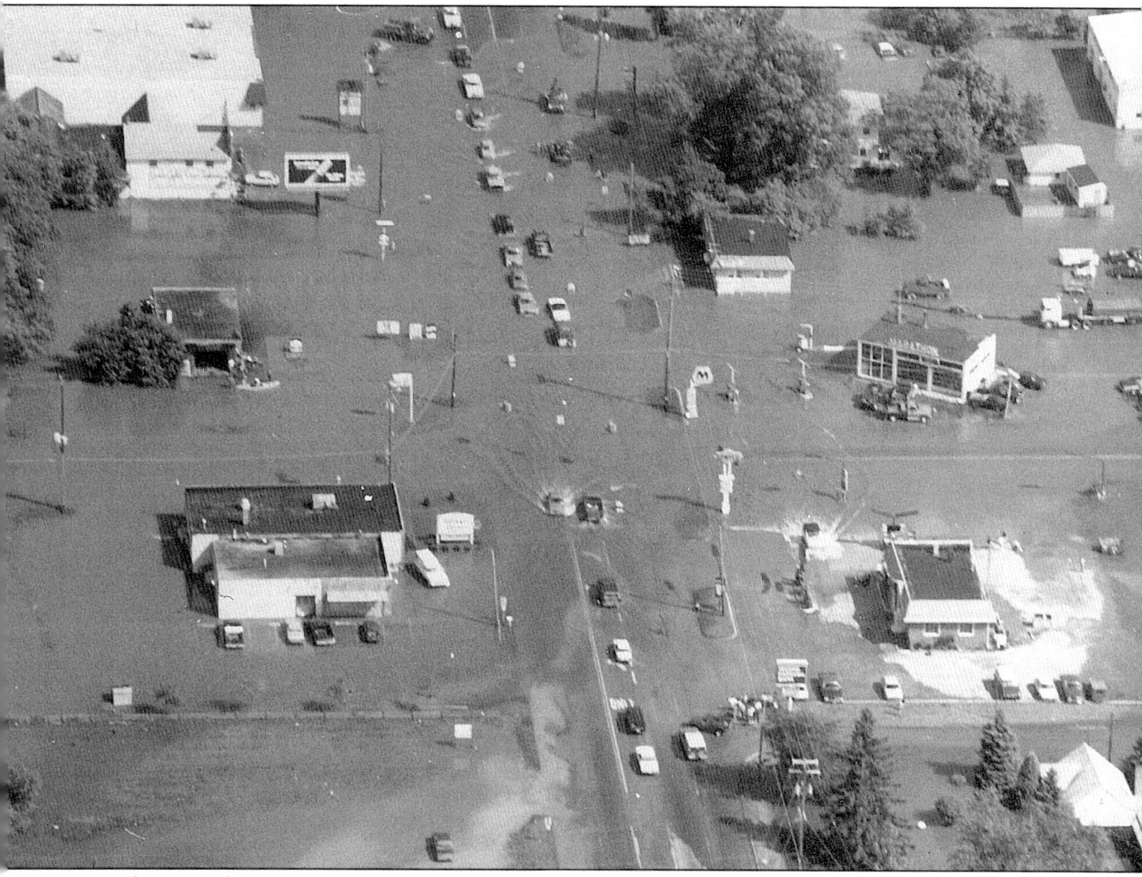

The Tittabawassee River rears its ugly head in this September 13, 1986 photo. Eleven to eighteen inches of rain fell in a 48 hour period creating one of the worst floods in recorded history. It is estimated that the Tittabawassee River swelled to 150 times its normal volume. This aerial view is looking east at the Gratiot and River Roads intersection. The "Great Flood" or "River of 86" made nearly every road in the township impassable, flooding homes and businesses, and drowning thousands of acres of crop land.

An annual "rite of spring" occurs when the Tittabawassee River overflows its banks, flooding the surrounding river bottoms and sections of River Road, making it impassable for several days. Residents have learned to cope during these annual high water periods, but none have ever matched the waters of the Great Flood of 1986.

Two

Agriculture Yesterday and Today

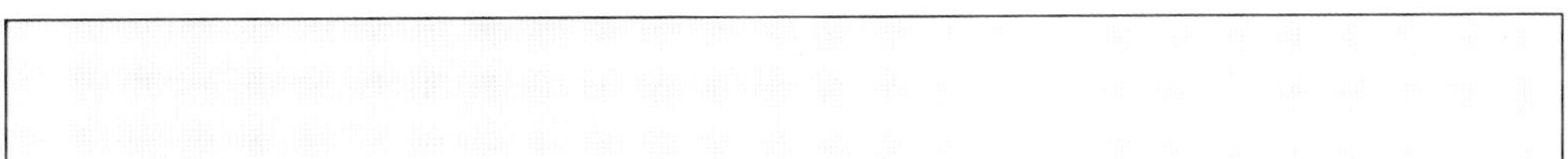

Edward and Thomas McCarthy, the township's first settlers, arrived in 1830. Europe's Great Potato Famine brought many settlers during the 1850s. They cleared the trees, dug drainage ditches, made the roads, built log cabins, and farmed the rich soil. Agriculture prospered. Farm houses, large barns, various livestock pastures, and fields dotted the rural landscape. Some of these farms, such as the Geddes farm pictured above, have become centennial farms, owned by the same family for one hundred years or more.

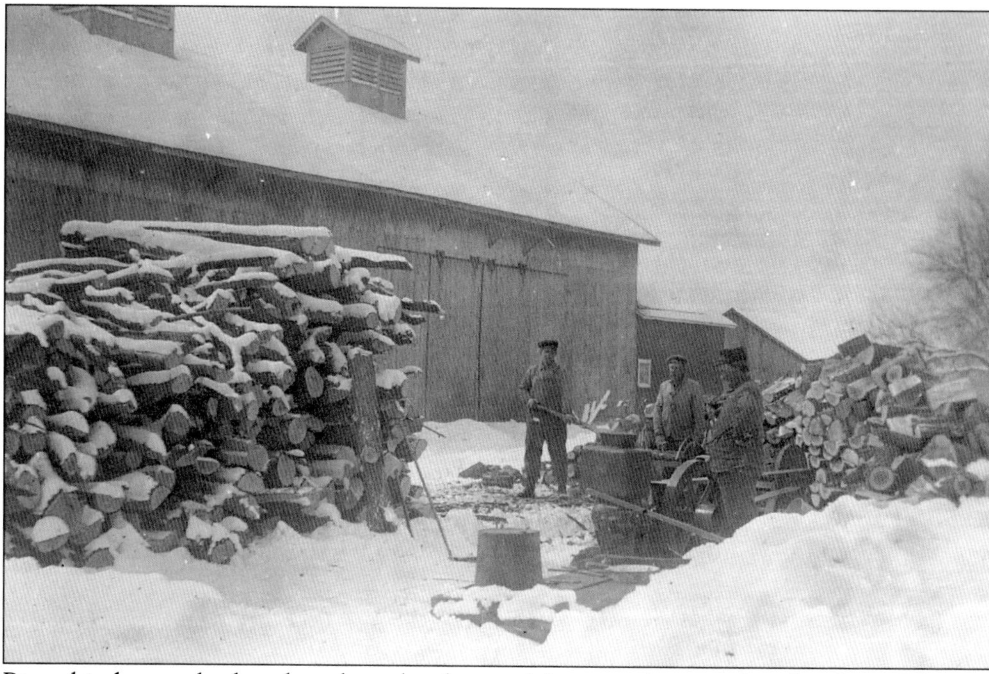

Pine, birch, maple, beech, ash, oak, elm, and basswood grew abundantly in Thomas Township. The early pioneers used those trees for building, cooking, and heating. Timber harvesting on individual farms continued into the 1900s. This gasoline powered "buzz saw," used for cutting firewood in 1915, is being operated by Walter Kluck, Arthur Kluck, and Herman Meyer on their Van Wormer Road farm.

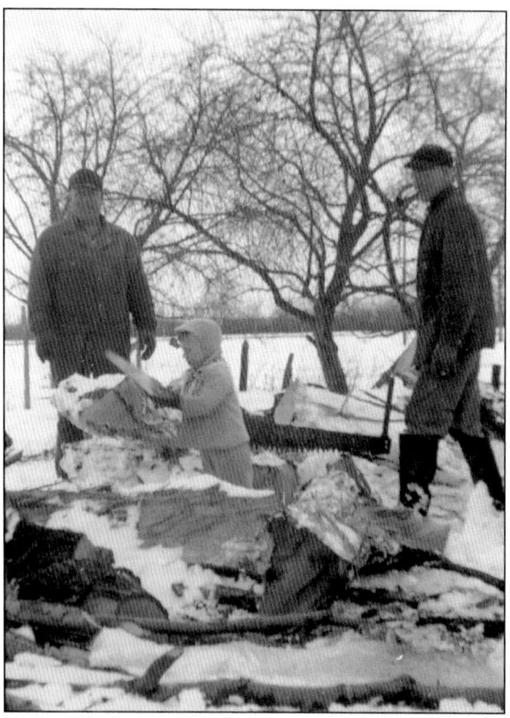

Richard Borm Sr. and his brother-in-law Norman Burk are using a two-handled cross-cut saw to cut firewood in this photo taken in the early 1950s on his Dutch Road farm. Richard Jr. in the center is also helping.

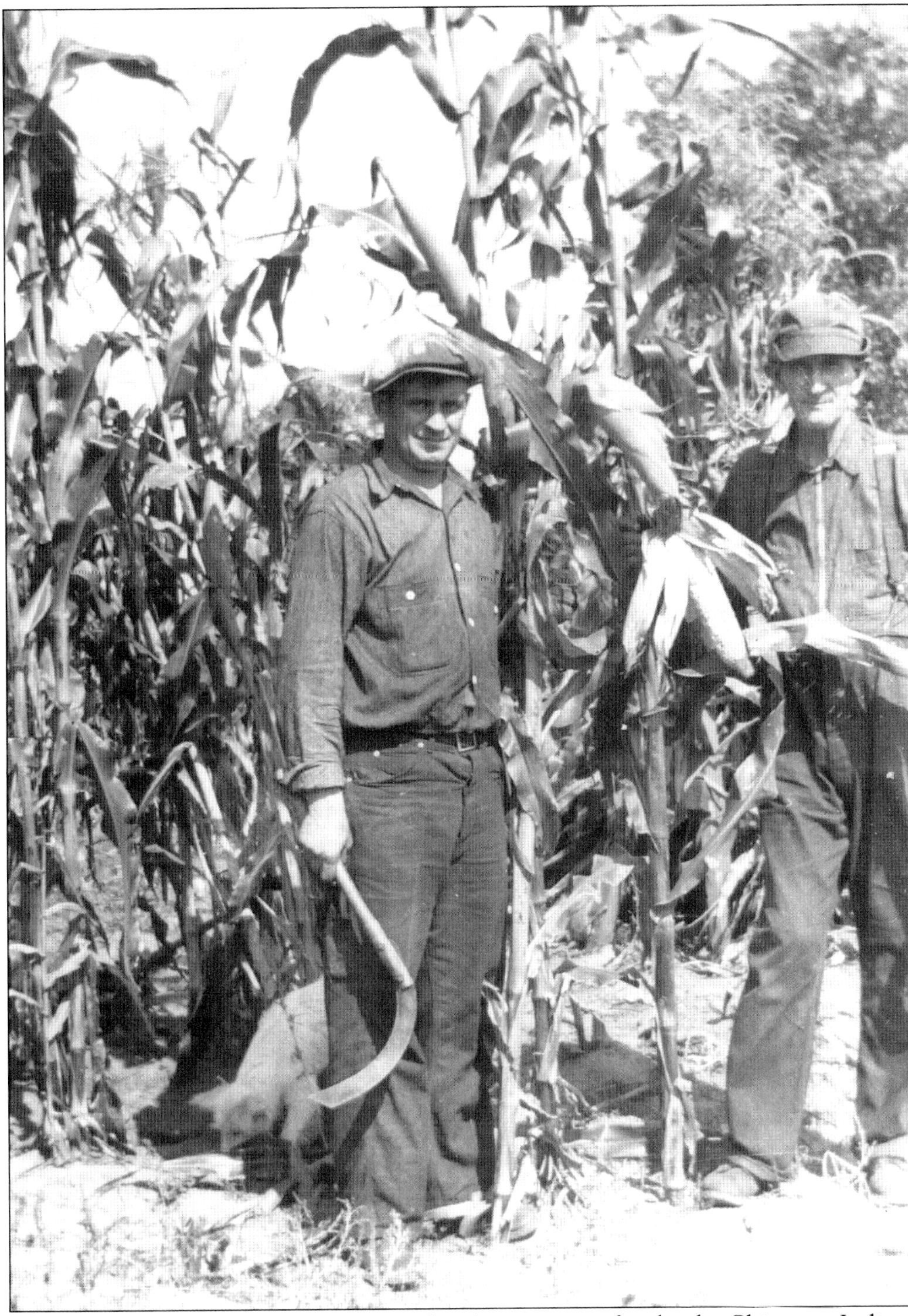

Corn has been grown in Thomas Township for centuries, first by the Chippewa Indians and then by the early pioneers. Tony Bugni and Am Roberts pose with the first hybrid corn planted in Thomas Township on their Bacon Road farm in the mid-1930s. Corn continues to be an important crop grown today by Thomas Township farmers.

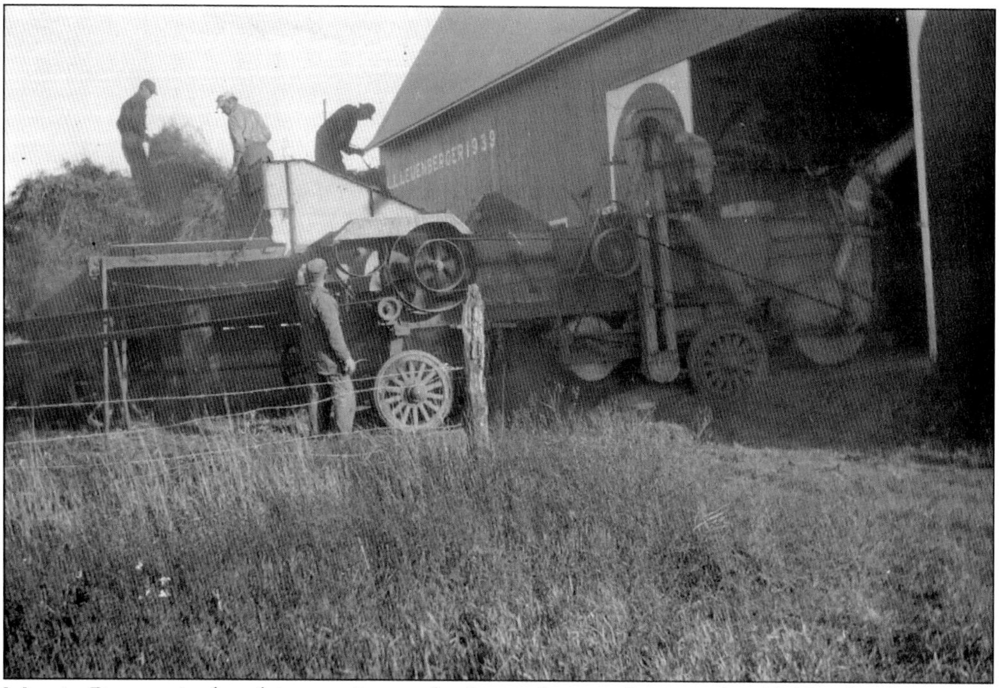

Martin Rueger is thrashing grain on the Leuenberger farm in the 1940s. At that time, most farmers did not own their own combines. Martin made the rounds to several farmers in Thomas, Saginaw, James, and Kochville Townships to thrash their grain. Because so much manual labor was involved, neighbors generally helped each other with the harvest.

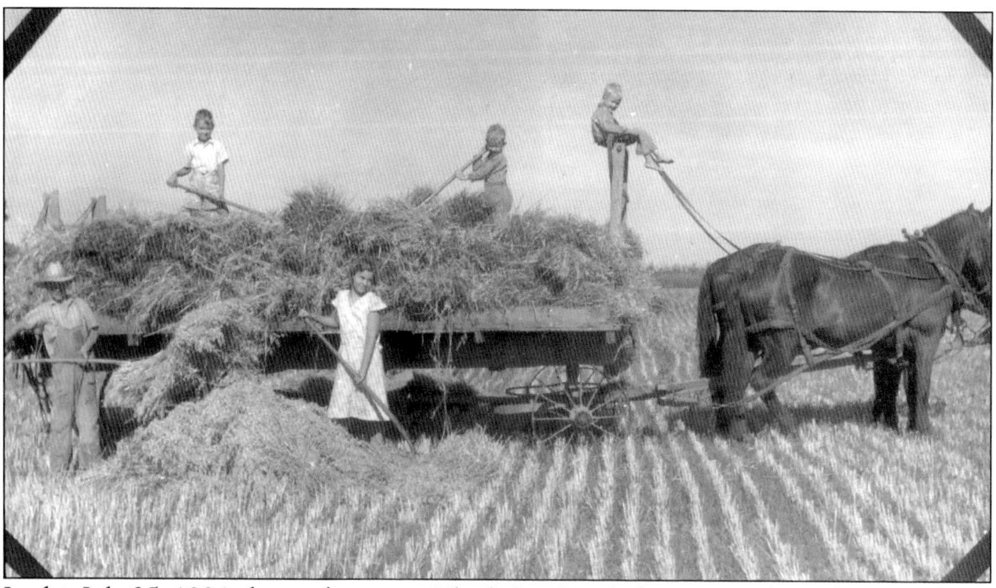

In this July 25, 1934 photo, the entire Kluck family is helping to pick up the oats which have been cut in the field. It will then be taken to the barn and forked into a thrashing machine. Pictured, from left to right, are Walter and Eleanor on the ground; Ed and Harold forking oats on the wagon, and Jerry Kluck holding the horse reins.

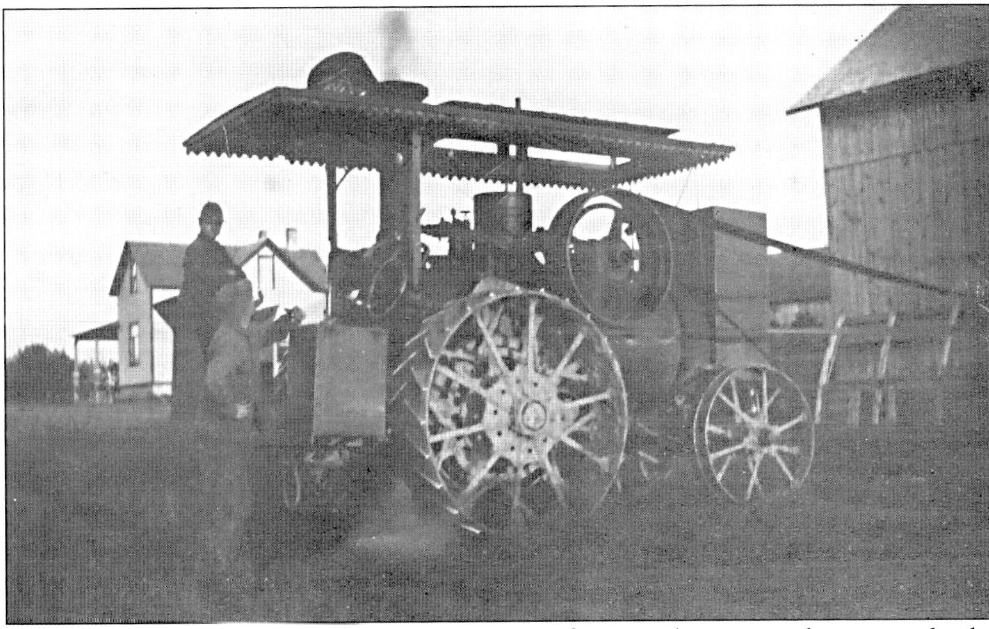

Wilbert Neuenfeldt operates the kerosene powered tractor that is providing power for the thrasher that was being used on the Lawrence Leuenberger farm on Summerfeldt Road about 1937. He also traveled to other farm fields, thrashing grain for several farmers.

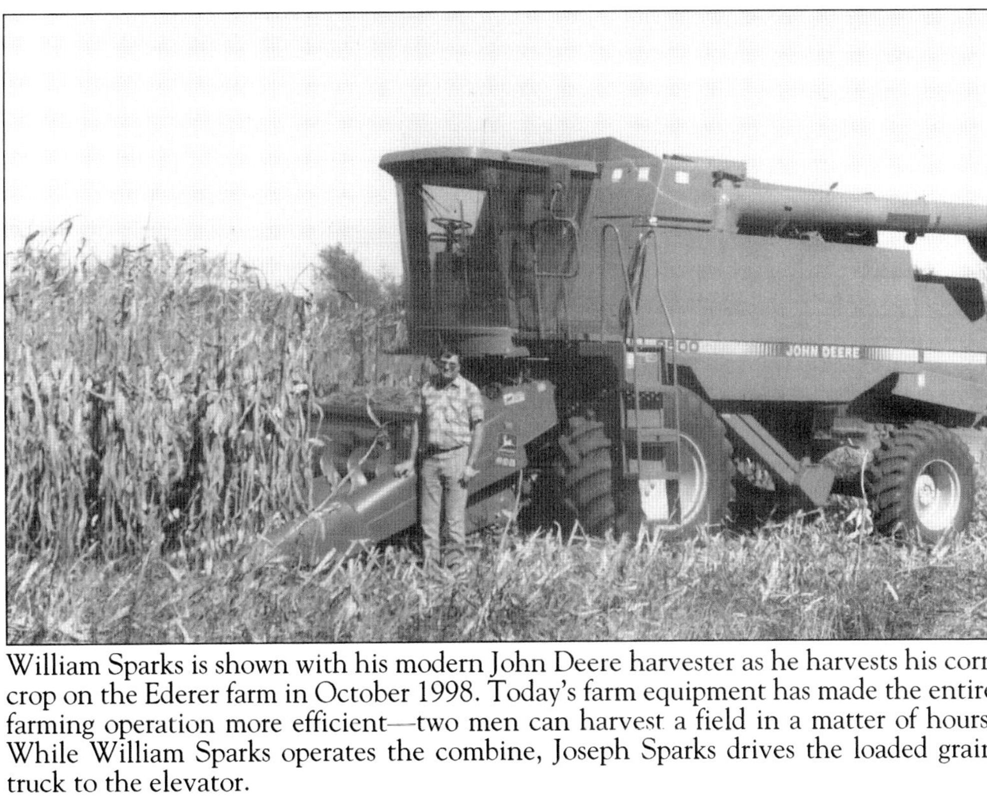

William Sparks is shown with his modern John Deere harvester as he harvests his corn crop on the Ederer farm in October 1998. Today's farm equipment has made the entire farming operation more efficient—two men can harvest a field in a matter of hours. While William Sparks operates the combine, Joseph Sparks drives the loaded grain truck to the elevator.

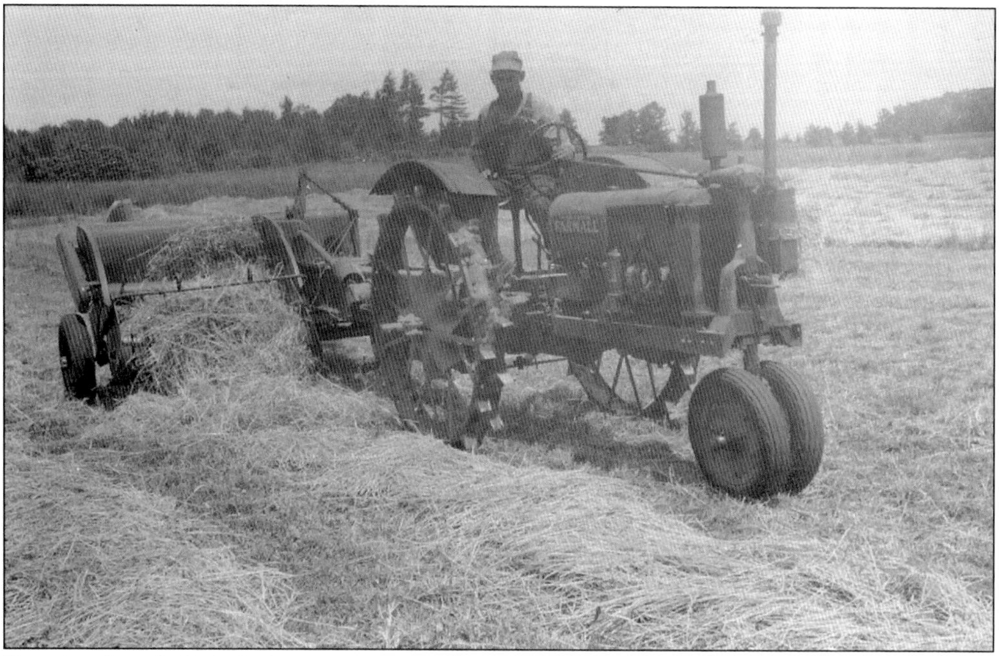

Farming has definitely become more efficient. Harvey Leuenberger is baling hay with the first International baler having a power takeoff to be used in Saginaw County in this 1950 photo. He is driving a Farmall tractor.

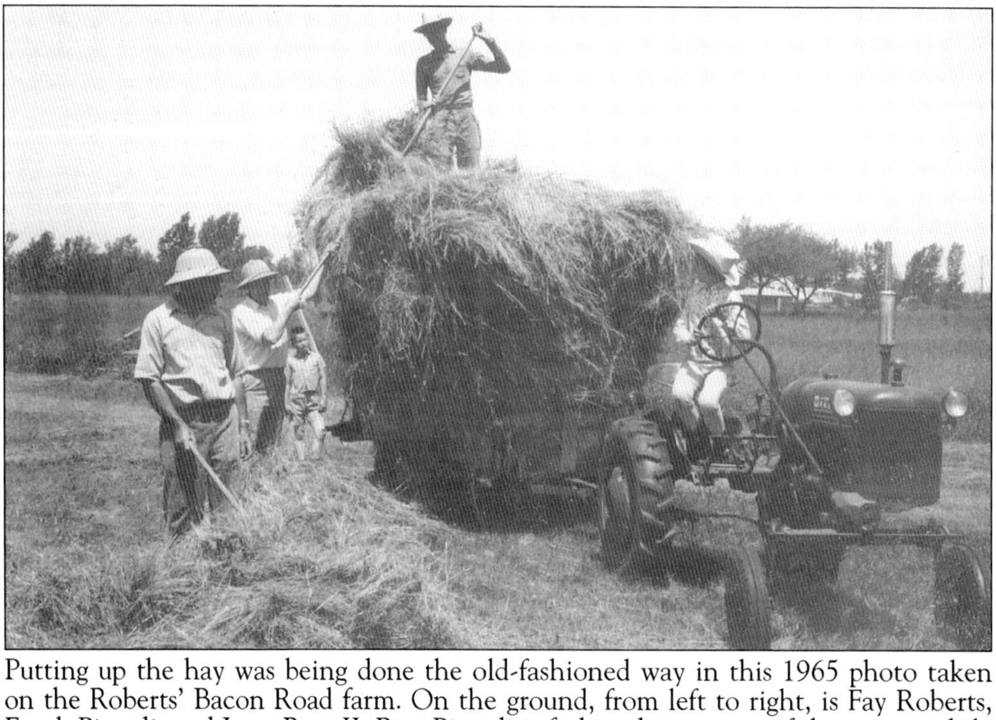

Putting up the hay was being done the old-fashioned way in this 1965 photo taken on the Roberts' Bacon Road farm. On the ground, from left to right, is Fay Roberts, Frank Picardi, and Jerry Baze II. Ron Picardi is forking hay on top of the wagon while Christine Picardi is driving the Farmall Cub tractor.

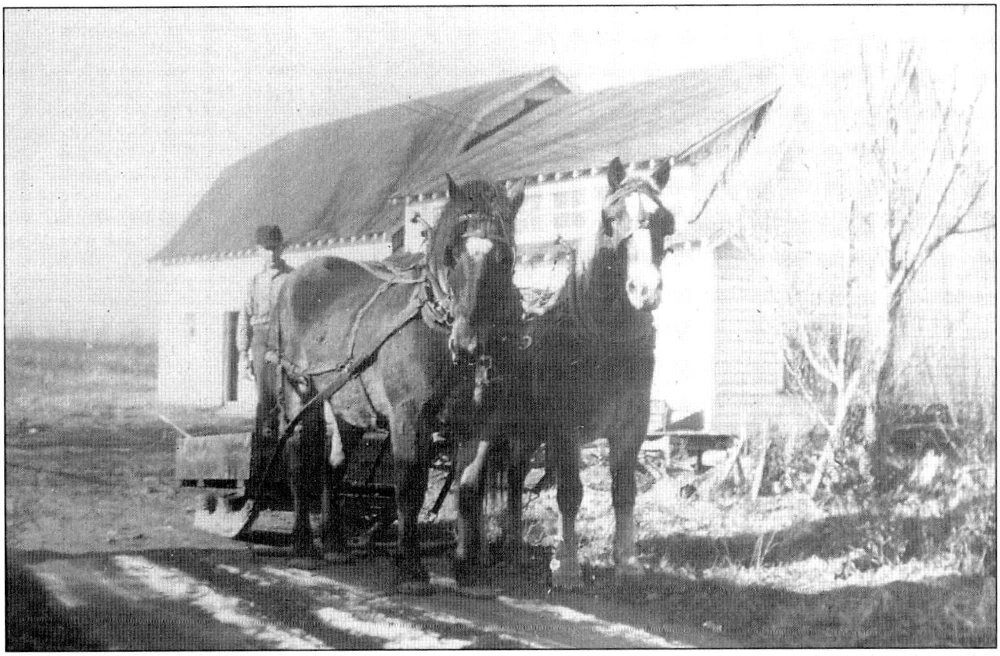

Teams of oxen and horses were used by the first pioneers to clear their land, make roads, and to farm. Draft horses were used by Thomas Township farmers as late as 1940 in their farming operations. Every farmer had at least one team of matched horses. Fay Roberts is pulling a sled with his team in the mid-1930s. His barn on his Bacon Road farm is in the background.

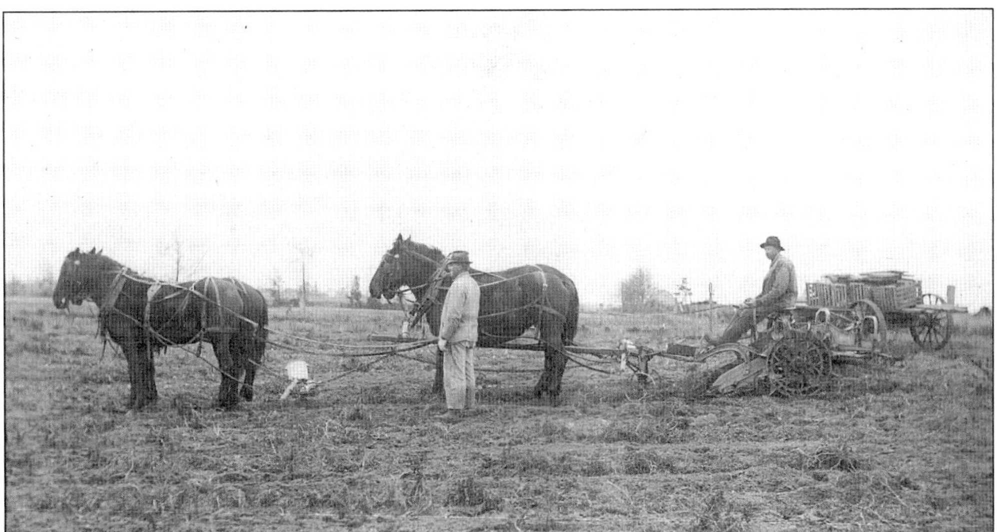

Walter and Arthur Kluck are pulling a potato digger with two teams of horses on their Van Wormer Road farm in 1919. The driver was able to sit while driving the horses. The potatoes were loaded into the wagon seen in the background.

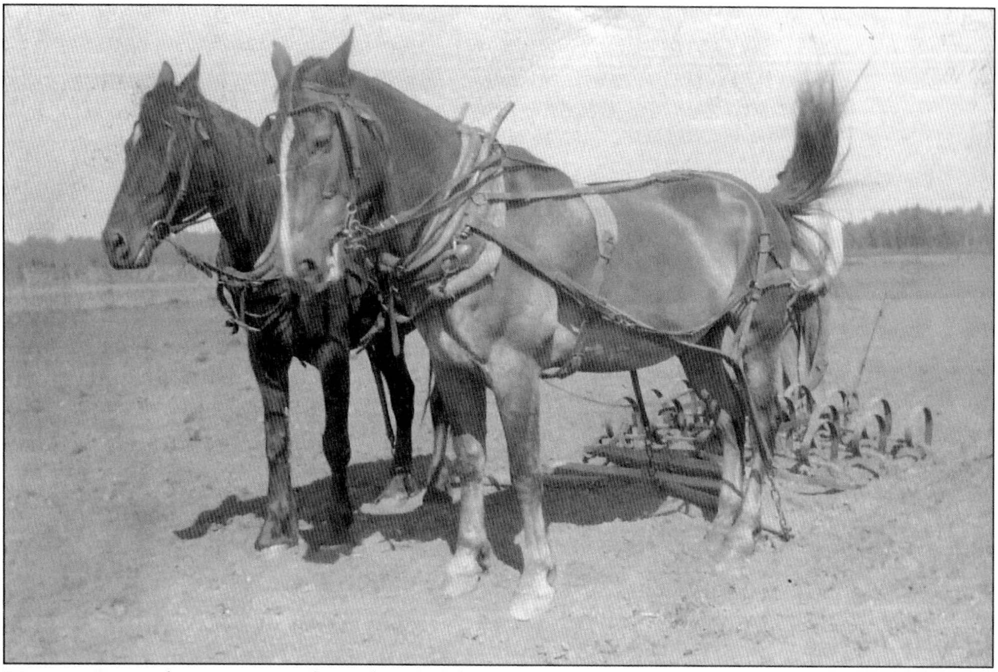

Harvey Leuenberger is working his field using a spring-tooth drag with his team, Bob and Baldy, in the 1930s. Most often a farmer had to walk behind the horses in the fields. All the while, the horse's tail is swishing back and forth, swatting at flies.

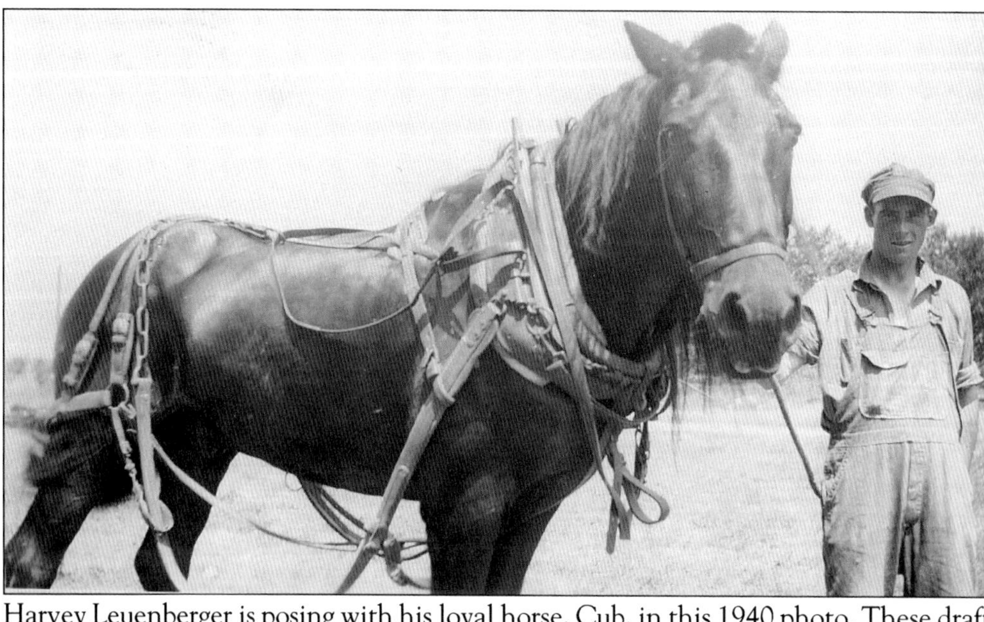

Harvey Leuenberger is posing with his loyal horse, Cub, in this 1940 photo. These draft horses were powerful, majestic, gentle animals who responded to their master's every command. Before beginning work in the field, a heavy set harness had to be put on the horse and strapped in place.

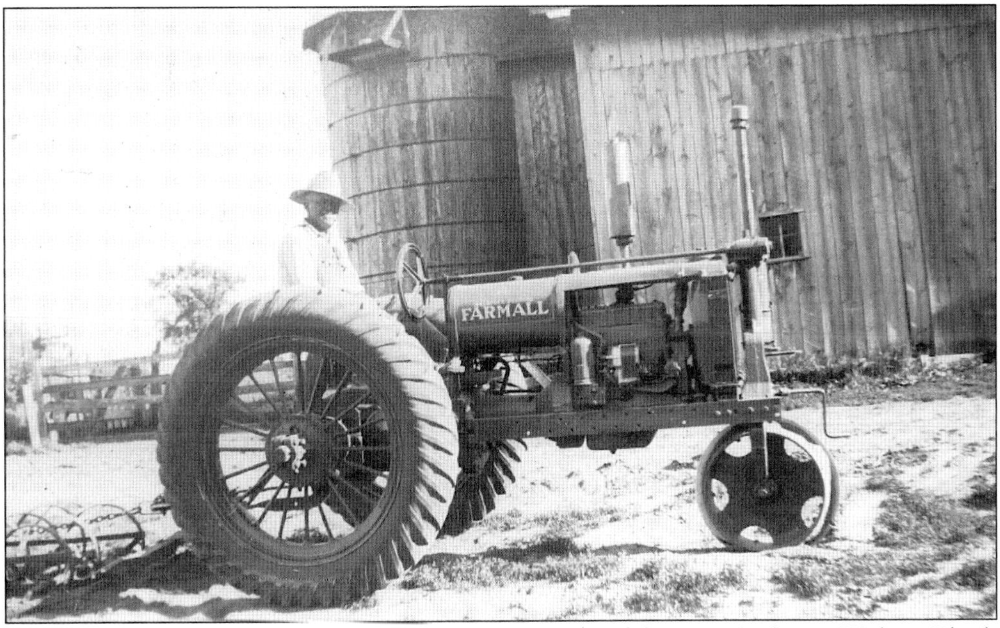

Horses were gradually replaced by tractors. In this May 1935 photo Walter Kluck proudly displays his new Farmall tractor. Work could now be done a lot faster than was possible with a team of horses.

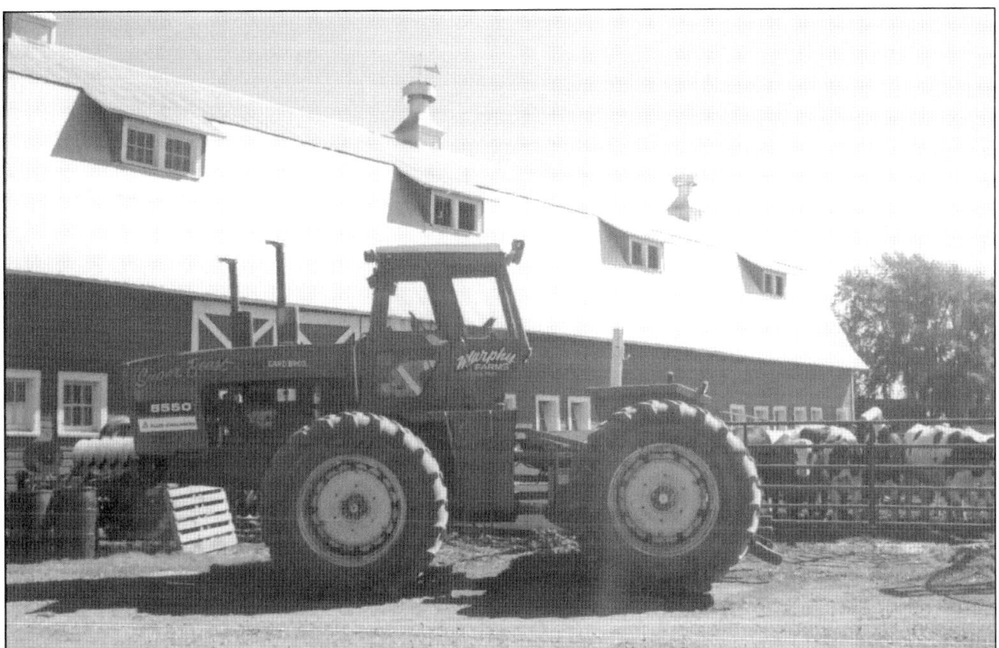

This modern tractor owned by Dean Murphy, in this September 1999 photo, is used today in his livestock and cash crop farming operation. It is much more powerful and efficient than tractors used 50 years ago.

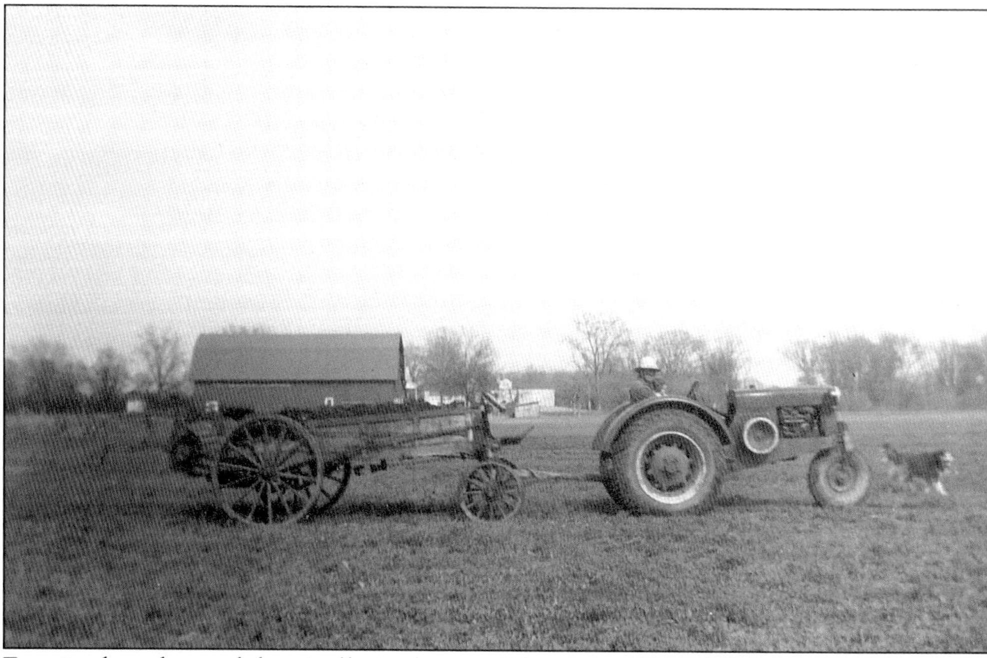

Farming has changed drastically in the past fifty years. Edward Ederer is working in the fields on his River Road farm with his first tractor, a 1937 Co-Op, in this 1940s photo. Faithful Shep, his dog, leads the way around the fields. His team of horses was still being used for some of the work.

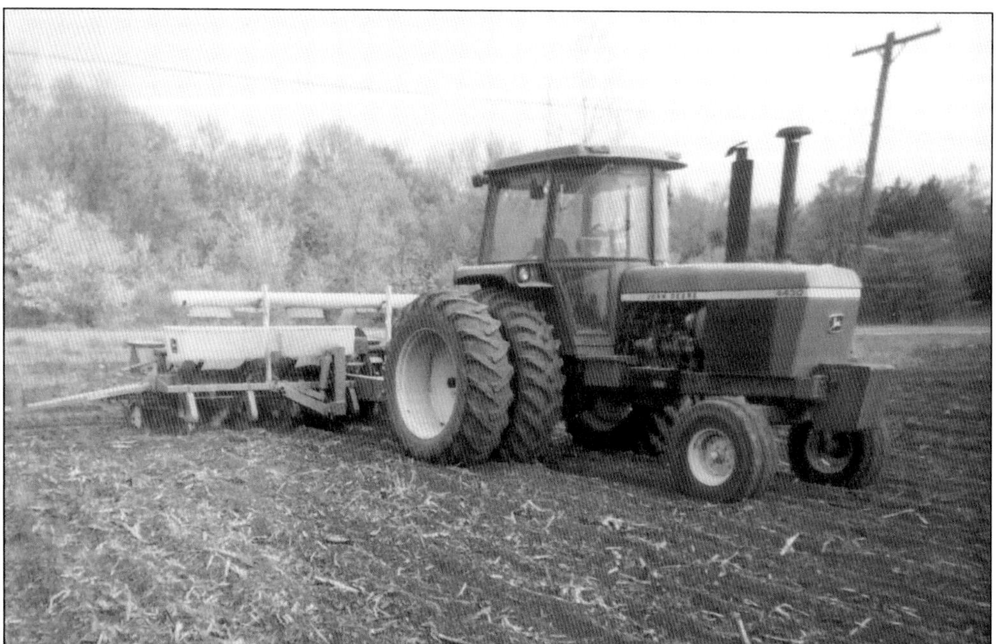

Bill Sparks is working the same field with his modern John Deere tractor in June 1999. He can now sit in an enclosed, air-conditioned cab which protects him from the sun and rain. The same farm work is now done in a fraction of the time required 50 years ago.

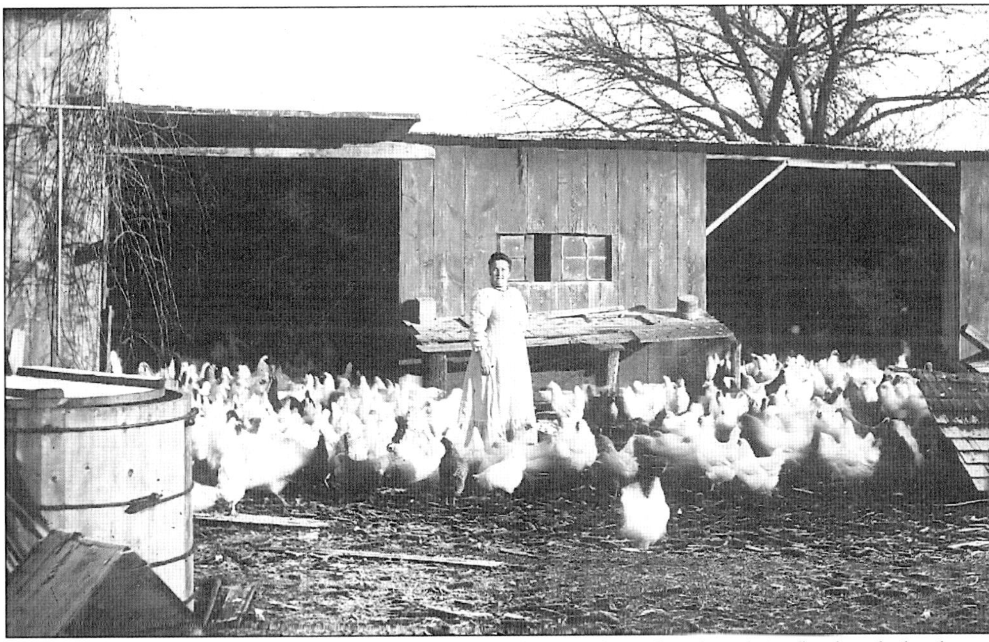

One of the farm wife's many duties was looking after the family's flock of chickens. Poultry has been raised in Thomas Township since the 1800s. Many residents would raise a few chickens in their back yards. Albertine Kluck is tending her large flock of chickens on her farm in 1918.

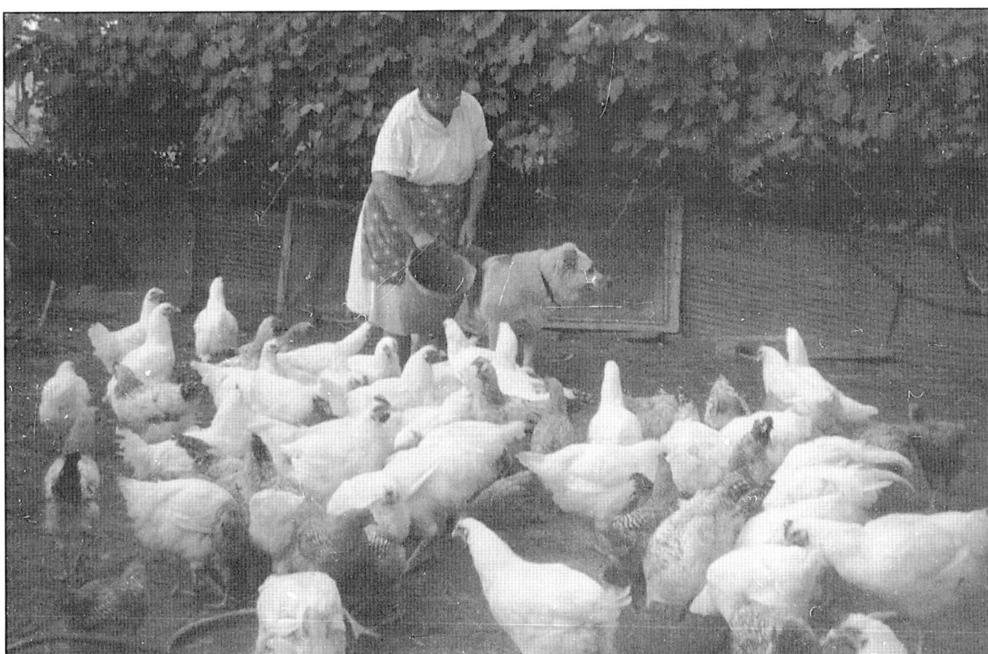

Erna Ederer is feeding her flock of young chickens on her farm in this photo taken in August of 1978. Her German shepherd, Penny, is also helping to round up the chickens for chow time.

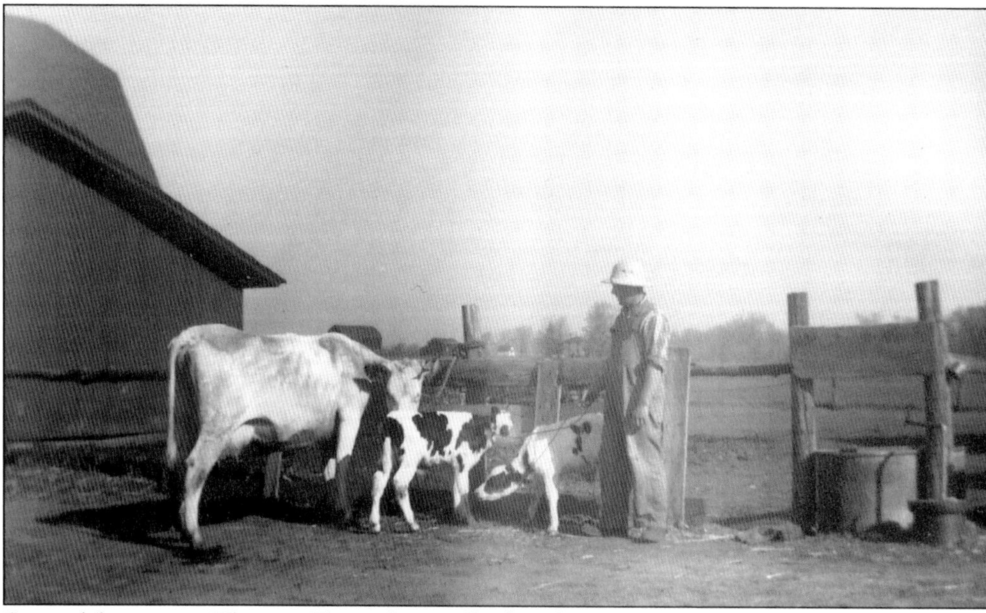

Several farmers in Thomas Township milked Holstein dairy herds. In this 1950s photo, Edward Ederer proudly shows a mother cow and her twin calves. Twins were rare and usually meant a photo session for the calves. The barnyard was enclosed with wooden fence posts. Some of the milk was bottled and sold to customers who came to the house. The rest was sold to Borden's Dairy.

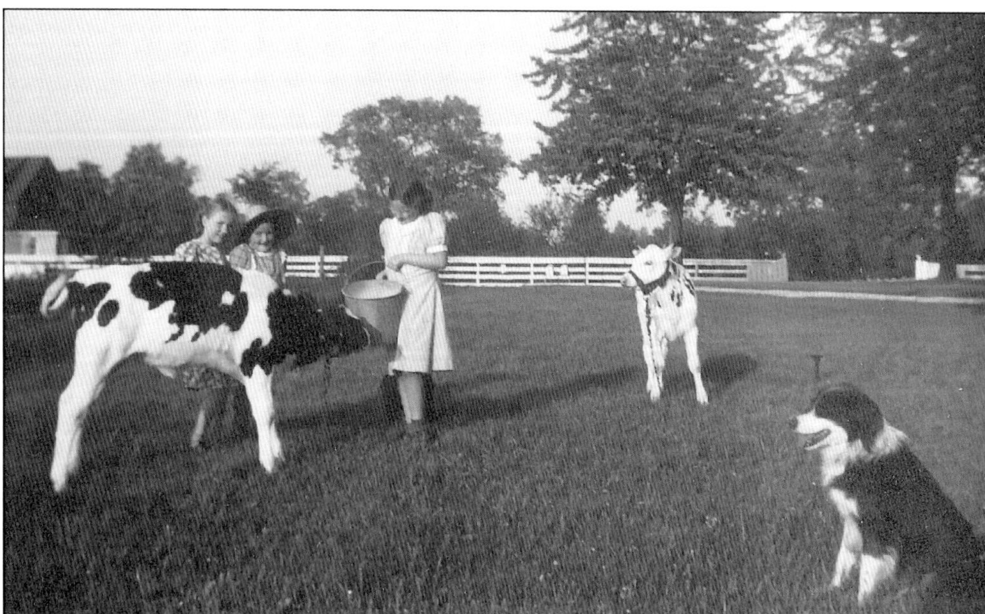

In this 1950s photo, these two calves have been weaned from their mother. Mary Lou feeds one of the frisky calves while Rose and Ruth Ederer and Chummy, the dog, watch. The calves were tied in the lawn to graze. The dairy cattle grazed in a pasture on the farm. Feeding the calves was a morning and evening chore usually assigned to the children.

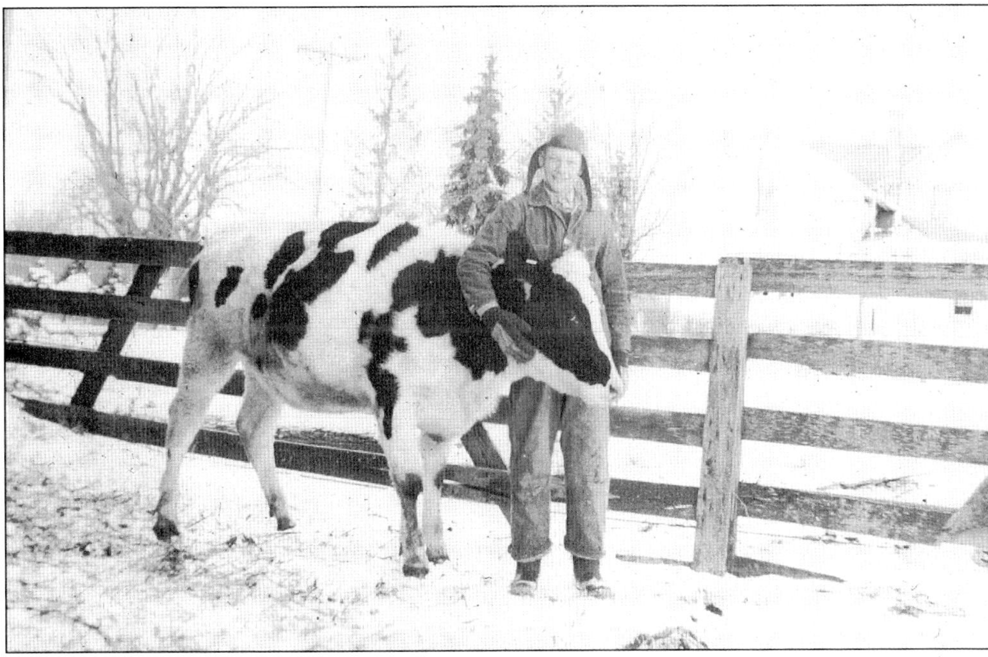

Ed Kluck is shown with his prize-winning Holstein cow, Bessie, in this 1930s photo. The barnyard is enclosed with a wooden fence. Walter Kluck milked a large Holstein dairy herd for years.

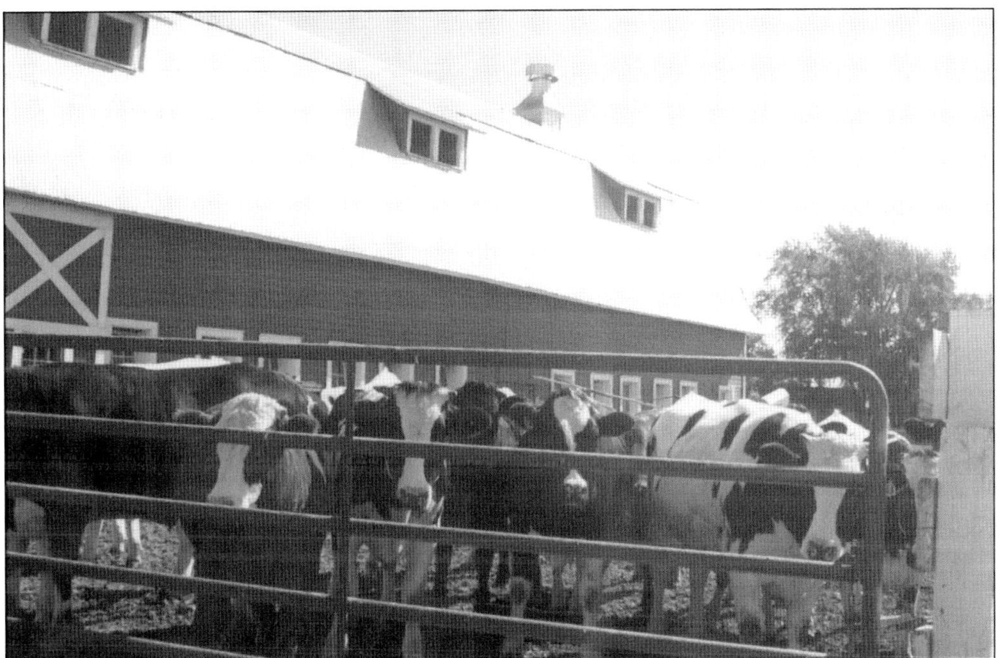

During the past twenty years, all remaining Thomas Township dairy farmers have phased out their dairy operations. Dean Murphy is one of the few remaining farmers who still raises cattle. He replaced his dairy herd with cattle raised as steers shown in this September 1999 photo. His cattle are in a barnyard enclosed with an iron fence.

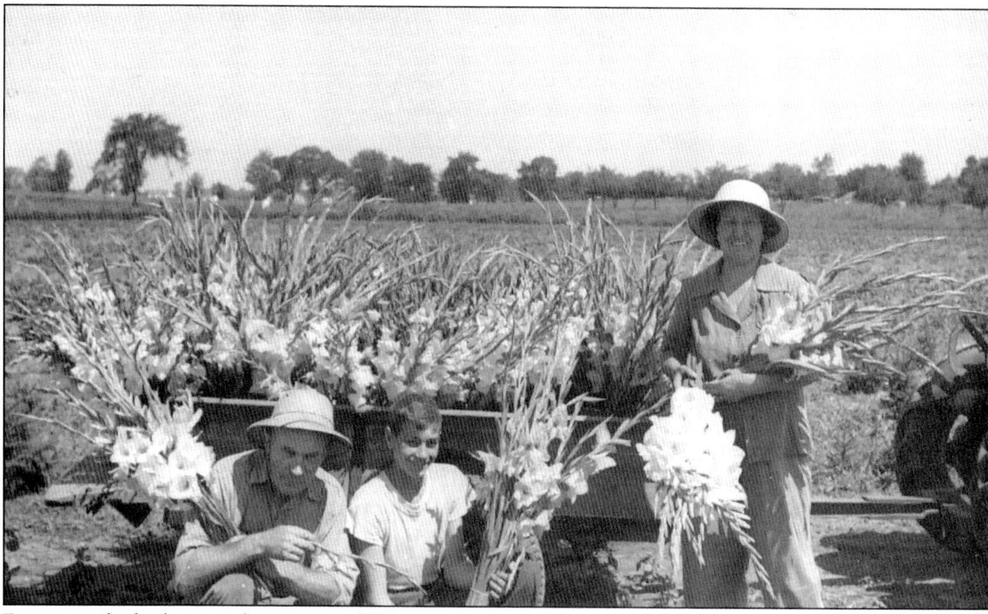

Raising gladiolus on the Fay and Eleanor Roberts farm required the entire family to help. The "glads" were raised on the land which is now Roberts Park. In this 1950 photo, the gladiolus are being harvested by Fay Roberts, Donnie Day, and Eleanor Roberts.

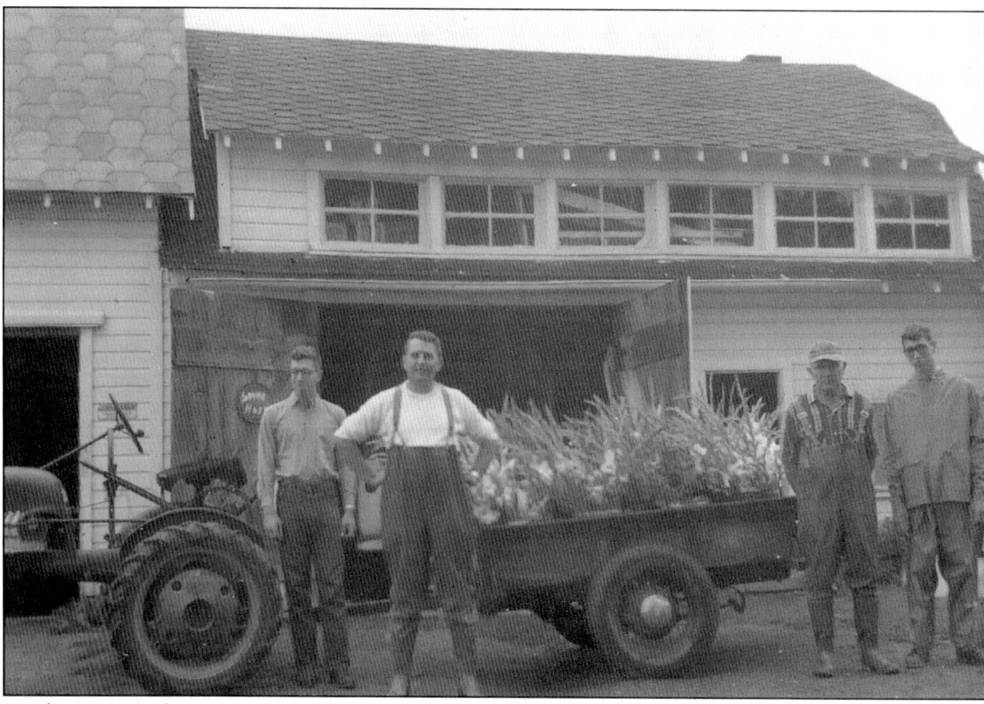

In this 1965 photo, a trailer load of gladiolus has been harvested by Ron Picardi, Paul Roberts, Fay Roberts, and Ken Picardi. They will be sold at Engel's Market, to local florists along Gratiot Road, and at the Saginaw Fairgrounds Farmers' Market.

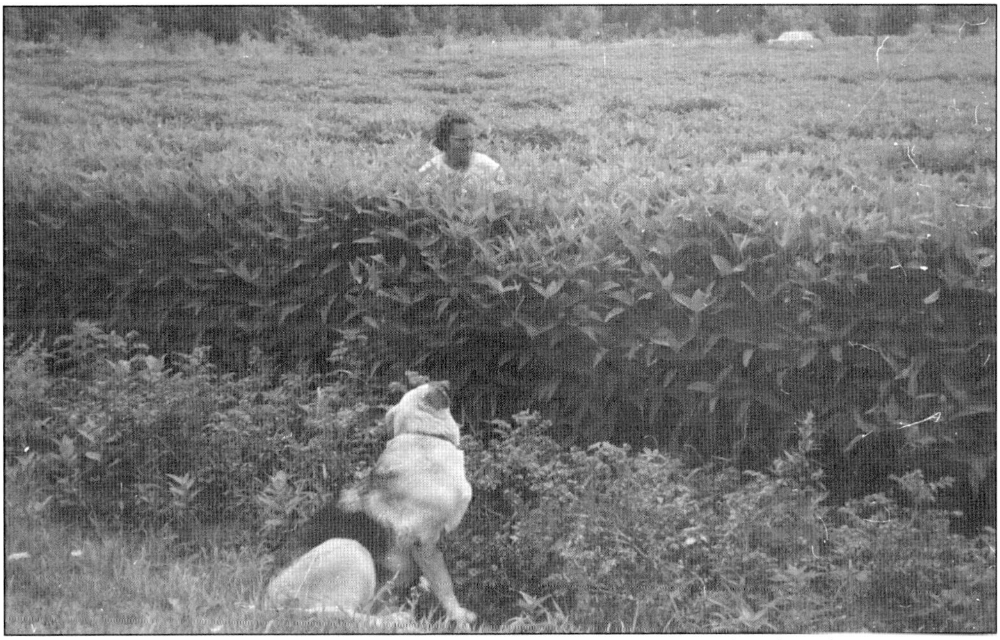

Acres of navy beans had been raised in Saginaw County for decades, prompting Saginaw County to be called "The Navy Bean Capital of the World." Almost every Thomas Township farm has raised navy beans. However, since the 1970s navy beans have been replaced with soybeans. Erna Ederer is standing in her soybean field in the summer of 1977. The plants are almost shoulder high. Penny, her dog, watches from the sidelines.

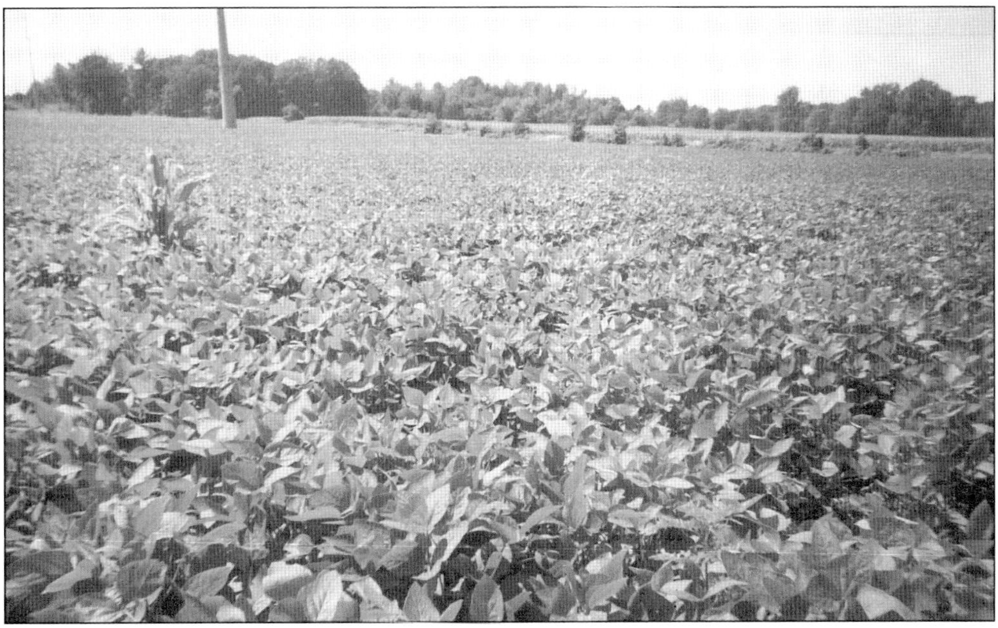

Today some of these soybeans are no-till as shown in this field on the Ederer farm in August of 1999. The beans are planted like wheat would be planted and are not cultivated.

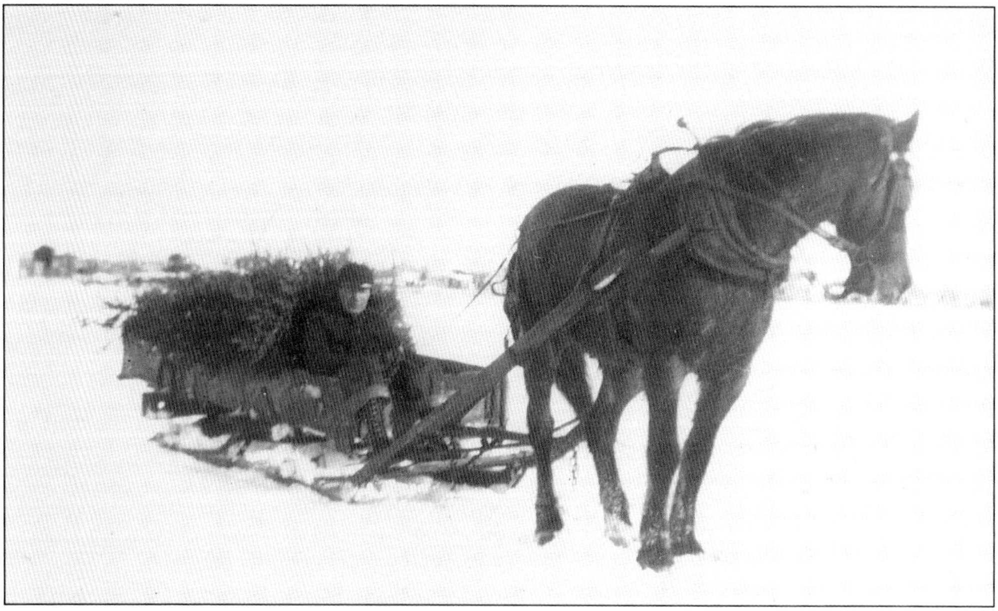

Fay Roberts has selected and cut his Christmas tree at the Kluck's Christmas Tree Farm on Van Wormer Road and is bringing it home to his Bacon Road farm in this scene from the mid-1930s. A trip to Kluck's Farm has become an annual pre-Christmas rite for many residents.

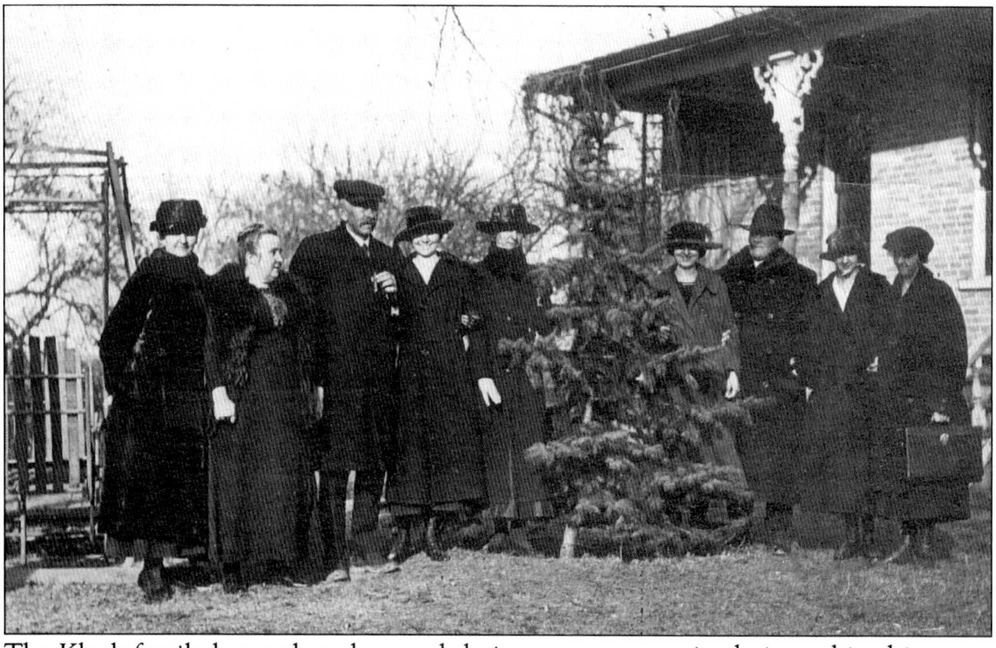

The Kluck family has gathered around their evergreen tree in their yard in this scene taken in February, 1921. Pictured, from left to right, are unidentified, Albertine Kluck, Fred Kluck, Frieda Kluck, unidentified, Clara Kluck, Art Kluck, and an unidentified couple. Walter Kluck began the nursery business, as a hobby, in March 1923. He began selling Christmas trees in the 1930s. Some customers have been coming annually to Kluck's Nursery for 50 years to select and cut their fresh Christmas trees.

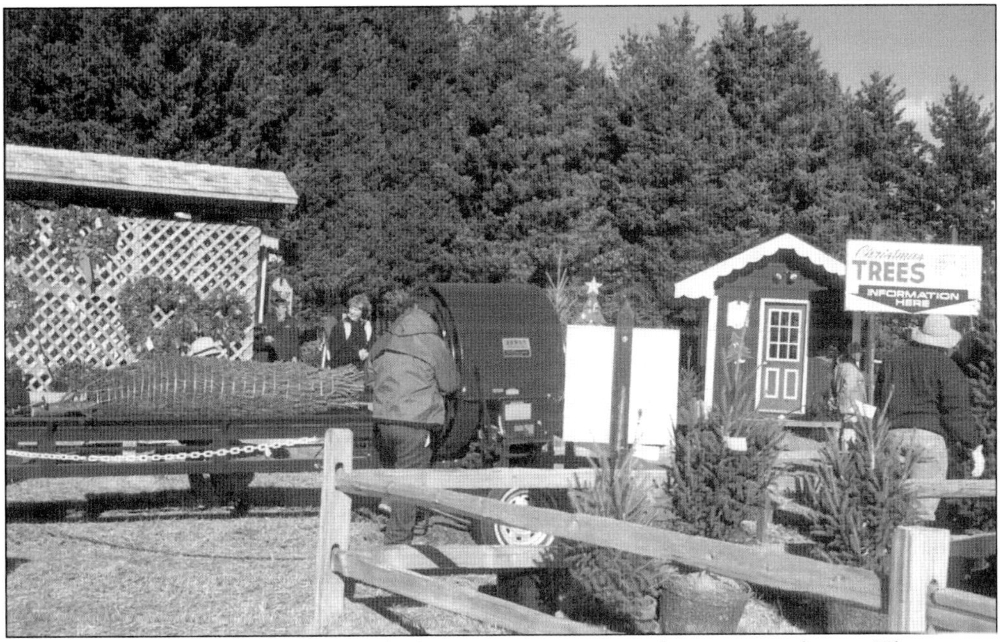

The Christmas tree harvest at Kluck's Nursery is a very busy time of year. The entire family and several employees are kept busy for one month before Christmas. In this scene, a customer has already selected and cut his tree and it is being wrapped by machine so that it can be easily transported home on his car.

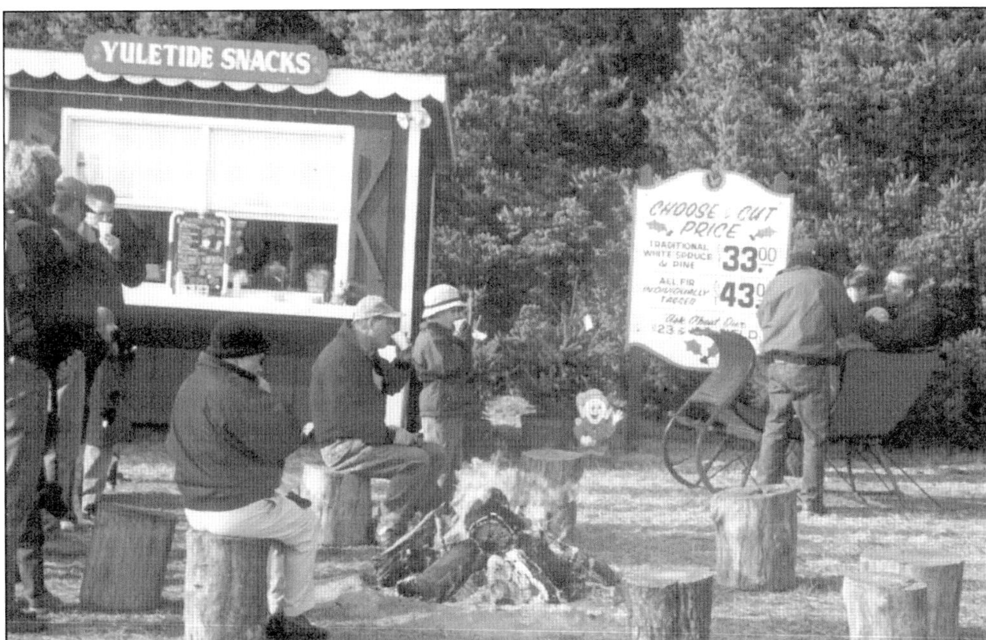

In this December 1999 scene, customers are warming up and relaxing with hot cocoa by the bonfire before leaving for home. Selecting a Christmas tree has become a pleasurable tradition for many families. About five thousand trees are selected and cut yearly at Kluck's by customers for their Christmas festivities.

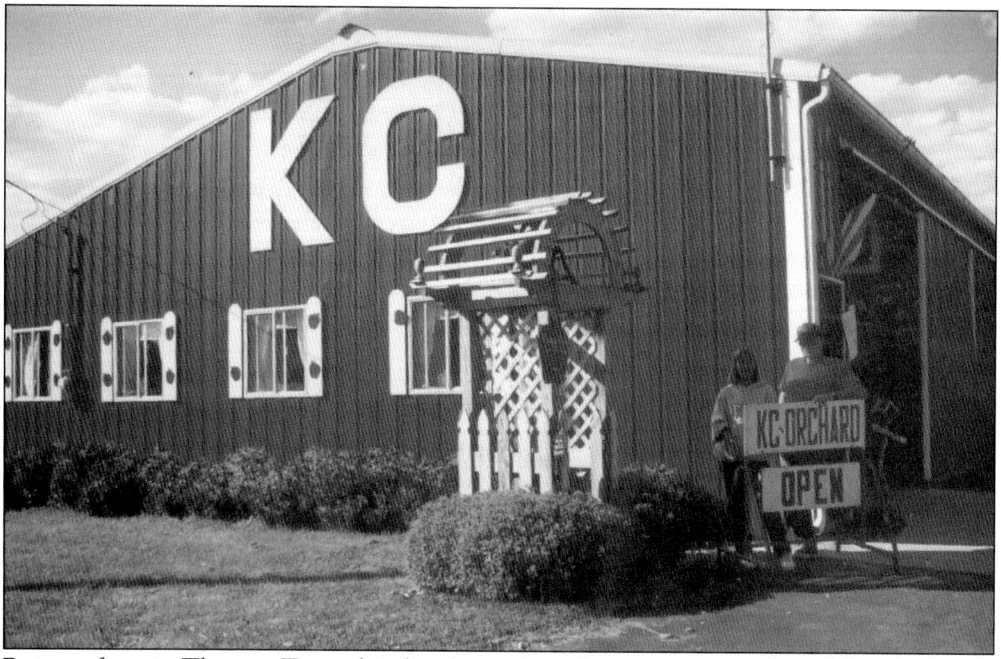

Raising fruit in Thomas Township has been done for centuries, gathered first by the Chippewa Indians, then by the early pioneers, and now by fruit farmers. The KC Orchard at 3595 North Thomas Road has been operated by Kris and Christine Wenzel since 1981. Christine and Fred Wenzel pose outside their apple-red store in September 1999. The store is open from August until Christmas each year to sell the apples harvested from their farm.

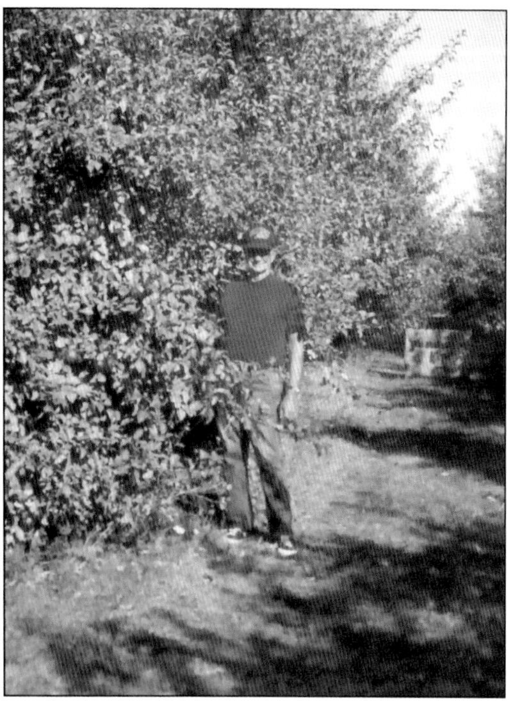

Fred Wenzel is shown picking some apples from one of the three thousand trees grown on the farm. There are 22 different apple varieties. Several acres of "U-Pick" pumpkins allow customers to select their own Halloween pumpkins.

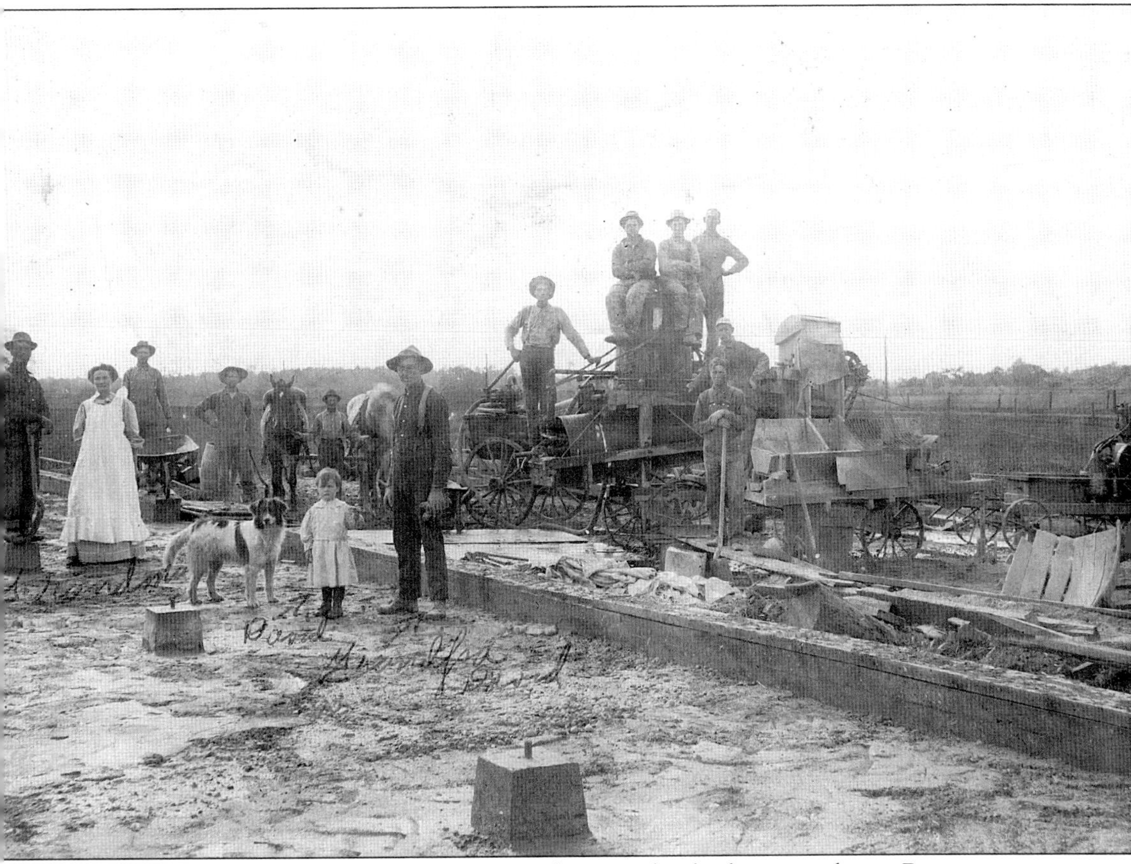

A farm in Thomas Township was not complete until it had its own barn. Barn raising was an event that brought family and neighbors together. While the men and teenage sons worked with their teams and muscles, the women and children were busy cooking for the large crew. With this united spirit and effort, the barn was soon finished. In the above photo, the Geddes family, friends, and neighbors are building their Geddes Road barn for the large dairy herd and teams of horses in 1911 for David Alex and Sarah Catherine Geddes, the second generation. The farm is owned by the fourth generation, Hector and Sharon Geddes. The barn still stands today.

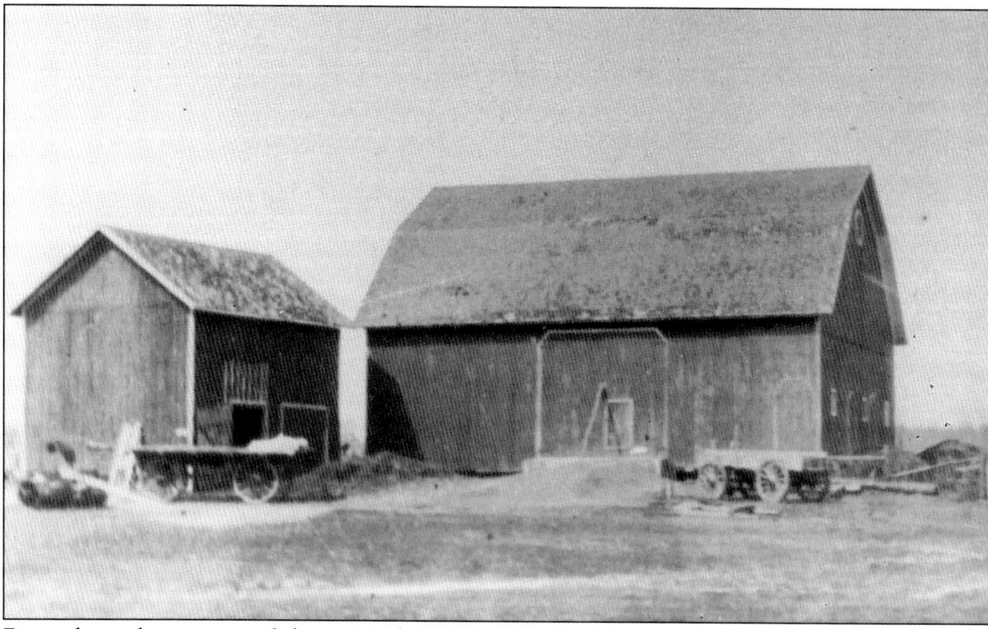

Barns have been part of the township's rural heritage since the 1800s. They symbolize the strength and endurance of our staunch farming forefathers. The photo of this dairy barn owned by George and Rebecca Dinning at 830 South Graham Road was taken in 1895. No two barns are built exactly alike. This barn is representative of the many constructed in the township during this time.

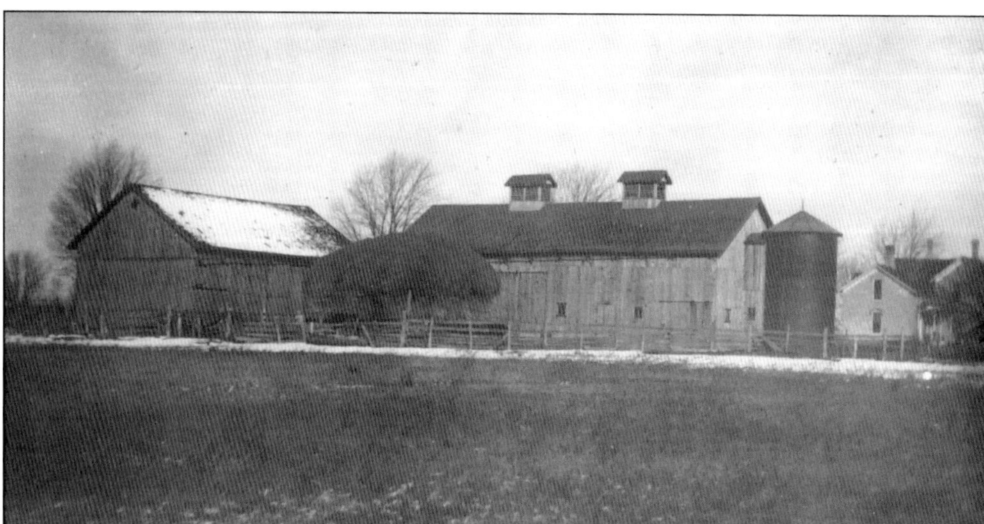

Fred and Albertine Kluck purchased their farm in 1907, shown here in 1919. The nails in this barn are handmade square shank. The Kluck farm today is owned and operated by the third generation Gerald and Sally Kluck and the fourth generation Tom and Karen Kluck.

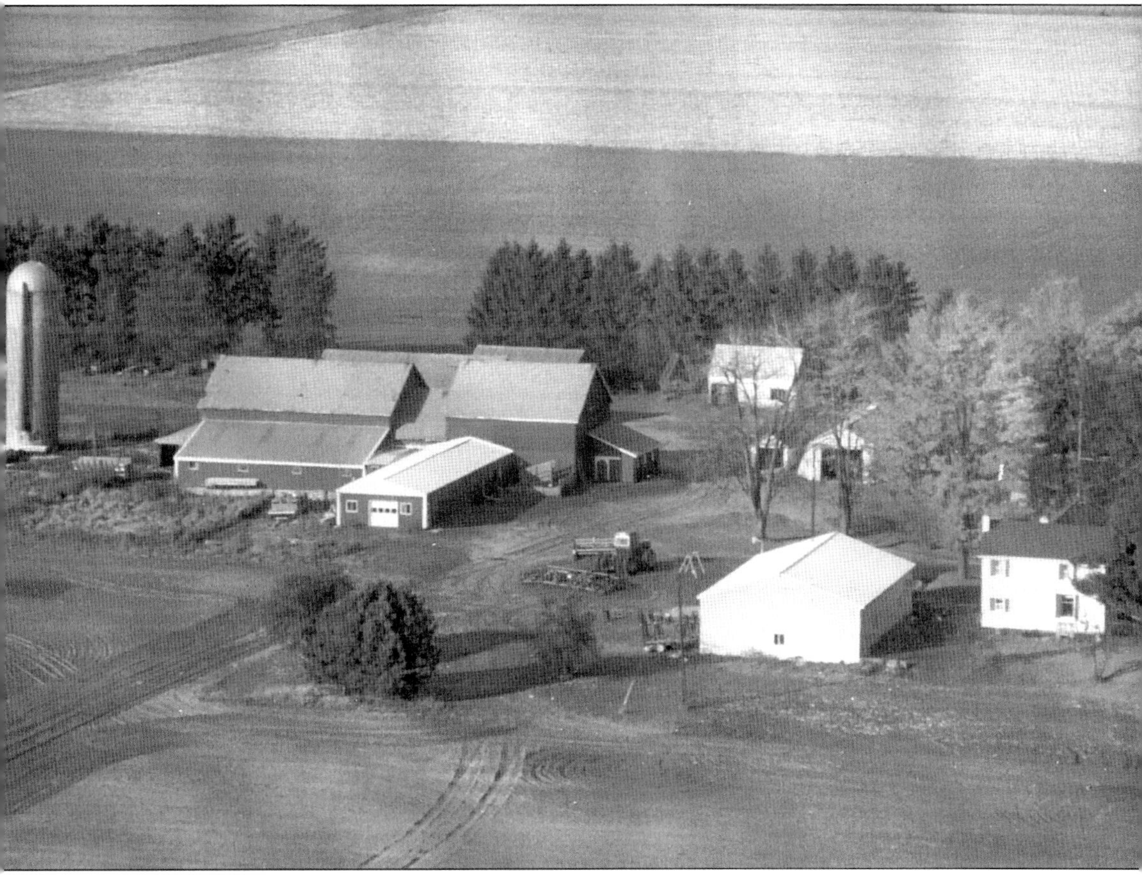

Johann Liskow obtained this farm in Section 23 from the government in 1853. His son, Ferdinand Liskow, took over the farm in 1872 and planted white pine trees in the center of the farm. The barn, which he built in 1872, stands in the middle of this late 1960s photo. The original sand-brick house, built in 1883, is shown in the lower right corner. It was torn down in 1988. This photo shows the other modern farm buildings which have been constructed for the dairy and cash crop farming operation. Today, this centennial farm is owned and operated by the fourth, fifth, and sixth generations—Ivan C., William, and Joseph Sparks. Stately white pine trees line the long driveway on the Geddes Road farm.

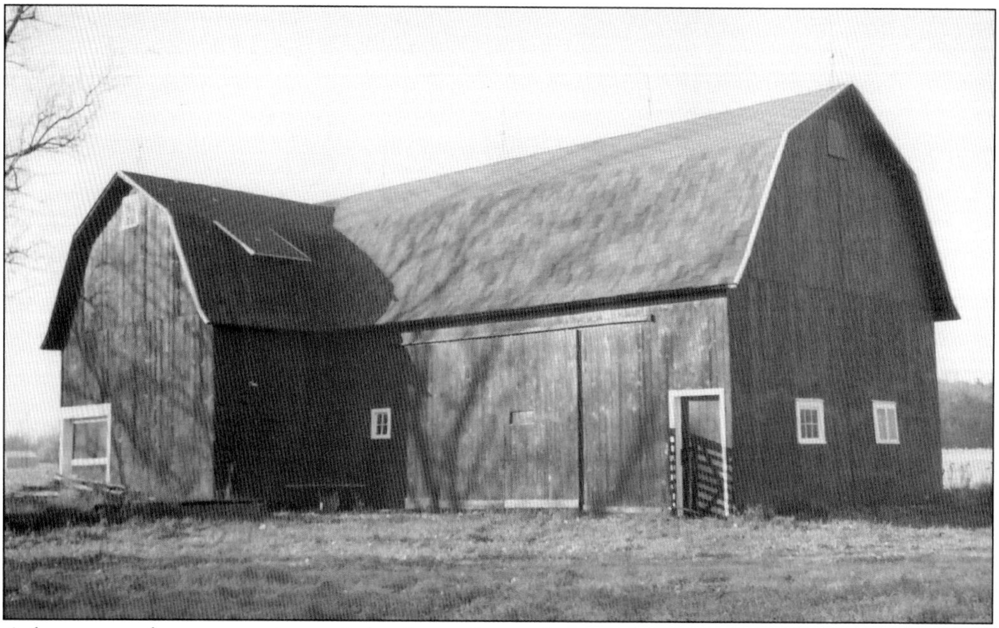

A barn was the centerpiece of the farm. Barns have become nostalgic; truly a work of art from times gone by. Joseph Ederer built many barns in Thomas, James, and Saginaw Townships during the late 1800s and early 1900s, building this barn for his own farm in 1907. The multi-purpose barn, owned by the third generation today, features horse stalls, cow mangers, livestock pens, granary, hay mow, and equipment storage.

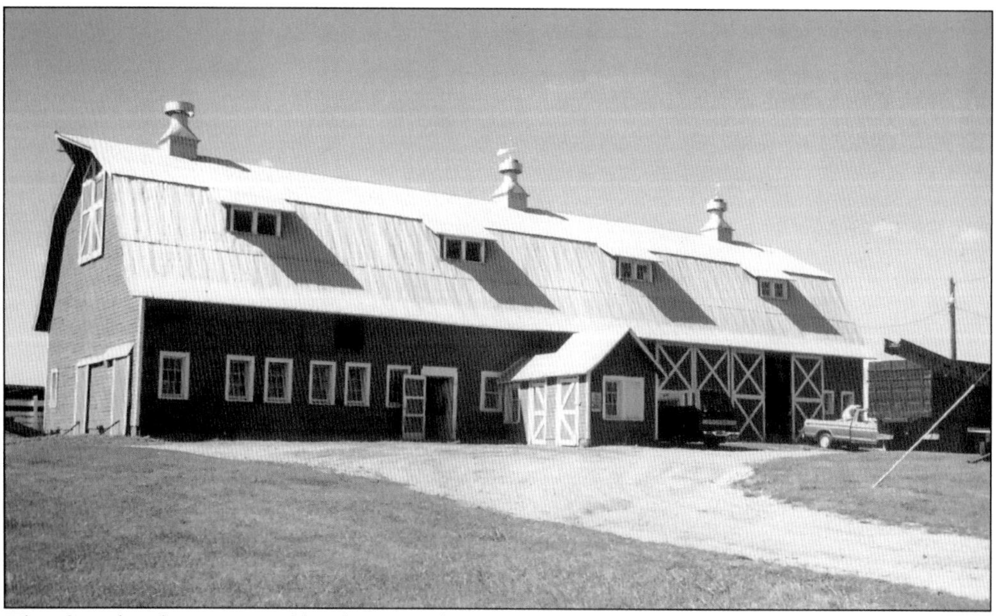

This farm has been owned by the Murphy family since 1895. The barn was disassembled and moved from Hemmeter Road in Saginaw Township to its present location on Lone Road in 1938. The large green barn was used for Murphys' large dairy herd for years. Its mows are filled with sweet-smelling straw and hay. Dean Murphy still uses this barn for his farming operation today.

Three

Main Street Business District

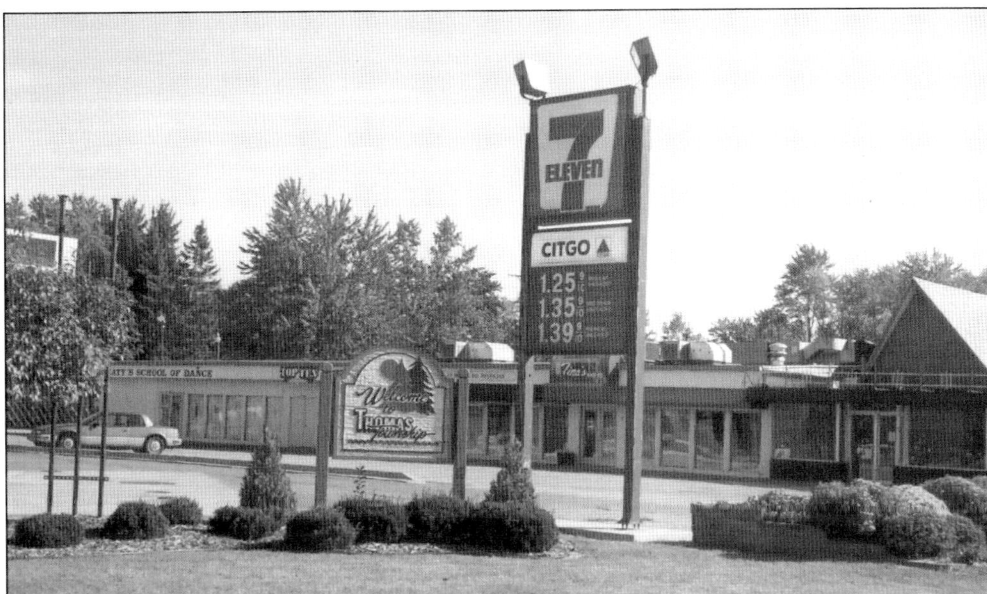

Travelers from Hemlock, Merrill, Alma, and other western villages stayed overnight in Shields before crossing the Tittabawassee River by ferry or toll bridge to continue their day-long journey to Saginaw City in the 1800s. A business district, known as Shields Corners, developed on Gratiot Road. Likewise, a mini-business district, called Frost Corners, developed on Frost Road. The unincorporated village of Shields has continued to develop with society's changing needs. It has become a commercial hub serving people for miles around.

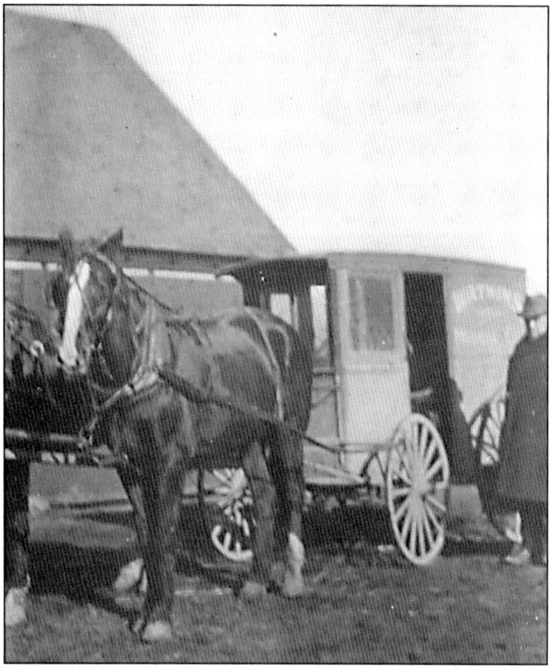

The "Watkins Man" stops at the Kluck farm in 1919 to peddle the wares so important to the farm household. The farmer's wife could make her selection of Watkins products: vanilla, liniment, baking powder and spices, dishes, and salves. The Watkins man stopped at many farms and houses along his route into Thomas Township. Automobiles eventually replaced the horse-drawn delivery trucks for the Watkins man who made regular visits to the township until the early 1950s.

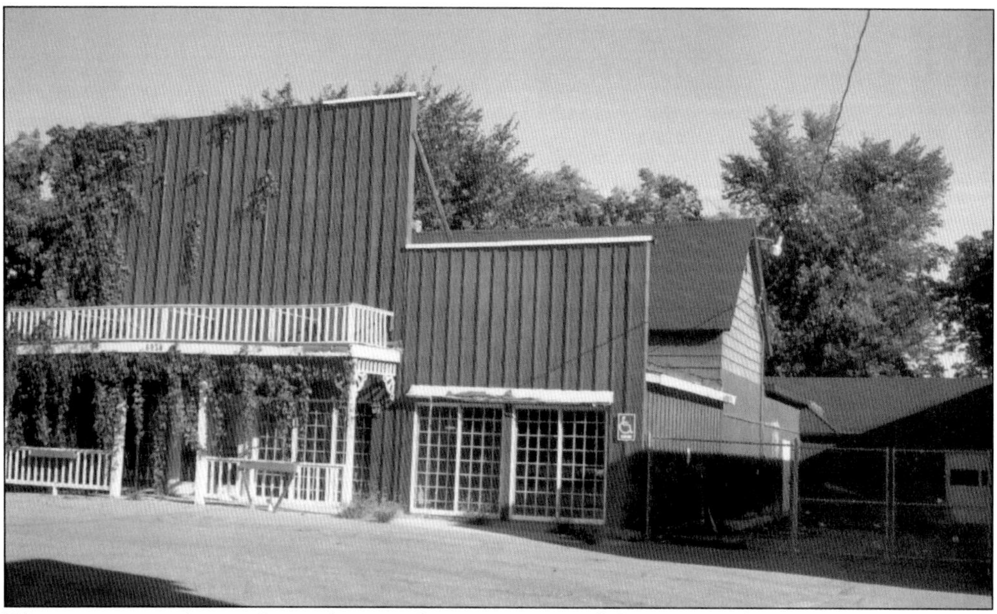

This structure, located on the northeast corner of Gratiot and River Roads, is the oldest surviving commercial building in Thomas Township. Built by Joseph Ederer around the turn of the century, it was a private residence before being converted into a grocery store and post office with a dance hall on the second floor. The store had several operators throughout its lifetime: B.W. Sayers, William Dodge, Joseph Halm, F.T. Rice, Fred Wegner, and August Wegner. It became a plumbing and heating store in 1957, then became Peter's Gun Shop, and finally God's Gifts and Our Talents. This Shields Corner store has served generations of township residents.

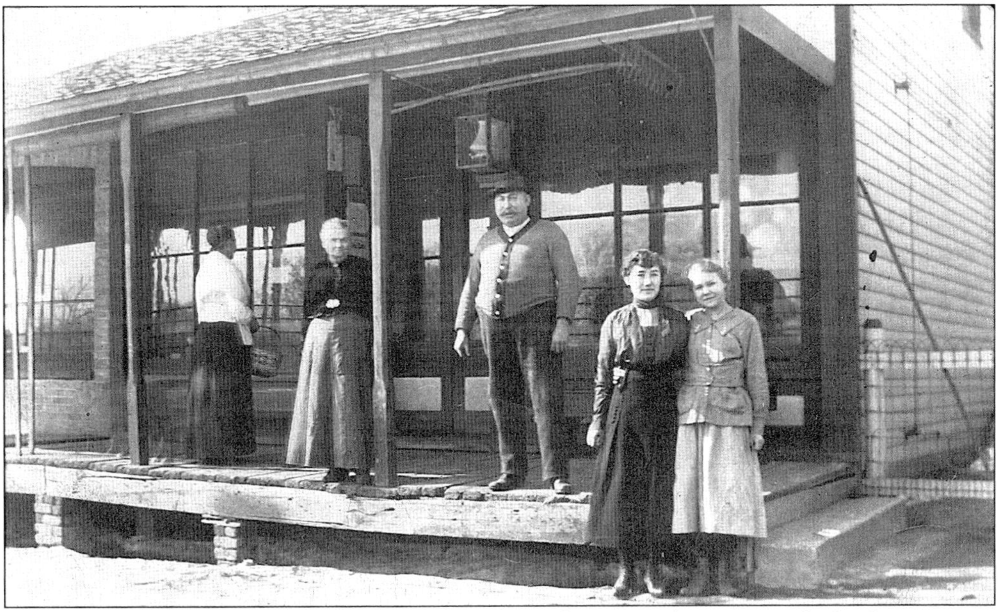

At one time, Frost Corners, at the intersection of Frost and Lone Roads, had two stores and a post office. It had a succession of owners from the 1800s—Jacob M. Wiltse, Bion Wiltse, and James Adams. Clarence Meade owned the store from 1901 to 1915. In this early 1900s photo, people have gathered at Meade's Hall to barter, shop, or visit with their neighbors.

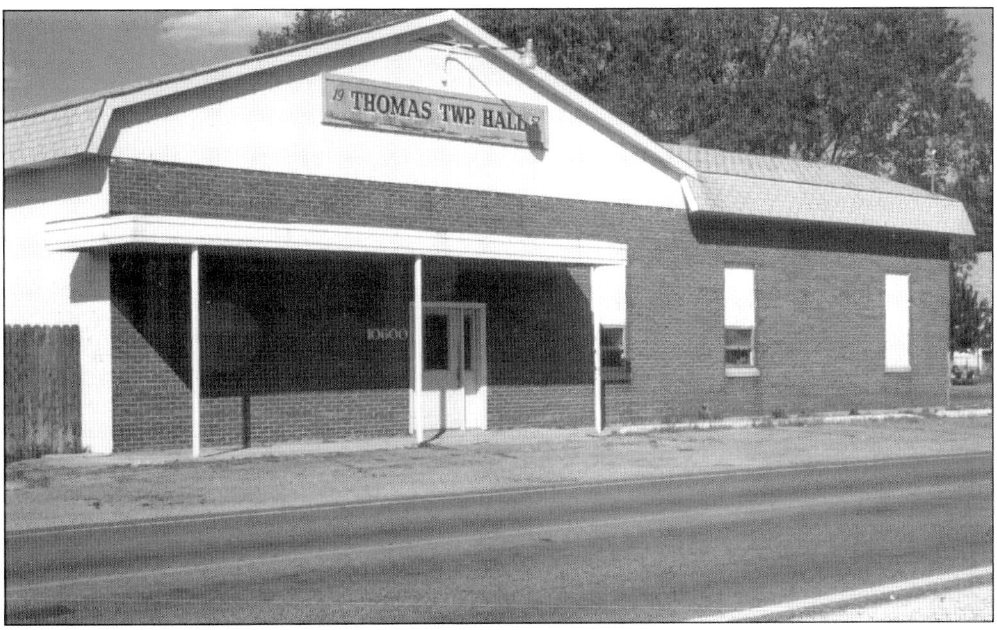

Frost Corners was a central location for many of the township residents. During the 1950s, the Thomas Township Hall was built on the Meade's Hall site. It was also a gathering place for voting, many enjoyable activities, and meetings for township residents until it was closed in 1994. It is now maintained as a storage site for the township.

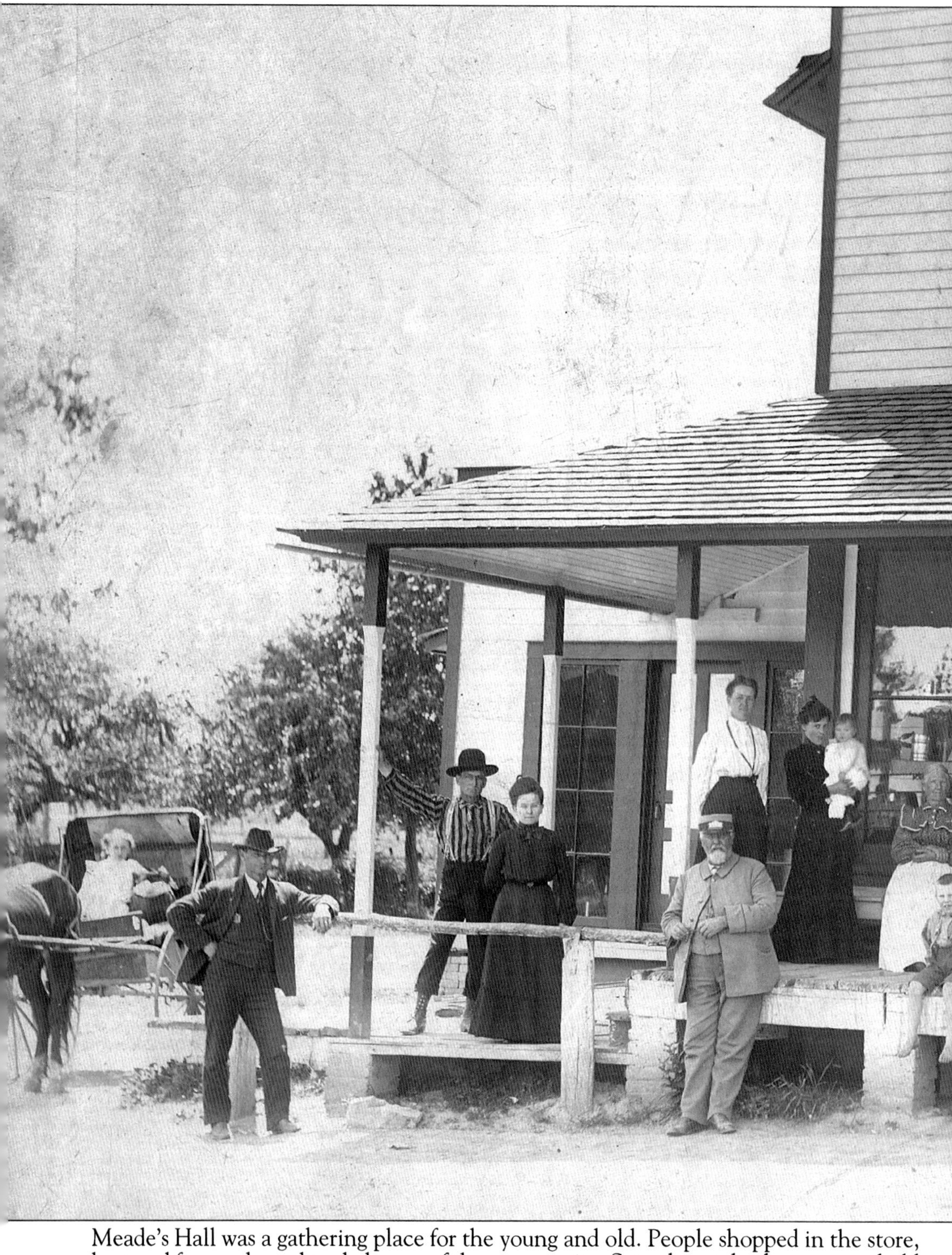

Meade's Hall was a gathering place for the young and old. People shopped in the store, bartered for goods, and traded news of the community. Saturday night dances were held for years in its second floor dance hall. After 1915, its owners were McGinnes, Russell,

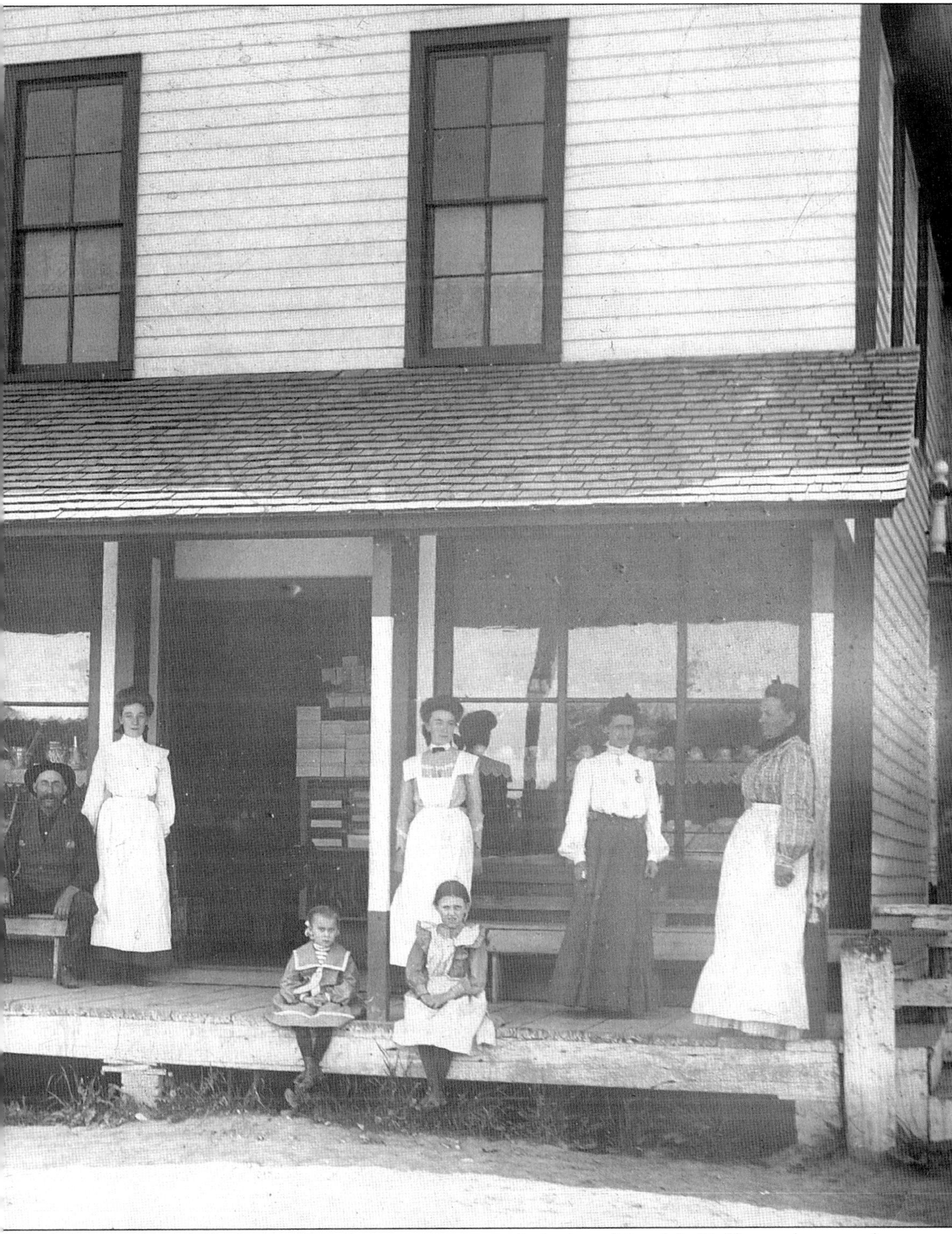

Adsit, and Joe Whelton. Nostalgic memories ended when Meade's Hall was destroyed in a fire on April 4, 1932.

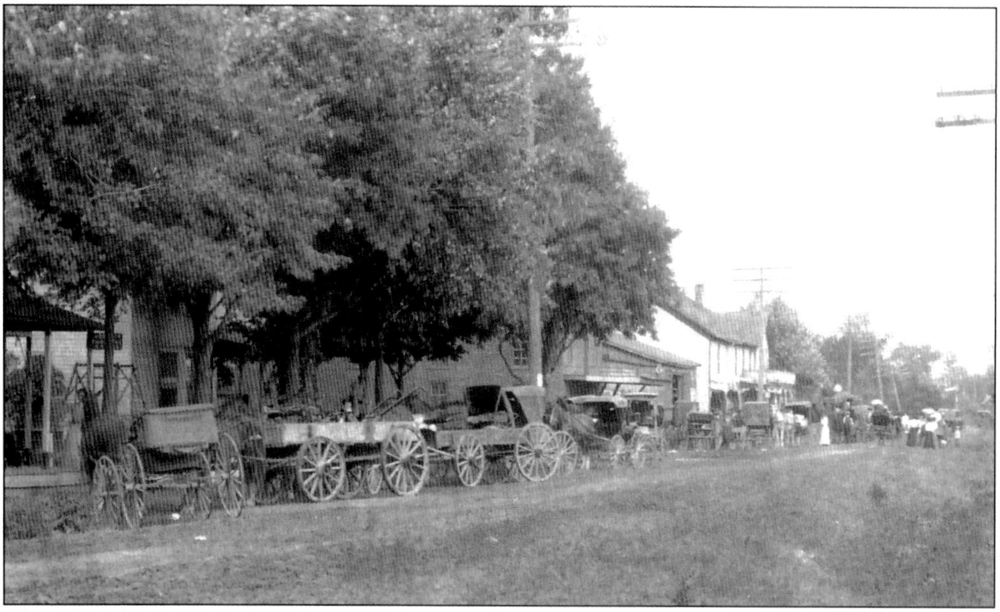

The Tittabawassee Boom Company constructed boarding houses for its men along Gratiot Road just west of the river. In the 1800s Shields became a stopping place for people traveling by horse and wagon from Alma, Merrill, and Hemlock. They stayed overnight in one of the two hotels before resuming their journey across the river. This August 4, 1909 photo was taken during the dedication of the new Gratiot Road bridge.

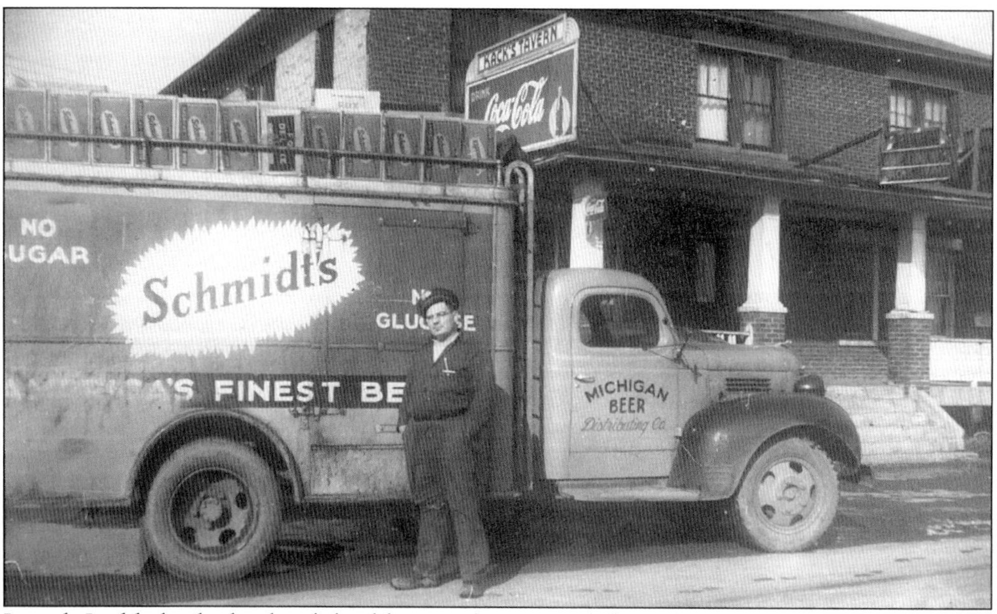

Joseph Leddy built this brick building with a second-floor dance hall in the 1920s after the original Shields Hotel was destroyed by fire in 1916. Some of the owners were J. Cavanaugh, Mr. Dittmar, Charles Adams, and George Schuch. Fred Wegner bought the building in 1944. He moved from his grocery's apartment into the Hotel and lived there until it was torn down. Art Noey's Appliances is on that site now.

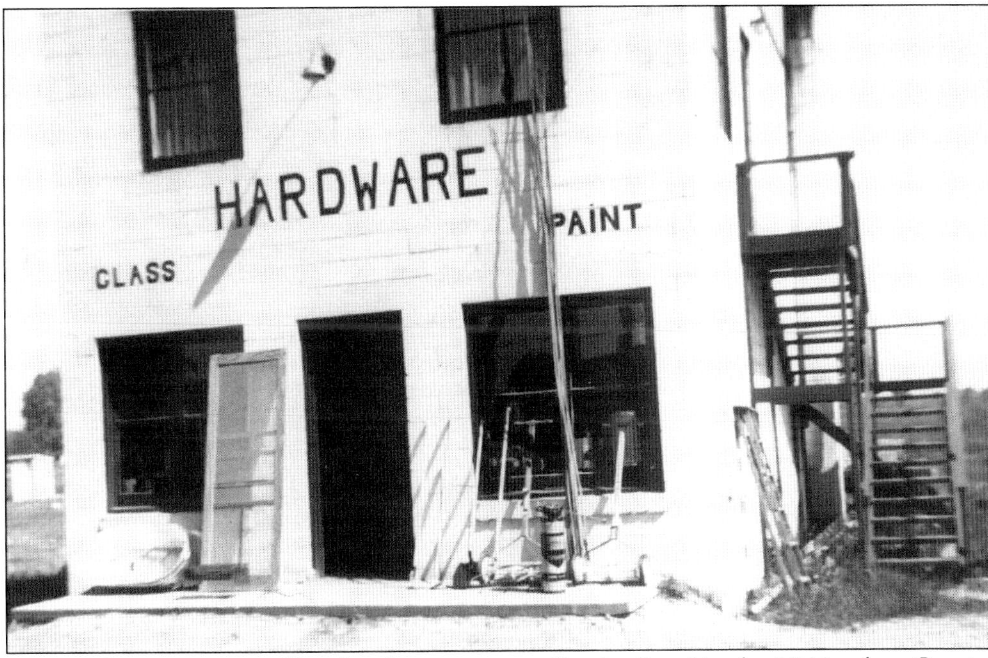

Neva Valentine operated her hardware store on Gratiot Road in the 1940s when Gratiot was still a two-lane highway. This photo was taken in June, 1949. An apartment was on the second floor. Customers could find everything they needed from screen doors to nuts and bolts and always received good old-fashioned personal service with a smile and a joke or two.

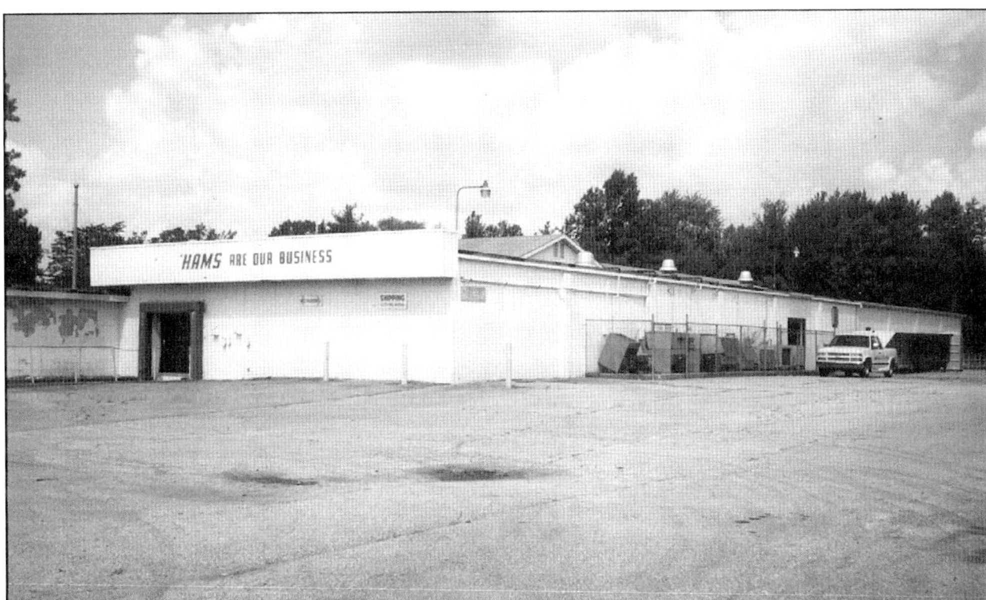

Paul Bunyan Hams, a meat processing plant, operated during the 1970s. This building was typical of the new type of construction occurring down Gratiot Road during this era and was enlarged numerous times as the business prospered. The building has been remodeled and is now occupied by the Stanley Steemer franchise.

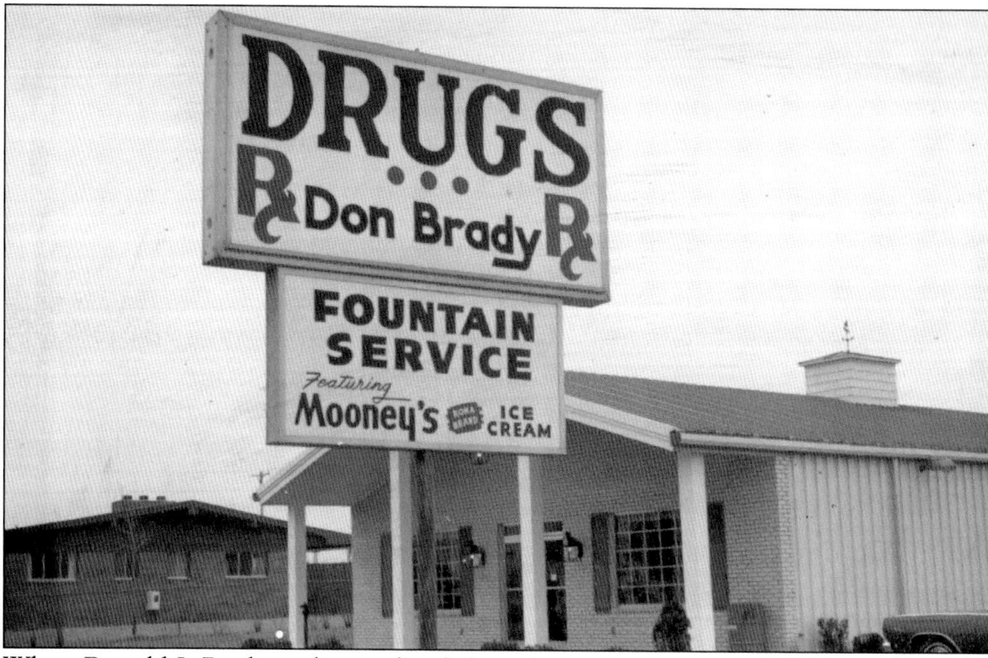

When Donald J. Brady took over his father's business in 1958, he moved it from 630 Gratiot to 7835 Gratiot Road. In addition to filling prescriptions, the drug store gave old-fashioned fountain service and friendly, personal service to its customers who could also pay their water and phone bills there. The drug store was sold to Hometown Pharmacy Corporation in 1998. The Grice family continues to give the same friendly, personal service today.

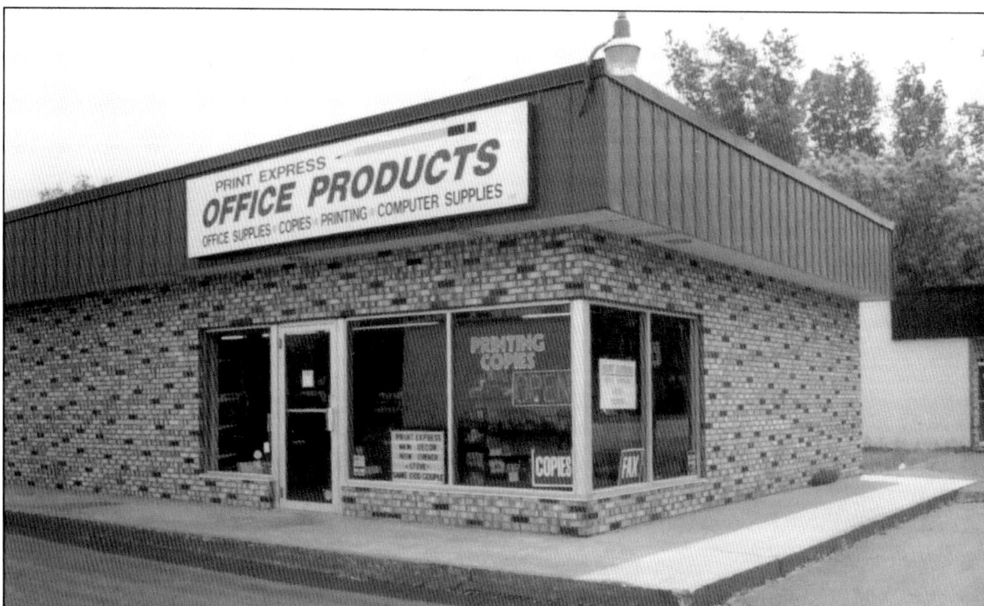

Reliable Print Express was started by Leonard Cliff 23 years ago. The Slasinski family purchased the business three years ago. Steve and Leann Slasinski do custom printing for area residences and businesses in their Print Express store.

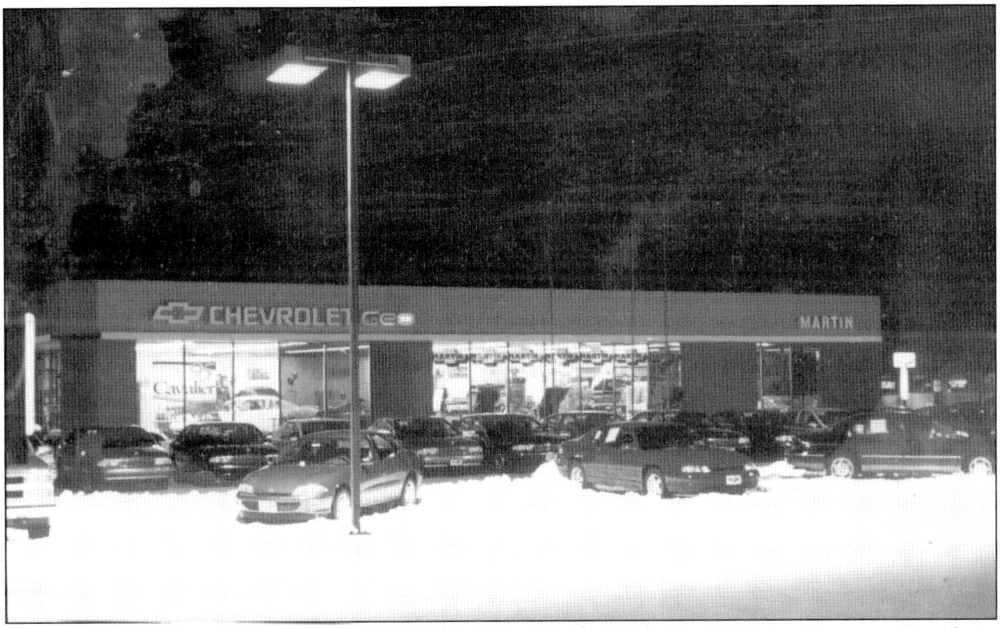

Beginning in 1914, Martin Chevrolet operated its business on Gratiot Road in Hemlock. Many township residents purchased their automobiles at this location. Bill Martin moved his business into Thomas Township at 8800 Gratiot near Kennely Road in the 1980s. It is now more centrally located to Shields' busy commercial hub.

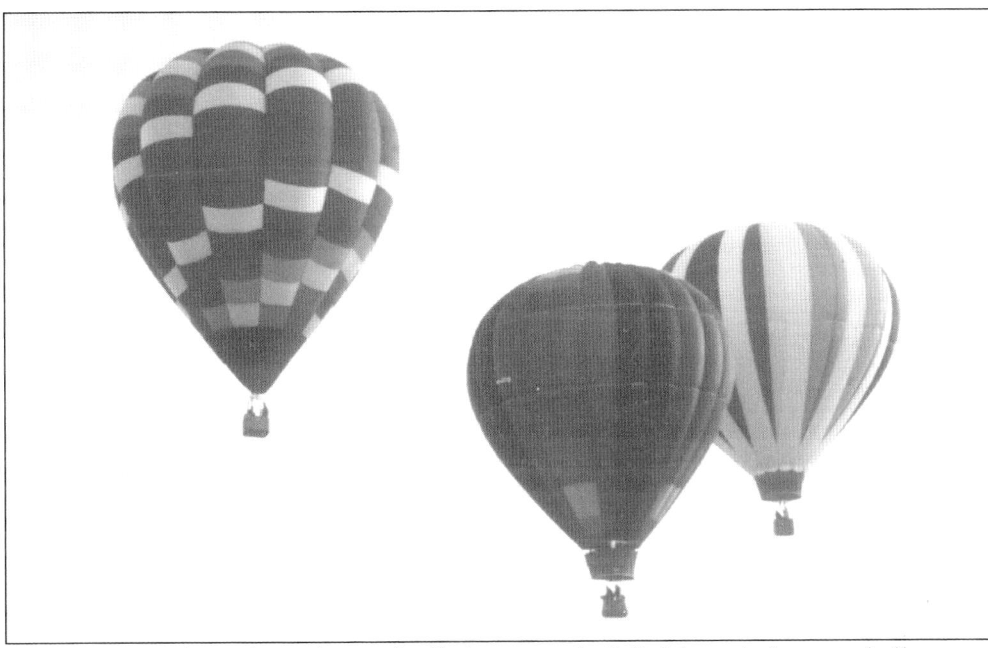

Township residents have been thrilled to watch Bill Martin's hot air balloons as they glide over nearby farm fields. Bill Martin shares his balloon hobby with the community. The brightly-colored balloons are launched in a field behind his dealership. A contestant of the WSGW radio station won a thrilling ride in the one of the balloons pictured above.

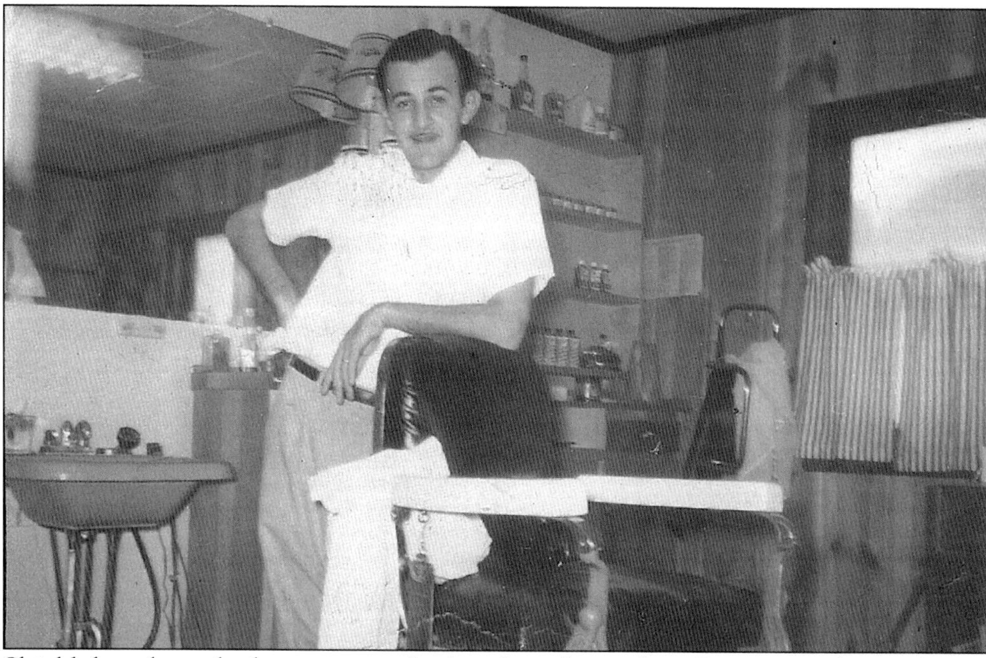

Shields has always had one or more barber shops located on Gratiot Road. Frank Pack is ready for a customer in his barber shop at 7855 Gratiot Road in this 1959 photo.

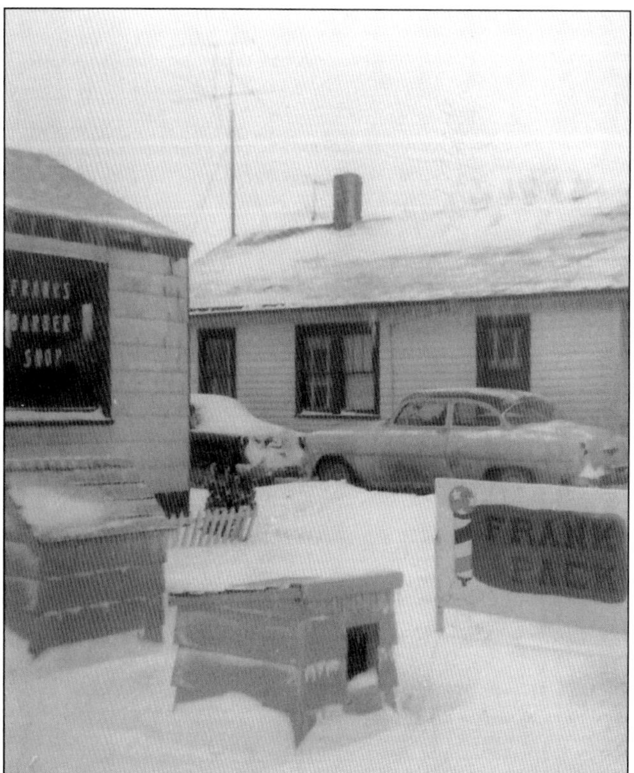

Pack's shop was located next to a private residence. Businesses were often located in residential neighborhoods during the 1950s and 1960s. Customers came for a hair cut and traded news of the community. A Farm Bureau insurance agent occupied the site in later years.

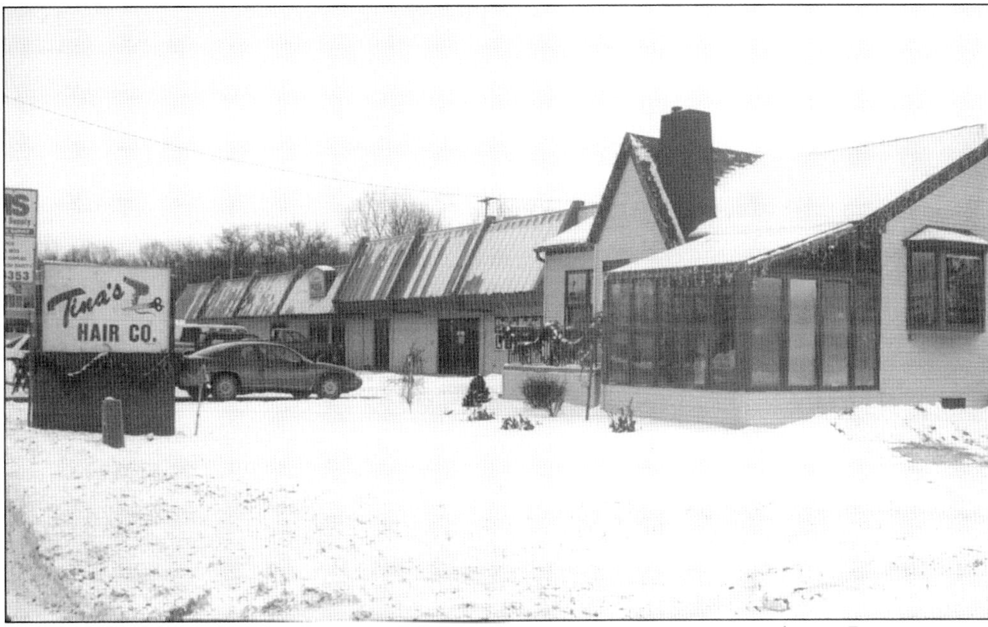

Mini-shopping malls, like the one shown here, have sprung up along Gratiot Road as residential homes have been converted into commercial shops. Tina and Steve Everett along with Pat Crampton have operated Tina's Hair Company since 1989 at 7962 Gratiot Road until new development compelled them to move to 6915 Gratiot on November 30, 1999. The renovated, former Pella Window store provides ample parking with an excellent, panoramic view of the neighborhood.

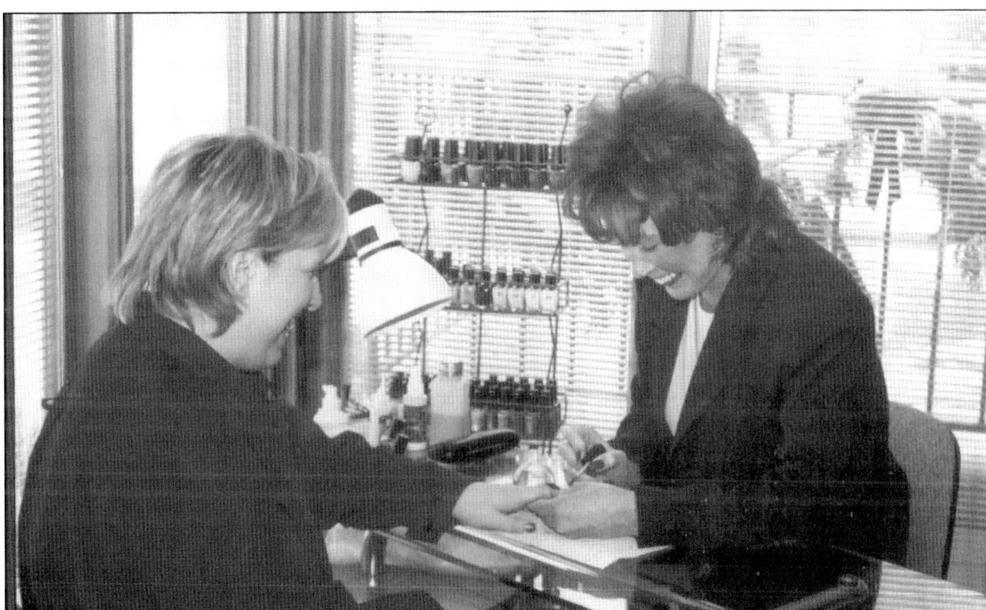

Tina Everett is giving her niece, Rachel Steinert, a manicure in her attractive hair salon's front room overlooking busy Gratiot Road in this January 2000 photo. Her salon will design the right look for men, women, teens, and children.

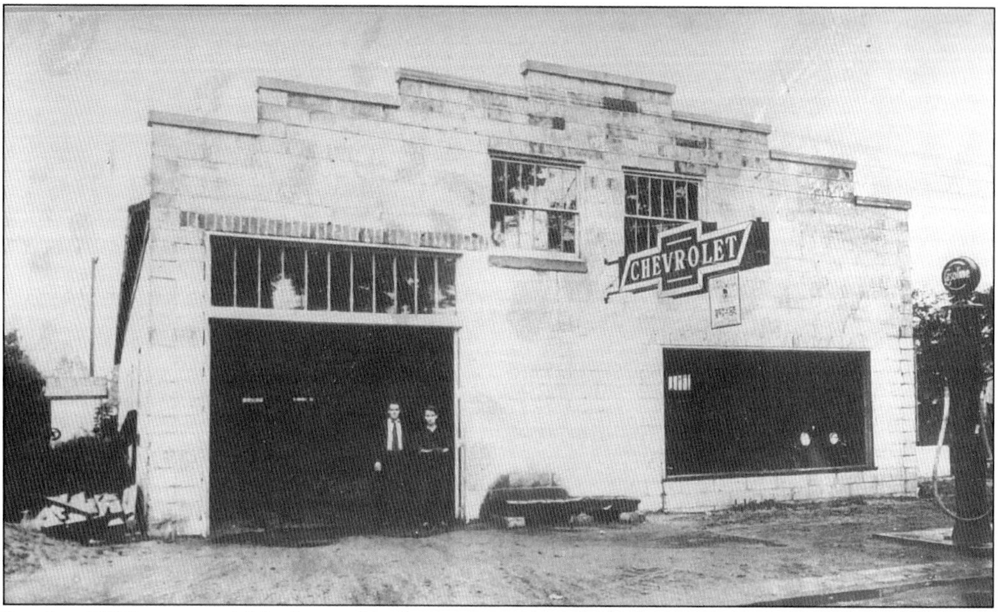

In the 1800s several blacksmiths shops were located along Gratiot Road for shoeing horses and fabricating tools for local farmers. With the coming of the automobile, they were replaced by numerous garages along Gratiot Road from Shields Corners to Hemlock. Martin Chevrolet repaired cars and pumped gas for decades at this Hemlock garage until moving its business to Shields.

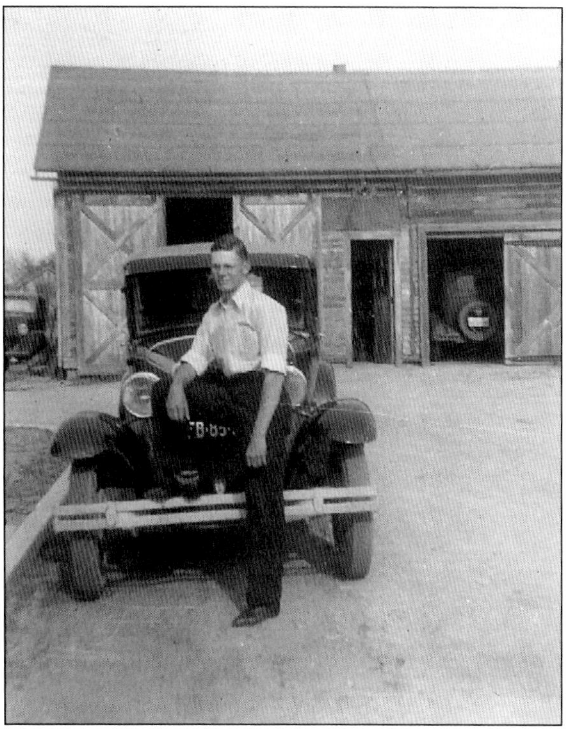

Art Fretter opened his garage in 1936 at 415 South River Road. He became known as the "jack of all trades," repairing all types of farm machinery, automobiles, and Swan Valley school buses until he retired in 1973. His shop was neatly lined with tools and parts only he would know where or what they were for. His nephew, Don Frederick, poses in front of Art's Garage in the late 1930s.

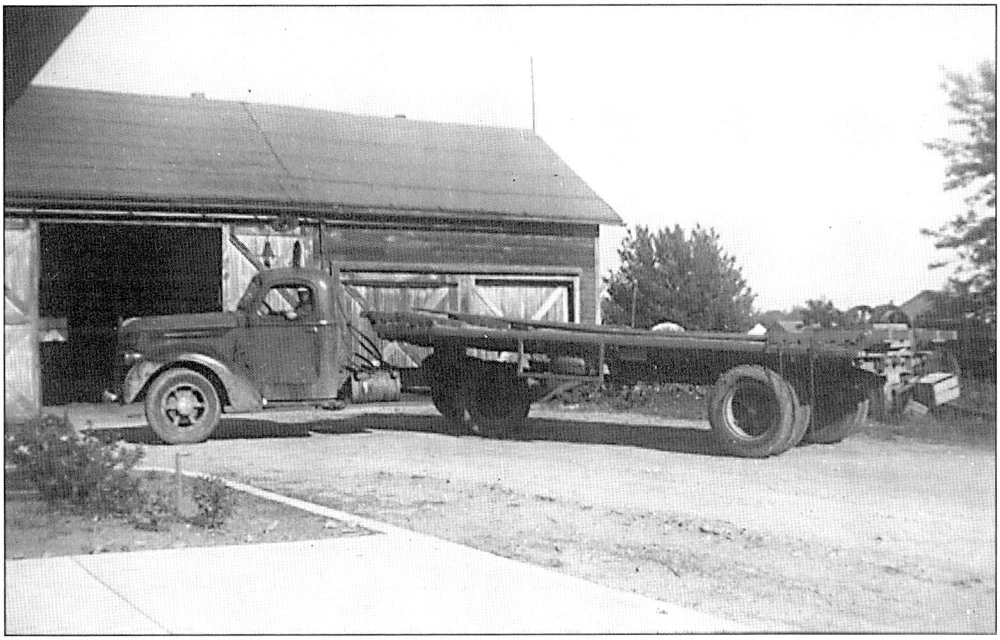

In 1915 the Miller City Tile Company of Findley, Ohio purchased the Sperry Brothers tile business in Section 36 on South River Road. The Sperry Brothers had originally manufactured clay bricks from 1895 until about 1906, when they switched to manufacturing tile. Such tile, installed by hand, was used for draining fields by area farmers. The Miller City Tile Company operated until 1941, when a fire destroyed the buildings. One of their trucks is shown in the above photo at Art's Garage. The photo below shows a truck driver and his load of clay tiles.

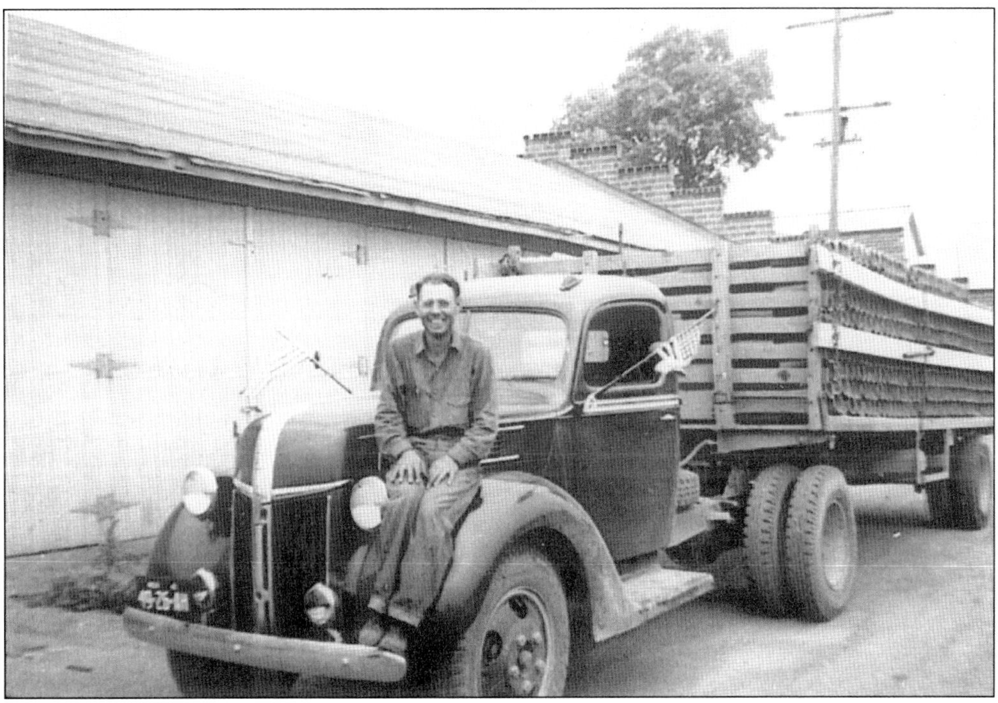

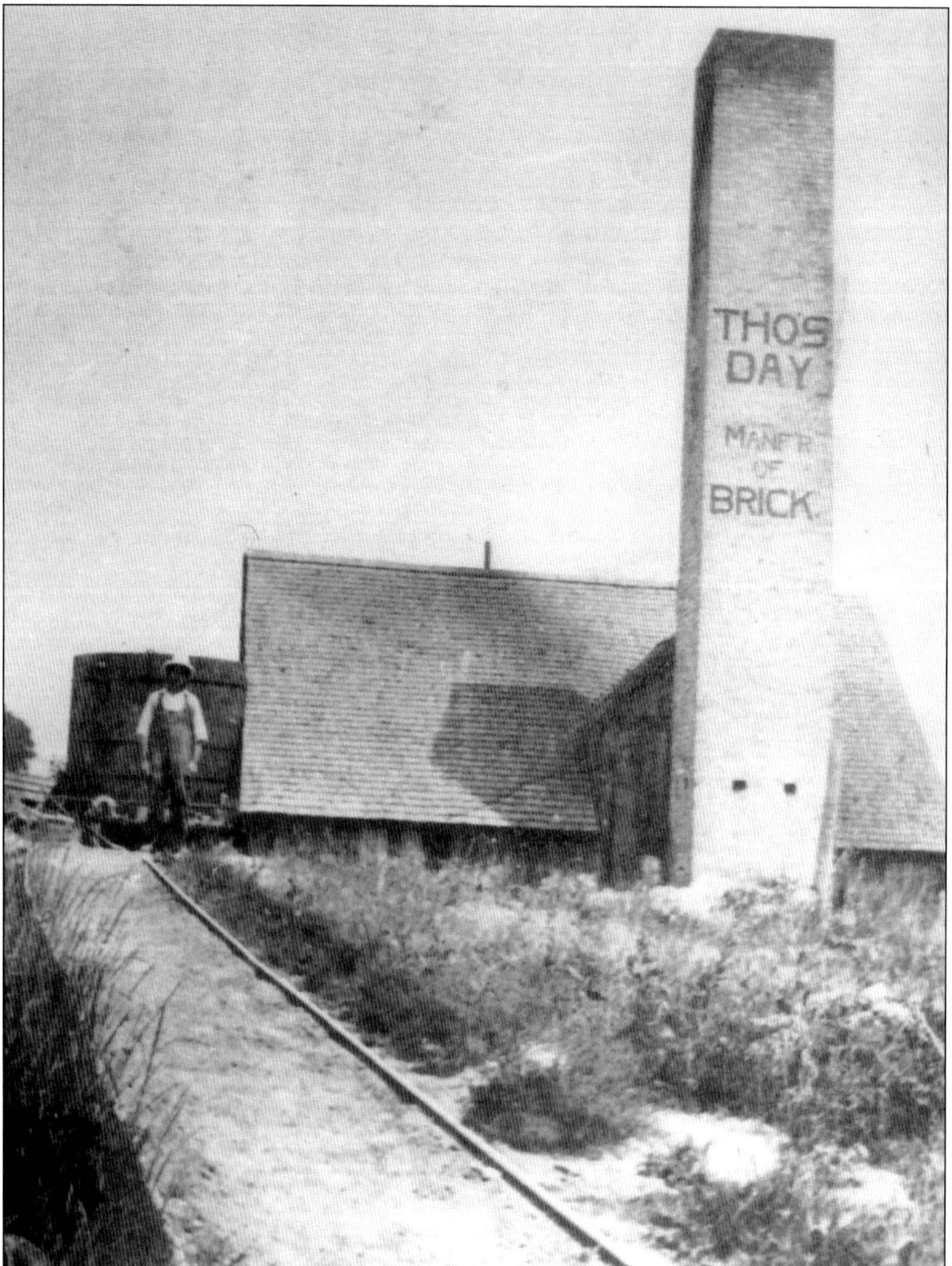

The manufacturing of clay bricks, starting in 1872, was an early Thomas and James Township industry. The Thomas Day brick plant, which was one of those industries, housed their clay pit on South River Road. Sections 14 and 36 in the township had the required type of clay needed for this industry. Horse-drawn dredges were used to dig the clay which was manufactured into bricks. They were sold for commercial use and shipped on river barges or transported by train through the Paines Junction Station to Saginaw.

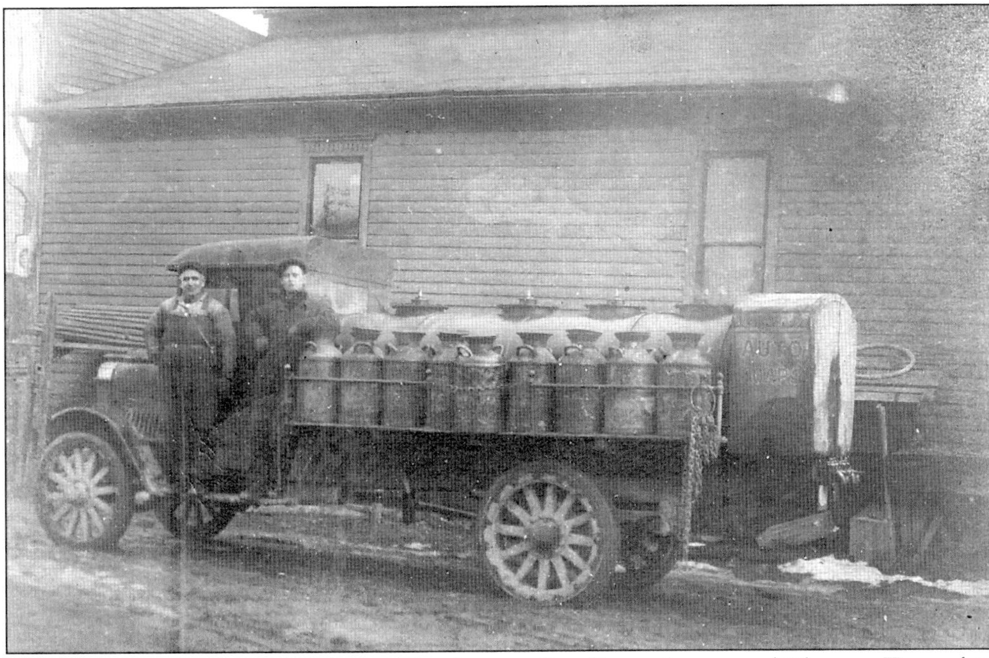

The Ditmar & Ruths Oil Delivery Truck was a familiar sight around Thomas Township as seen in this late 1930s photo. Fuel oil used for cooking and heating was delivered to businesses and residential homes in containers shaped similar to milk cans.

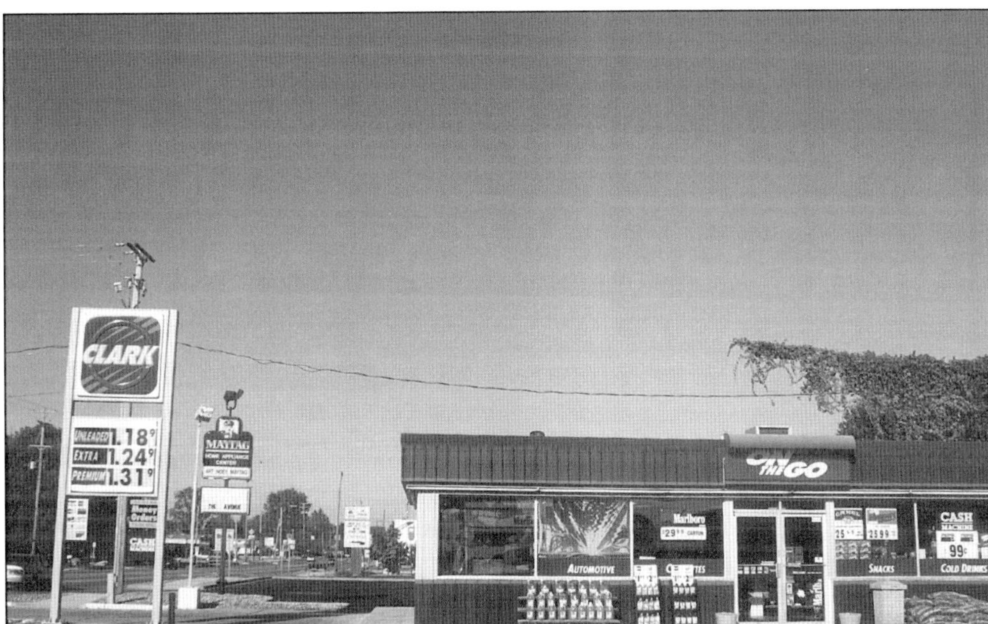

Clark Gas Station occupies the site next to the former Shields' Hotel. Located a short distance west of the Gratiot Road bridge, it is one of 800 stores owned by the Clark Oil Marketing Company. Denny and Bernie run the business which has both self-serve gas pumps and a small party store. It is a busy spot serving many customers daily.

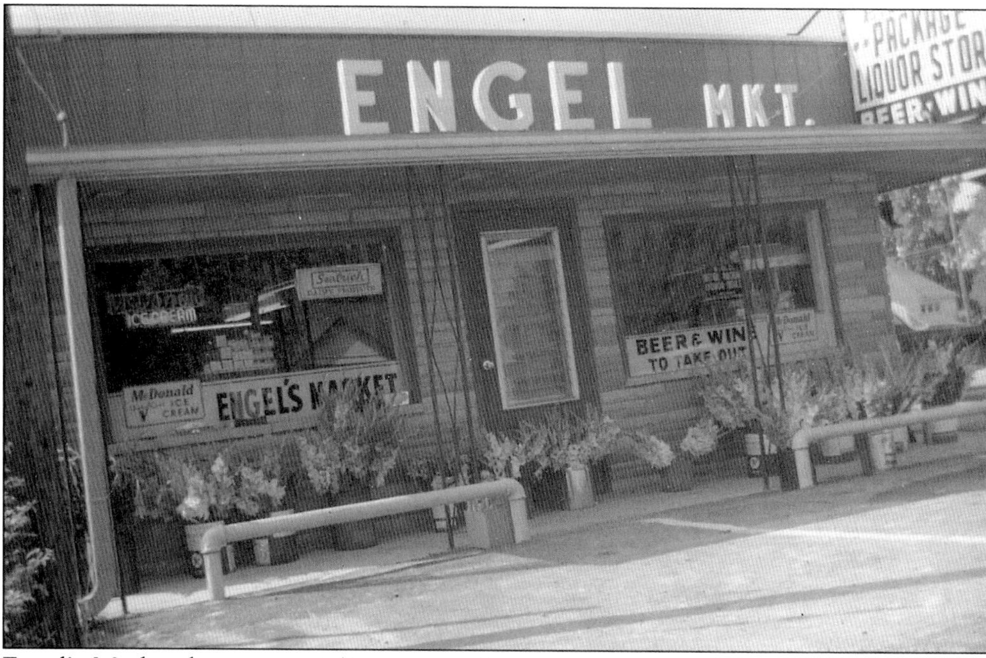

Engel's Market began in 1952 in a small building at 7365 Gratiot Road and then eventually expanded. The above photo, taken in the late 1960s, shows the gladiolus raised on the Roberts' farm for sale. The Engel family, and then Wayne Engel, operated the neighborhood market for years, selling a complete line of groceries and liquor while giving friendly, personal service to its many customers. It is now occupied by Panorama Video.

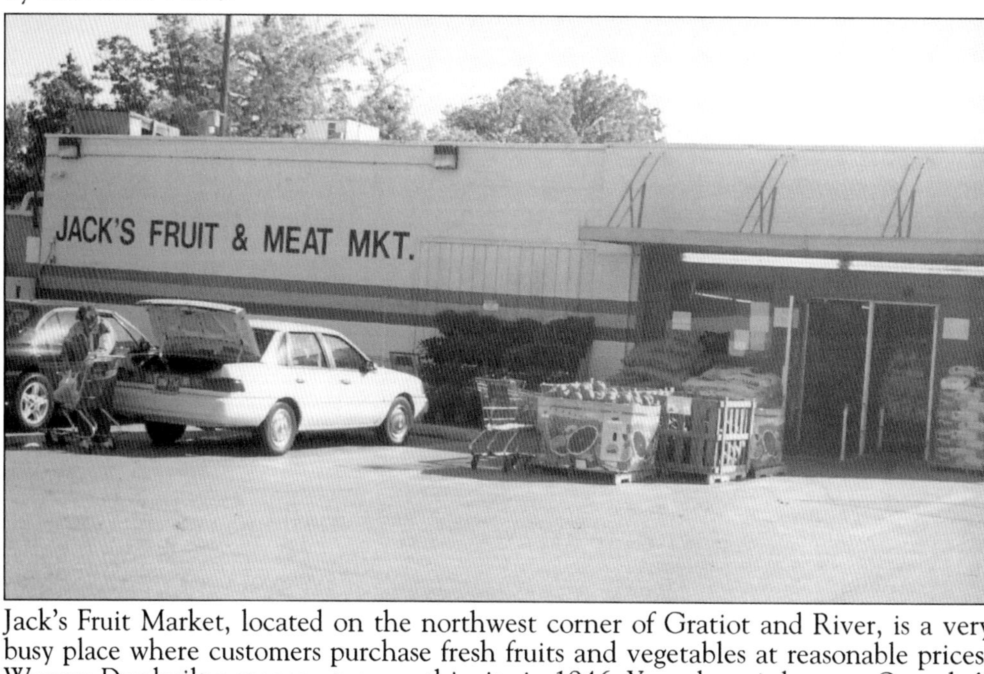

Jack's Fruit Market, located on the northwest corner of Gratiot and River, is a very busy place where customers purchase fresh fruits and vegetables at reasonable prices. Wyman Day built a grocery store on this site in 1946. Years later it became Ottersky's Variety Store, then Uncle Bob's Restaurant, and now Jack's Fruit Market.

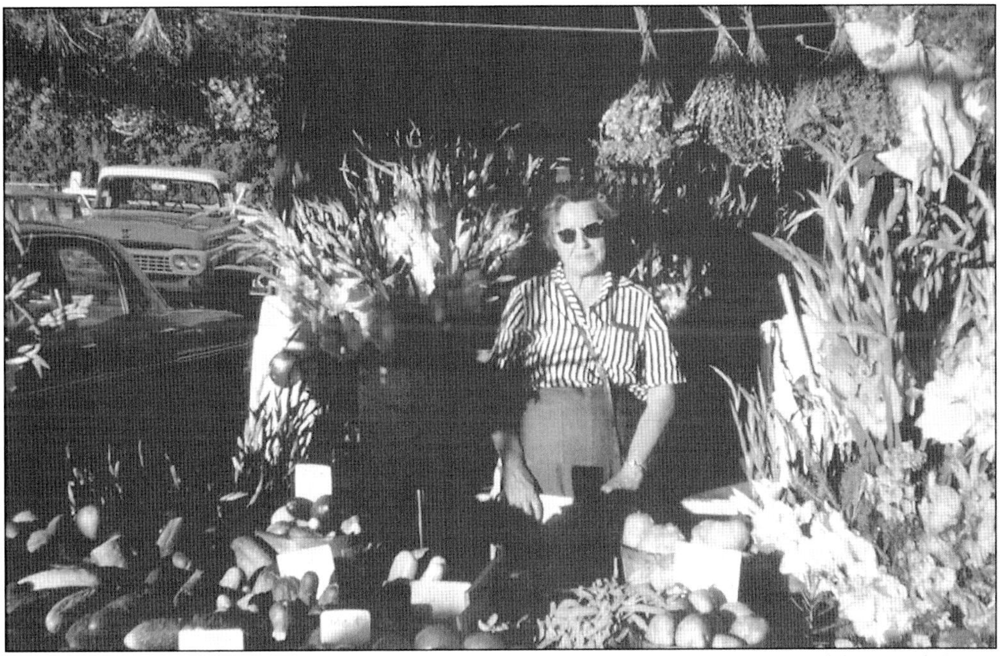

Eleanor Roberts, shown in this 1960s photo, is selling flowers, vegetables, and fruits raised on her Bacon Road farm. With her truck garden farming operation, the entire family helped to grow and harvest the produce. She sold her produce at the downtown Saginaw market and later at the Saginaw Fairgrounds Farmers' Market or at road stands on Gratiot Road.

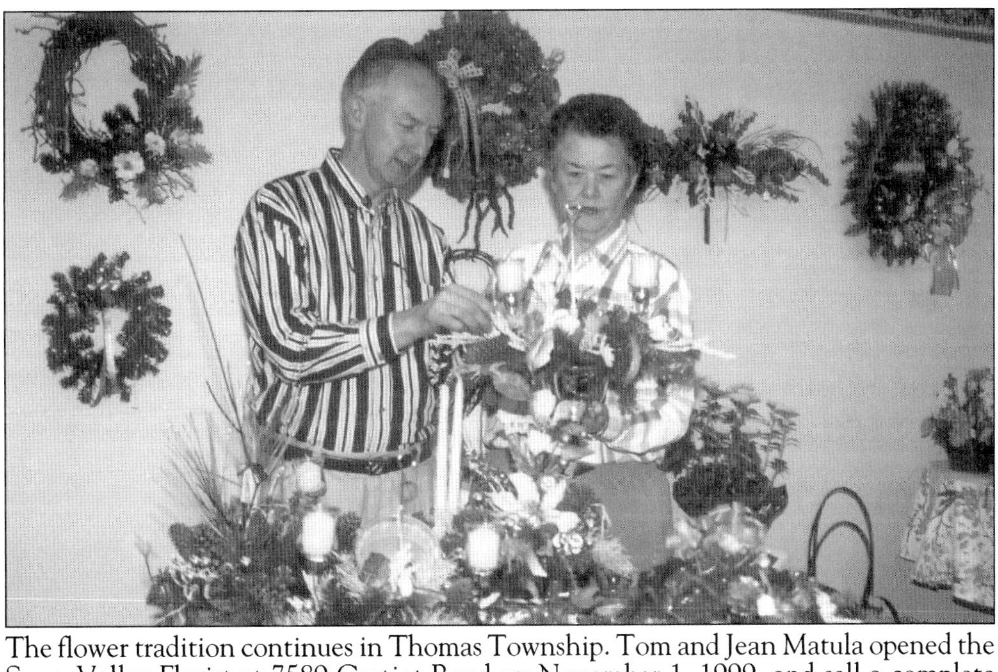

The flower tradition continues in Thomas Township. Tom and Jean Matula opened the Swan Valley Florist at 7589 Gratiot Road on November 1, 1999, and sell a complete line of flowers for home, commercial, weddings, funerals, and special occasions. They give prompt and personal service to their many customers.

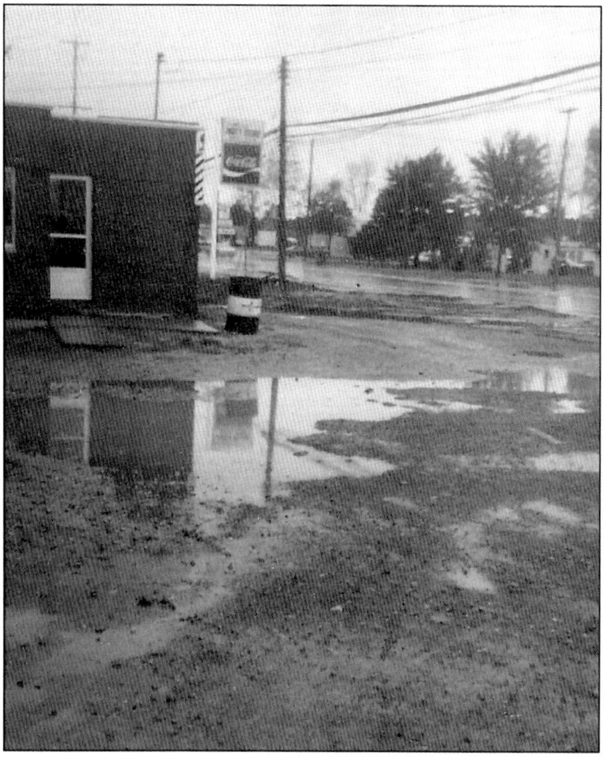

This 1960s photo, looking out on Gratiot Road at the intersection of Harcourt, shows a Gratiot Road when residential houses and large shade trees lined most of the highway. Water pockets and mud holes were a common sight along the roads that ran parallel and intersected with Gratiot Road.

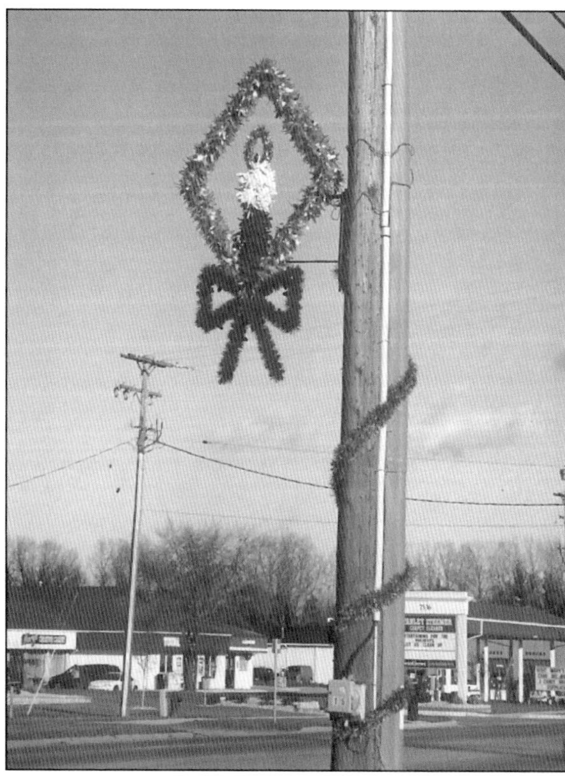

Residential housing has been replaced by businesses as shown in this December, 1999 photo of Gratiot Road. The Christmas candle decorating the power pole is a community project of the Thomas Township Business Association. Originally organized as the Shields Civic Association in 1978, businessmen coordinated their efforts to make the Shields' business district a better place to shop. The Association sponsors the annual Gratiot Road Christmas lighting and the Spring Beautification Day.

Four

Growth, Development, and Expansion

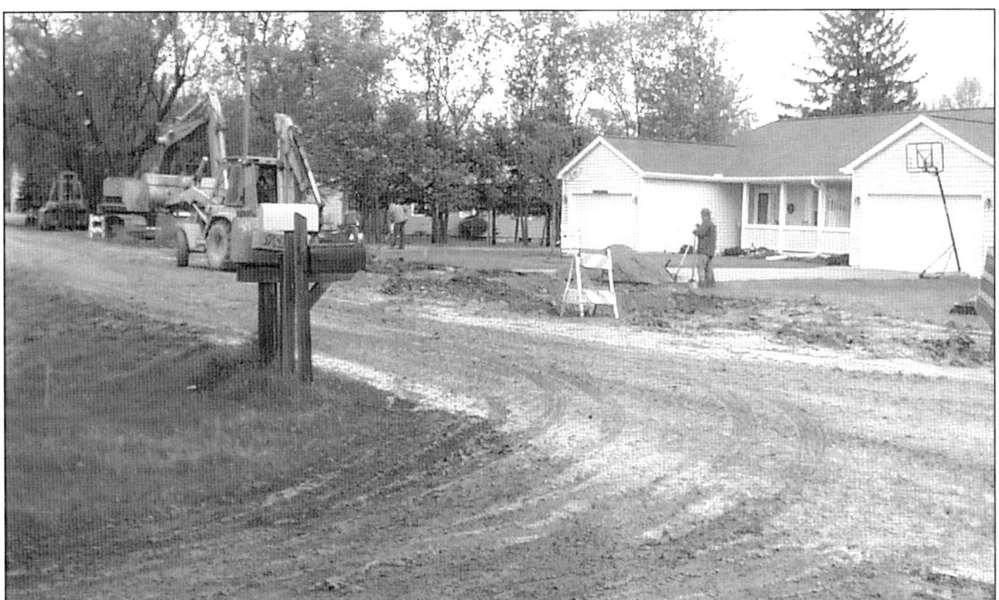

New development began in the 1950s with construction of a new four-lane Gratiot Road Bridge and the widening of Gratiot Road, followed by water and sewer construction. Despite the increase in population, the township retained its rural atmosphere until the 1960s when subdivisions were constructed, creating a gradual change in the township from a rural to a suburban community. Construction of the Companion Drain, improvement of Bacon Road, and the development of Pondview Estates are shown in this photo.

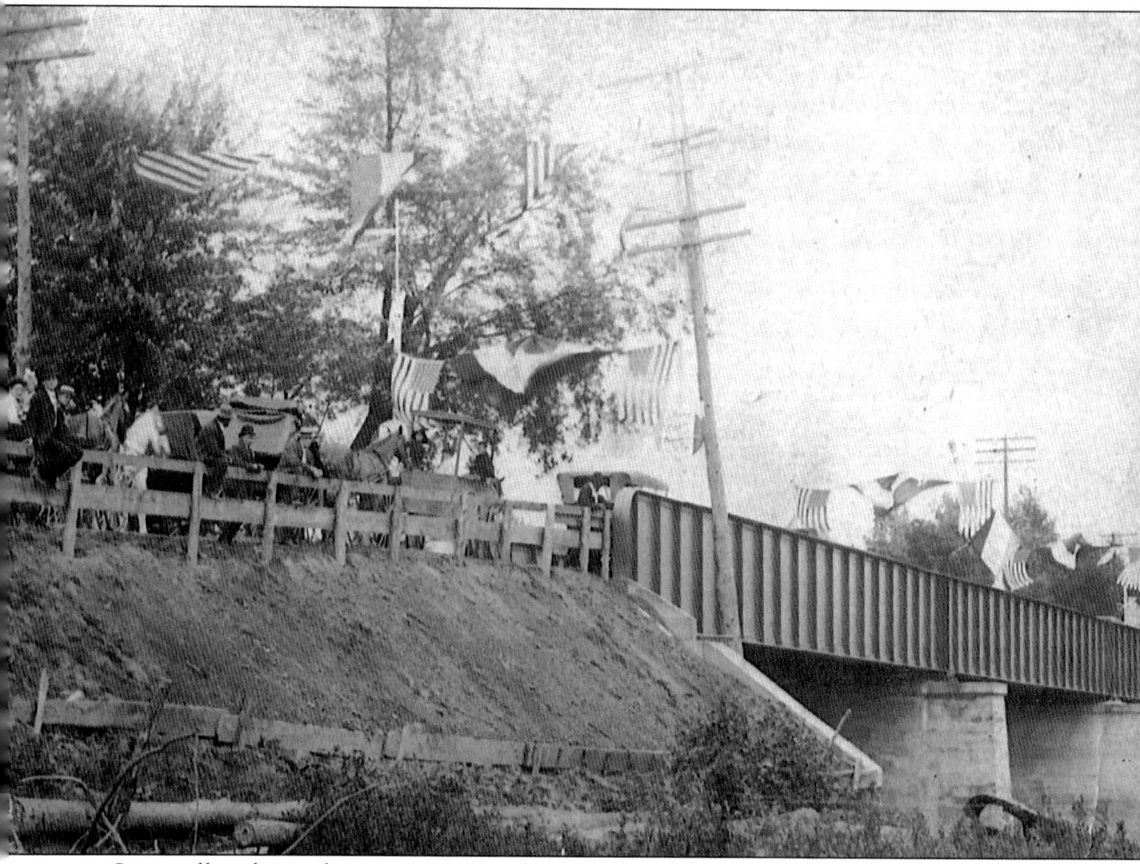

Originally, the only way to cross the Tittabawassee River was by Wiltse's Ferry at Bryant's Trip or by Kapitan's Ferry near the present Tittabawassee Road Bridge. The Tittabawassee Boom Company helped to construct the first State Road Bridge (now known as Gratiot Road) in 1870. This bridge became the gateway to West Side Saginaw. The planked Gratiot Road extended 30 miles into six different towns. The Paines Company built a new toll bridge in 1875. Rates were a penny for foot traffic, a dime for a horse and rider, and twelve cents for a wagon to cross. In 1904, the deteriorating old bridge would frequently collapse into the river. Tolls were abolished in 1906. Saginaw businessmen raised funds for the construction of a new bridge in 1908. The above photo shows the bridge dedication which was sponsored by the West Side Business Association on August 4, 1909. Farm families came for miles around in wagons decorated with flags, banners, and lanterns. There were races, contests, and prizes all sponsored by West Side businessmen. A new era of communication was opened.

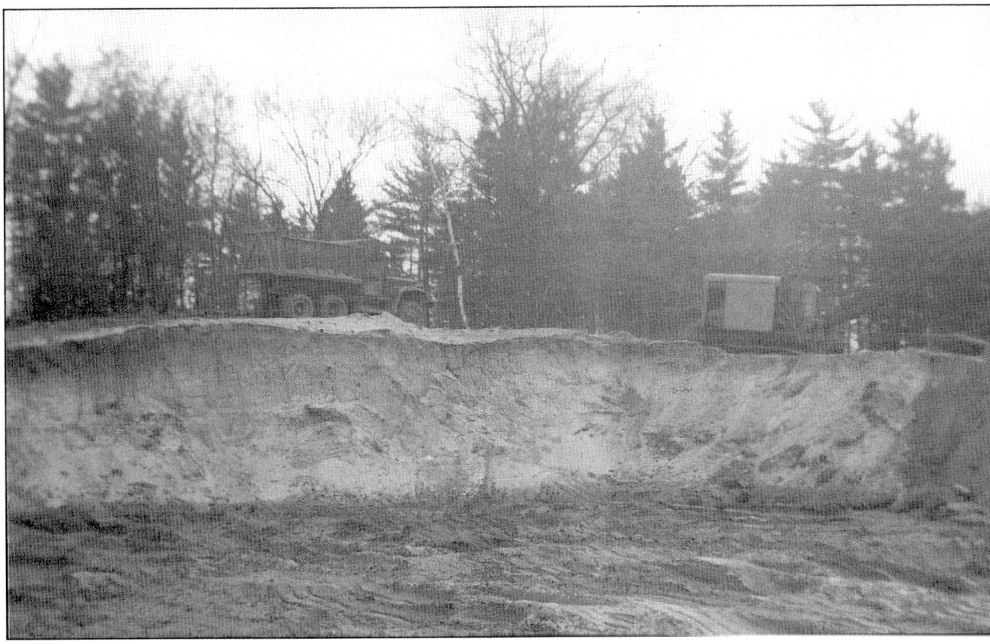

The narrow Gratiot Road Bridge was becoming congested with the increasing daily traffic. A new Gratiot Road Bridge was begun in 1952 and completed two years later at a cost of $1.5 million. Sand used in construction for this bridge was removed from large sand hills on the nearby Borm and Ederer farms. These 1952 photos, taken on the Ederer farm, depict the large remaining pit and the grader leveling off the remaining sand.

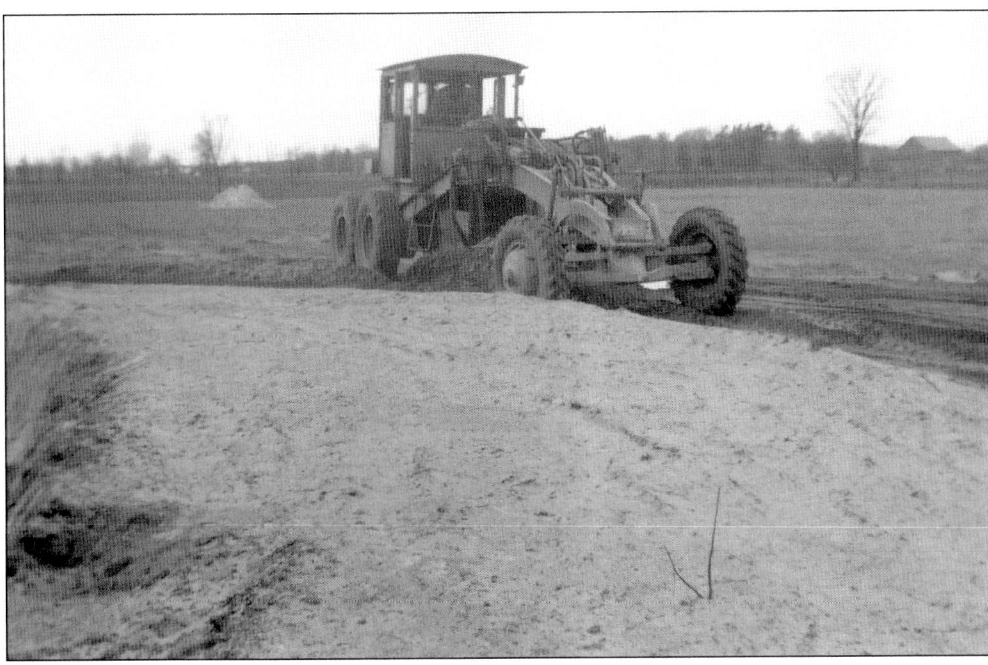

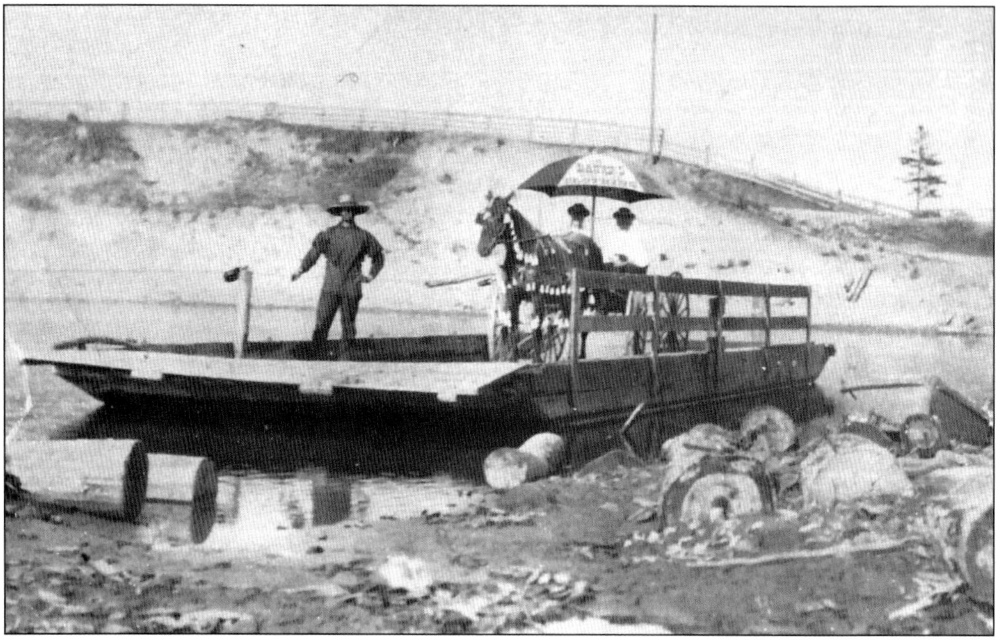

A cable ferry was often used for crossing a river until a bridge was constructed. Martin Kapitan, seen here in the 1880s, pulls on the cable attached to each side of the riverbank to bring the barge and its passengers, including their horse and buggy, to the opposite side of the river. This ferry, near the present-day Tittabawassee Road Bridge, was abandoned about 1909. Wiltse's Ferry also operated at Bryant's Trip.

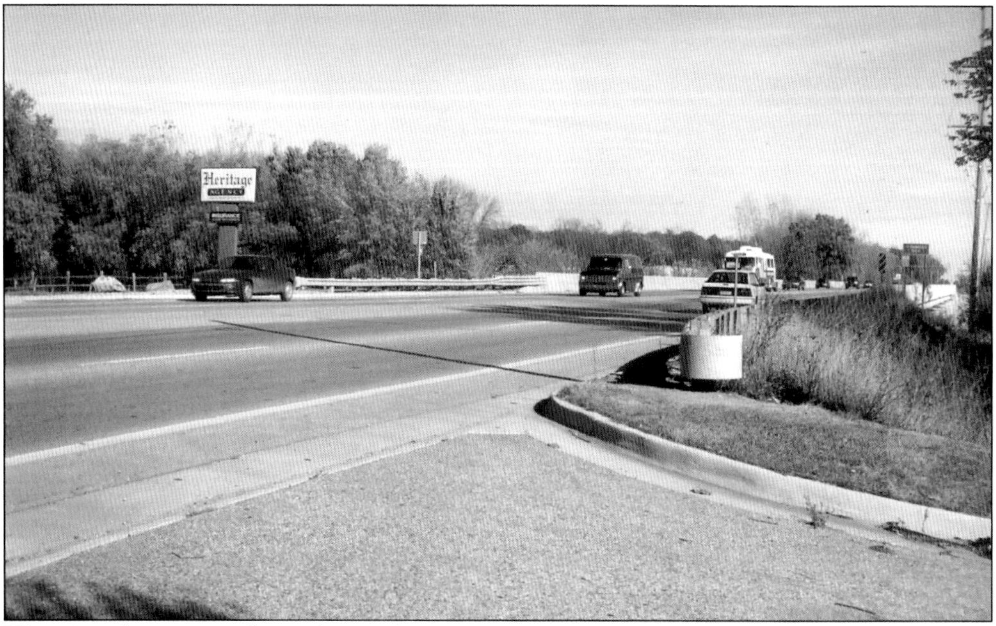

This October, 1999 photo shows the present Gratiot Road Bridge. This style of bridge construction has been used in other bridges crossing the Tittabawassee River, such as the State Road Bridge which was originally built in 1912 and rebuilt several years later. The Gratiot Road Bridge continues to be the main thoroughfare into Saginaw.

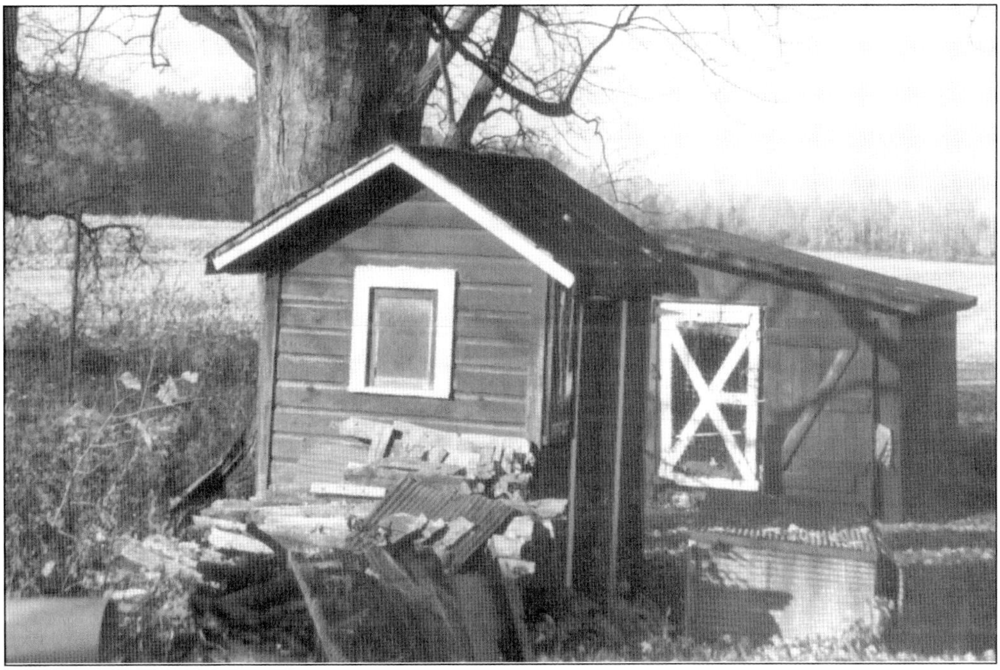

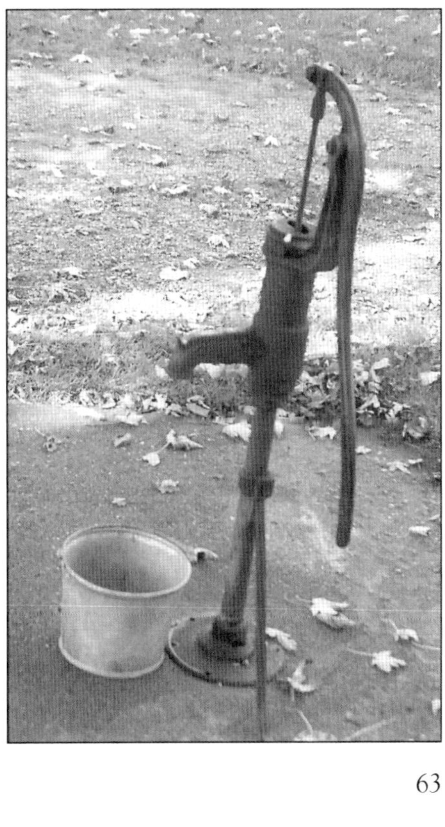

Every township homestead, farm, school, and business built in the 1800s until the 1950s had both an outhouse in its back yard and a hand pump in a well by the back door. Joseph Ederer built this outhouse and dug the well on his farm in 1907. Flowered wallpaper graced the outhouse walls and lace curtains decorated its window during its glory days. Although it stands idle now, the outhouse is a reminder of those nostalgic days when people lived without indoor plumbing and water. The still-working hand pump is a reminder of how far our modern-day conveniences have progressed.

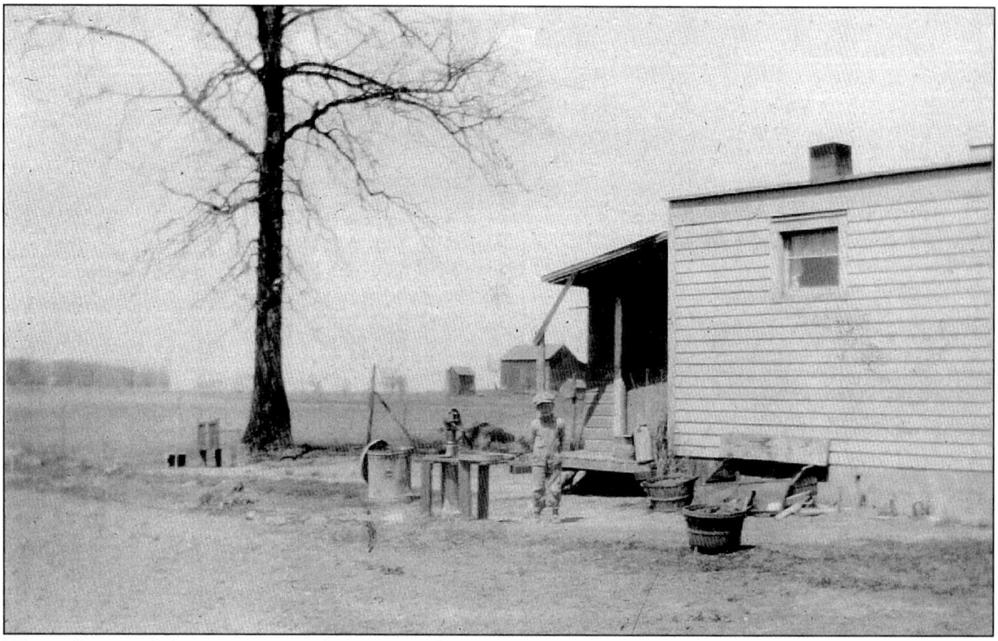

This photo of the two-room homestead on Bacon Road was taken in the spring of 1930. Ralph Roberts is the child near the hand pump. There is a root cellar for storing food under the side of the house. A neighbor's shed and outhouse are in the background. The old oak tree, now much bigger, still stands today.

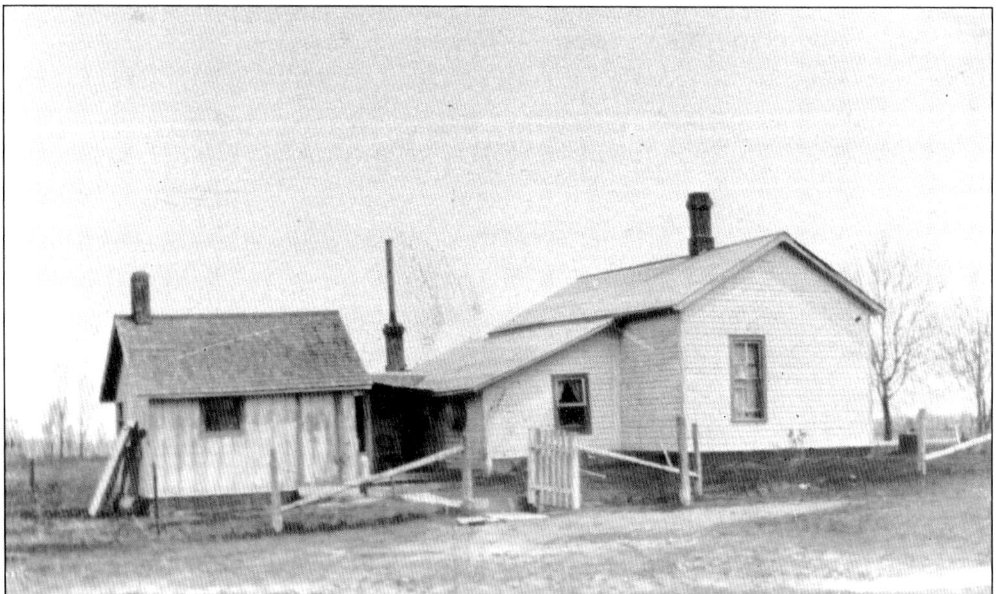

In this 1895 photo of the rear of the Dinning house with its attached lean-to kitchen at 830 South Graham, the hand pump can be seen on the right. The outhouse and hand pump were essential items for houses built until the 1950s. Electricity was not available until the 1930s for most homesteads. The outhouse and pump were located some distance from each other in the back yard.

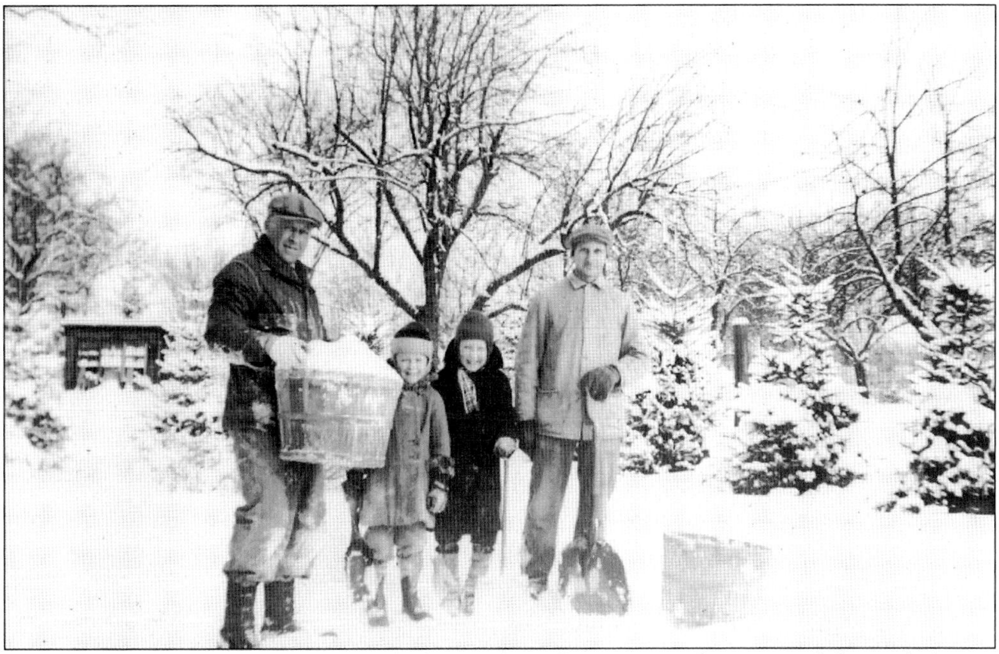

Because well water was often brackish or salty, almost every homestead depended on a cistern to store rain water for washing dishes and clothes and bathing. The cistern was generally in the basement or an underground storage tank. The water would be hand pumped into the kitchen sink. Walter, Gerald, Harold, and Ed Kluck are shoveling new-fallen snow into their cistern to replenish a low water-level in this 1936 photo.

Frieda Kluck is hanging up the family's laundry in this 1918 photo. Monday was usually designated as washday for most families. Doing the laundry was an all-day event; clothes were washed and wrung by hand,then hung outside to dry. With the 1930s and coming of electricity to most rural homes, washday became easier as clothes could now be washed with electric Maytag wringer washers. However, the housewife still depended on good weather to dry the clothes outdoors before she began her weekly laundry.

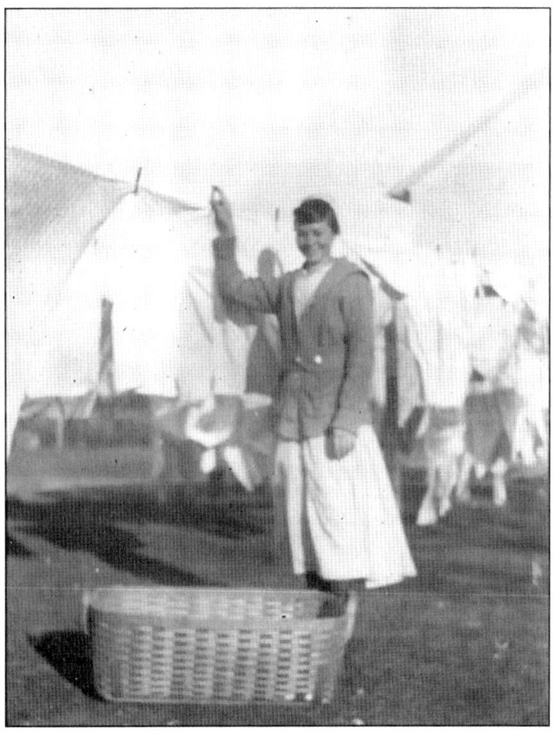

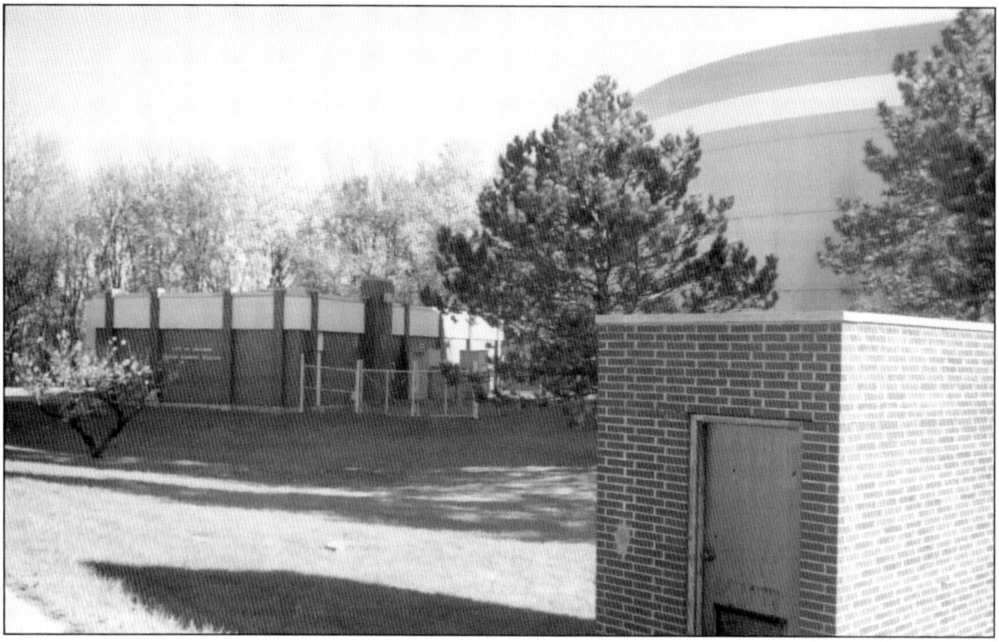

By 1954 it was evident that the township needed a reliable water system since residents had to dig their own wells, and good drinking water was often difficult to find. The Francis Engineering Company prepared the plans, bids were taken, and revenue bonds were raised. Construction of the new water system was started in 1958. Eight years later, the township connected to the Saginaw City water system. The above photo shows the City of Saginaw pumping station and the large reservoir near the Tittabawassee River's south side. Water pumping stations were built on Frost and Graham Roads.

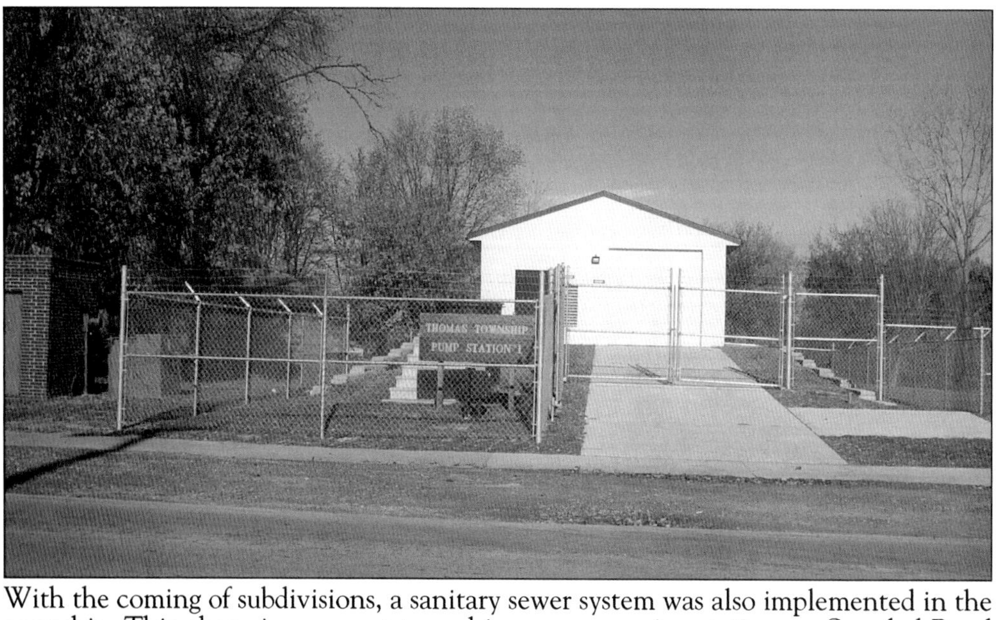

With the coming of subdivisions, a sanitary sewer system was also implemented in the township. This photo is a current township sewer pumping station on Stroebel Road near the River Road intersection.

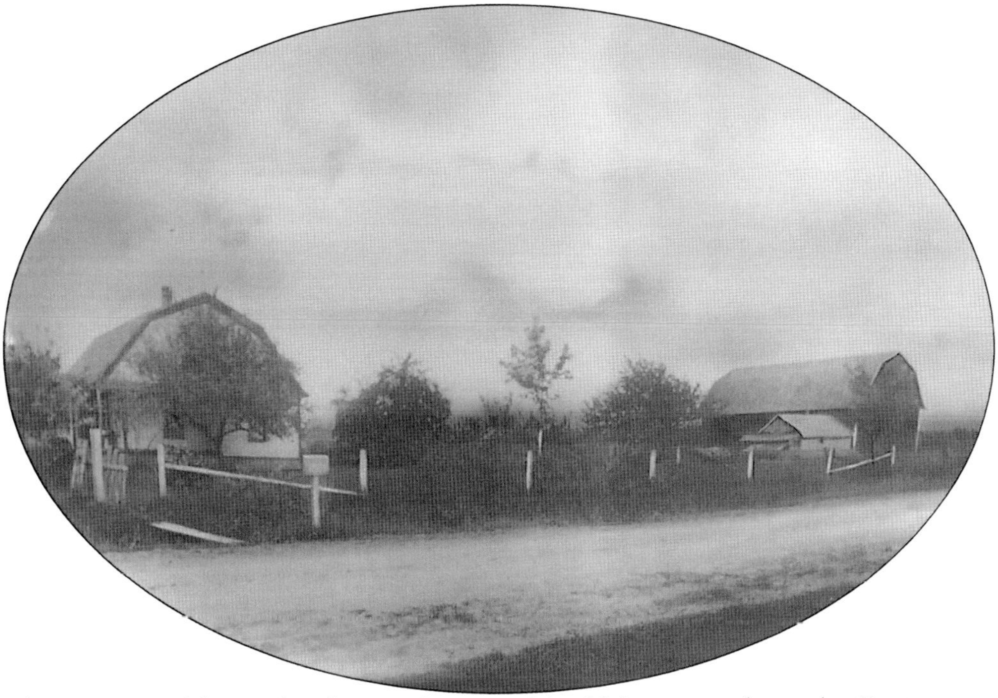

This painting of the Fischer farm at the turn of the 20th century shows the Gratiot two-lane dirt road. Residents were responsible for maintaining sections of their road. A horse-drawn post office buggy delivered the mail. Yards and fields were fenced in to keep cattle from straying into the roadway. The Chippewa Indians called Gratiot Road "Rainbow Trail" since it stretched across the entire state from Lake Michigan to Lake Huron.

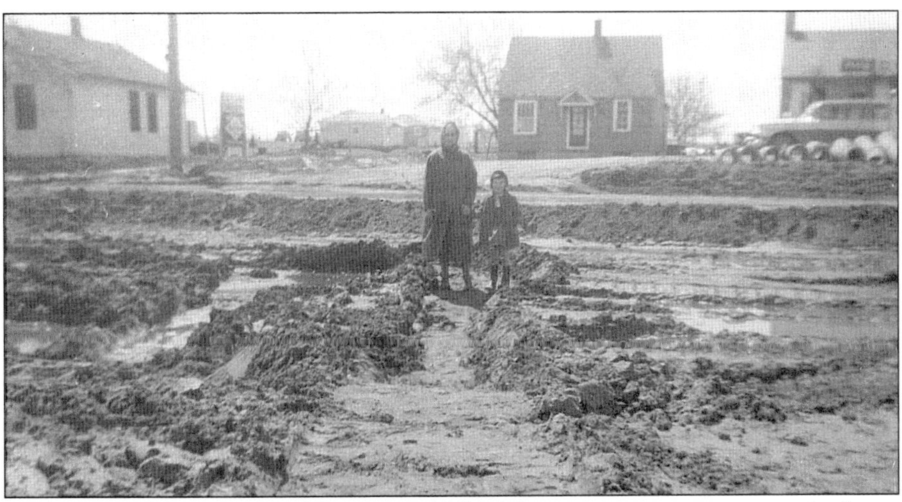

The widening of Gratiot Road began in 1954. The immense project required surveys, the purchase of right-of-ways, the cutting down of a number of large trees, digging out the old planked road, installation of new drainage and storm sewers, and months of construction. Neva Valentine and her daughter are shown in this 1959 photo when Gratiot Road was being expanded into a four-lane highway. The new highway was completed in 1959 and opened up faster communication with outlying towns.

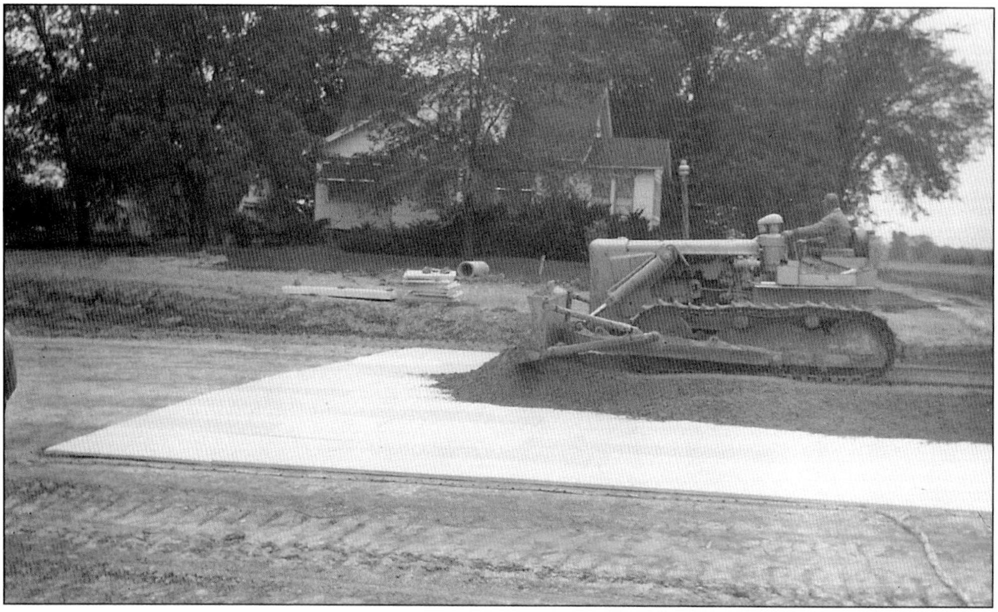

North Graham Road was paved with a new experimental styrofoam. In the above 1970s photo, a bulldozer is pushing a sand subbase over the styrofoam. In the bottom photo, Dick Ward is holding a piece of the styrofoam and a "thermocouple," which was placed in the sub grade. This experiment was a test for a low cost solution to keep paved rural roads from breaking up during the spring thaw.

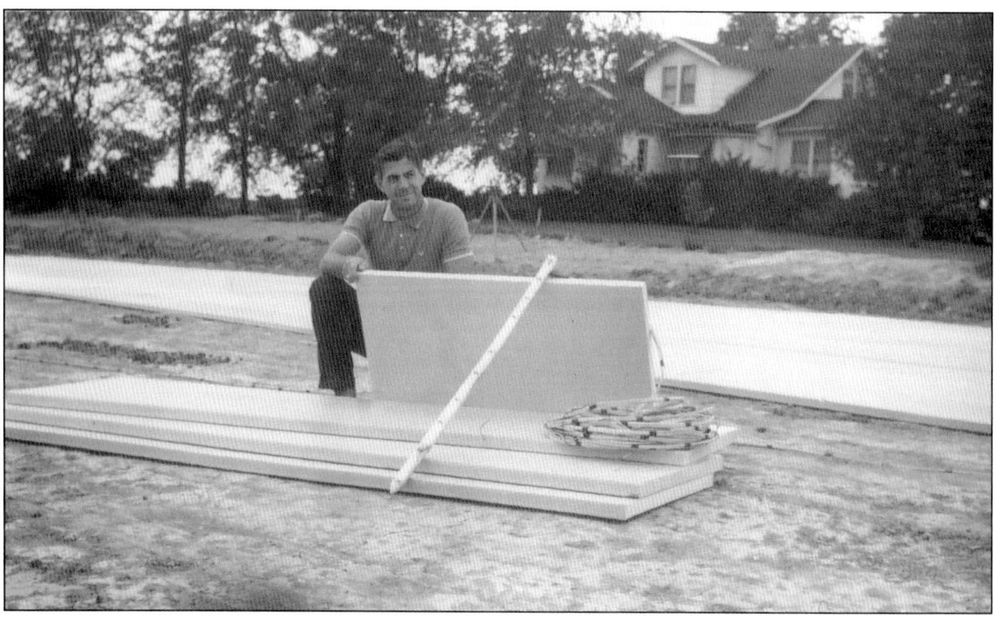

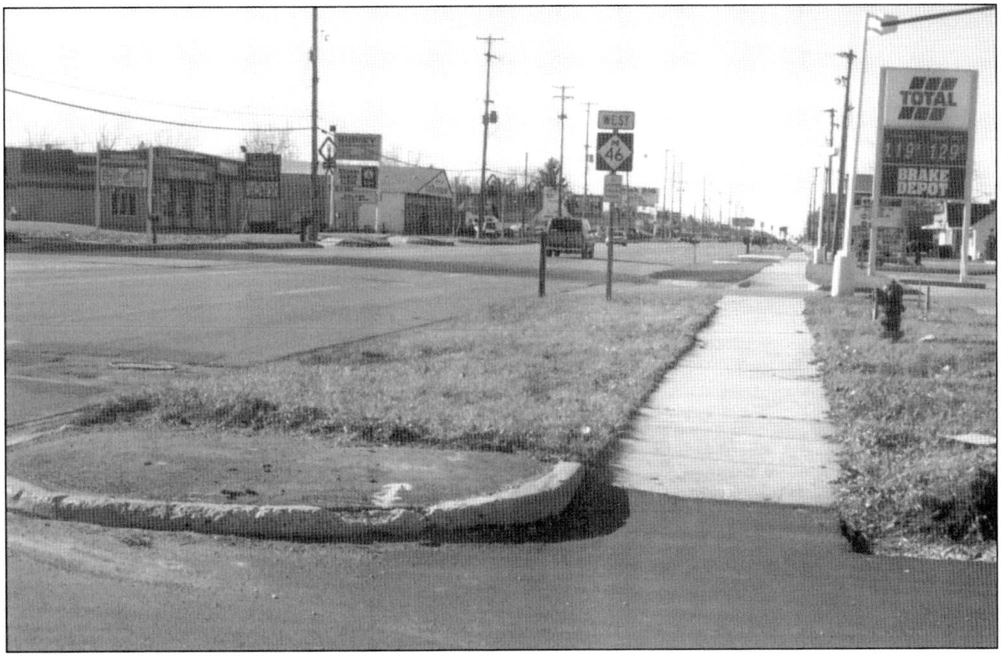

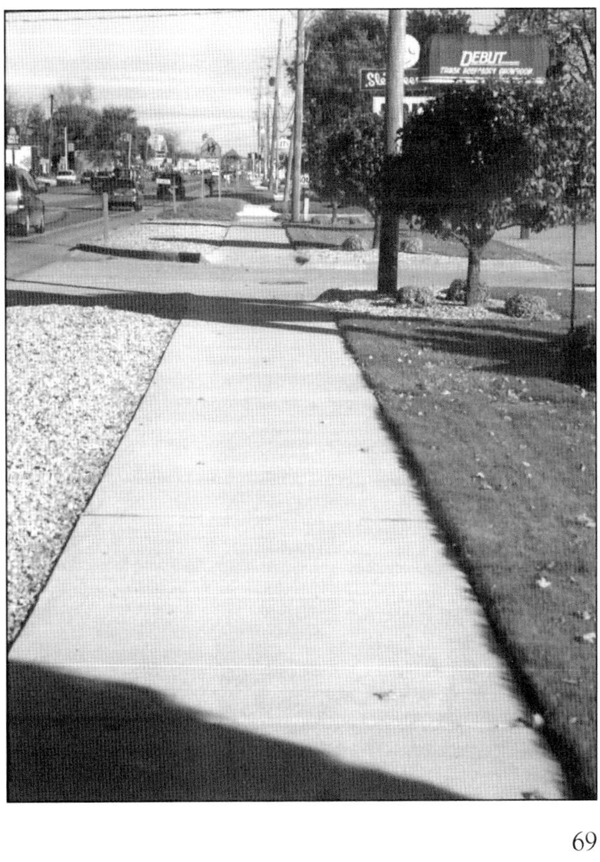

Interest in constructing sidewalks in Thomas Township began in 1979, although funding only became available in 1991. Since then over 12 miles of sidewalks have been built in the township. In these two views of sidewalks running parallel to Gratiot Road, the busy highway is evident. The sidewalks have made a tremendous improvement to businesses and residents along the Gratiot Road corridor. It is now much safer and easier for local residents to walk to their favorite establishments. The sidewalks also serve a recreational purpose, as adults and children can walk, jog, run, and ride their bicycles during lunch hours, evenings, or anytime without the interference of heavy traffic.

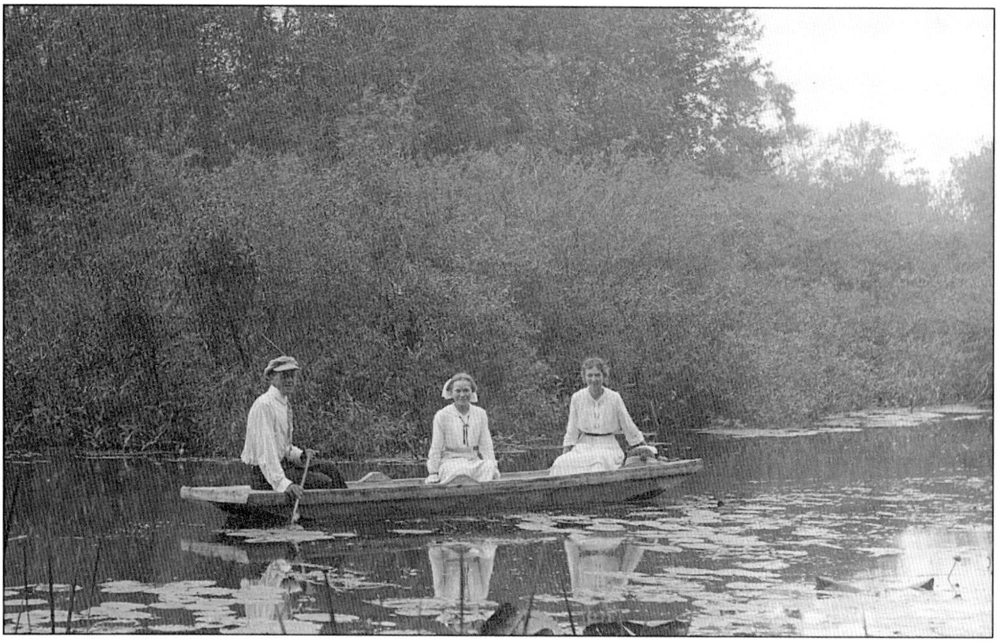

Swan Creek drains a considerable portion of Thomas Township and empties into the Shiawassee River. The creek has been beneficial to Native Americans, lumbermen, and farmers throughout the centuries. As evident in this pair of 1919 photos, boating was a pleasurable pastime on a Sunday afternoon. In the above photo, Frieda Kluck and Vera Zorn are being paddled down the creek in a canoe while the bottom photo shows Walter Kluck picking water lilies on Swan Creek on a Sunday afternoon.

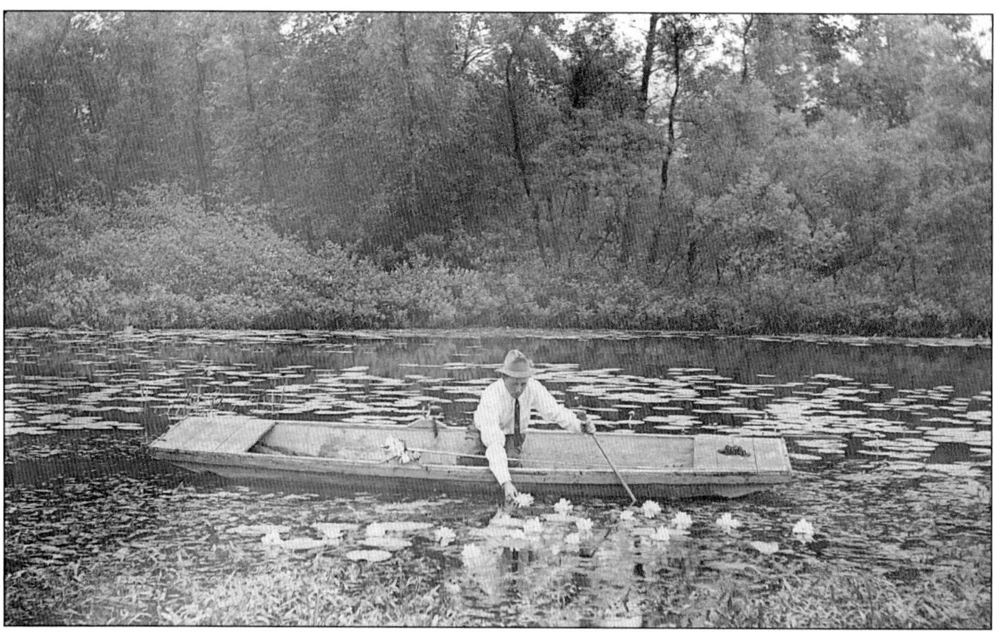

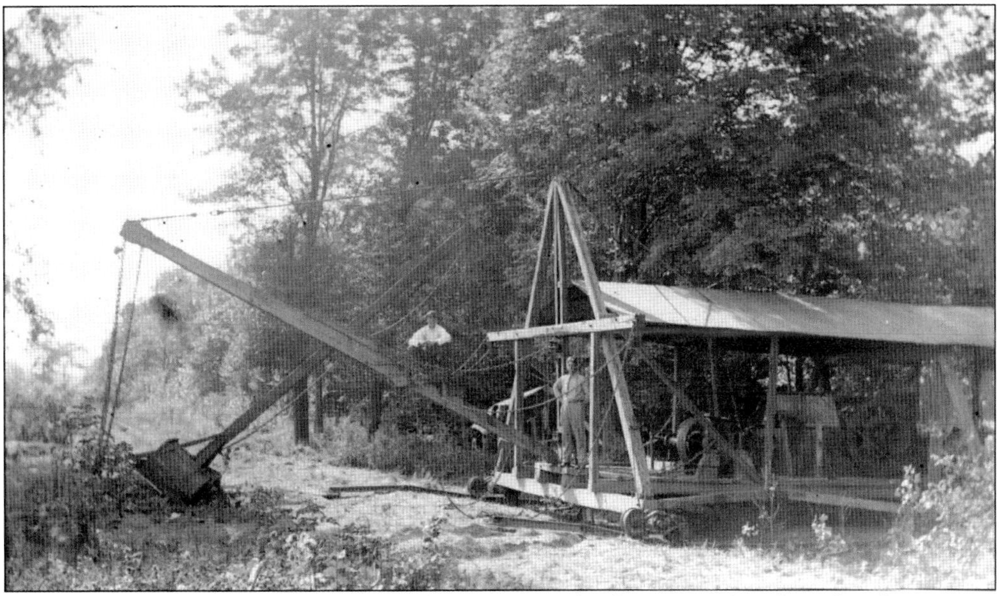

In the above photo a dredge is at work in 1919 to dredge Swan Creek and make it more passable for river traffic and drainage. This type of equipment was used to dredge many drainage ditches in the township and the clay for brick manufacturing.

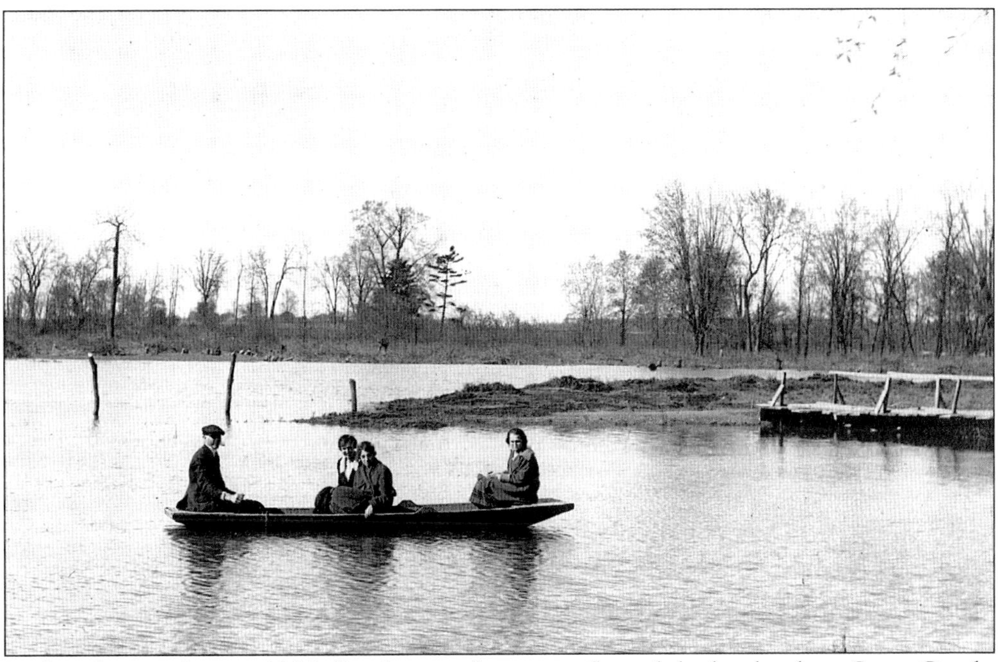

In this photo, taken in 1919, flood waters have overflowed the banks along Swan Creek. Spring floods often spilled over the banks of the Tittabawassee River and the streams which drained the countryside. The Kluck family is out inspecting the flooded areas.

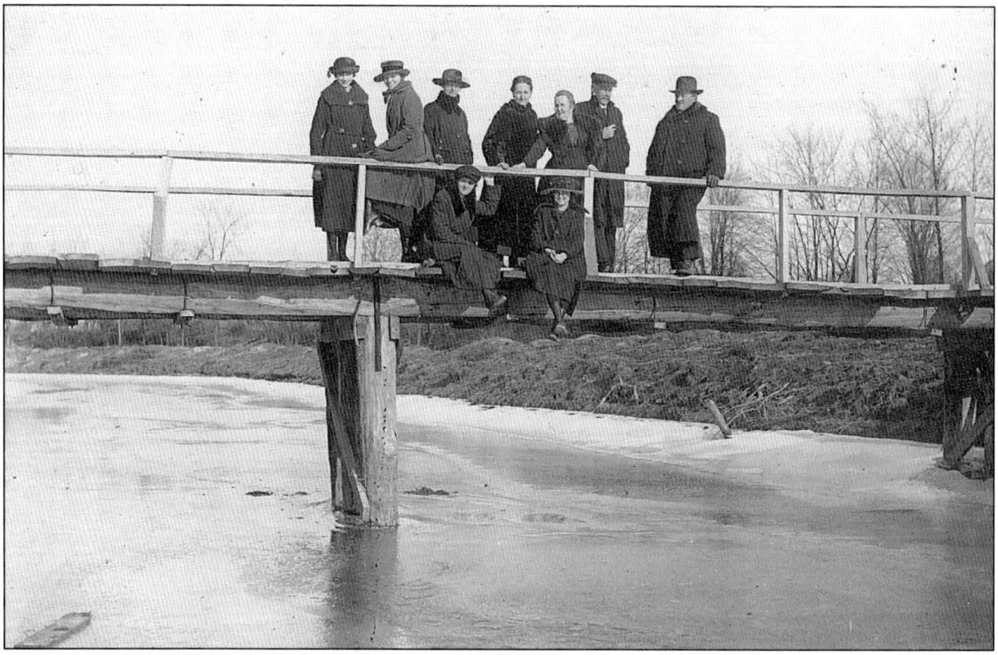

Walter and Fred Kluck built this bridge over Swan Creek so they could reach their farm land on the other side. Pictured in February, 1921, from left to right, are unidentified, Frieda Kluck, two unidentified, Albertine Kluck, Fred Kluck, Arthur Kluck, and two unidentified (sitting) crossing their private bridge. The Kluck family has maintained and used this bridge for their tractors and equipment since it was built.

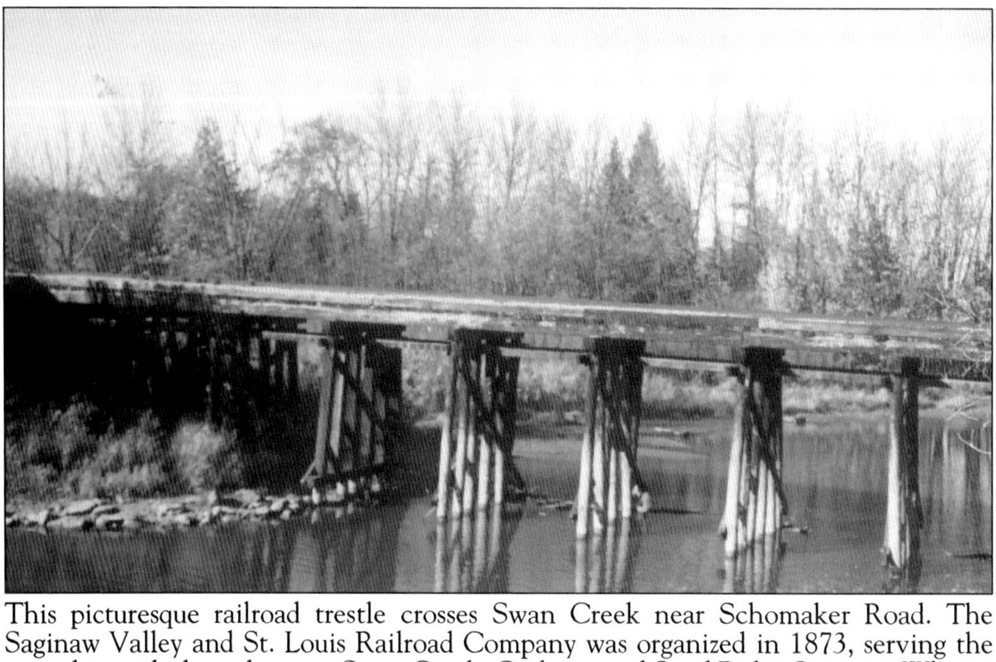

This picturesque railroad trestle crosses Swan Creek near Schomaker Road. The Saginaw Valley and St. Louis Railroad Company was organized in 1873, serving the township with three depots—Swan Creek, Graham, and Sand Ridge Stations. When a flag was displayed, the train stopped to pick up passengers or freight. In 1947 the railroad merged with the Chesapeake and Ohio which uses the tracks and trestle today.

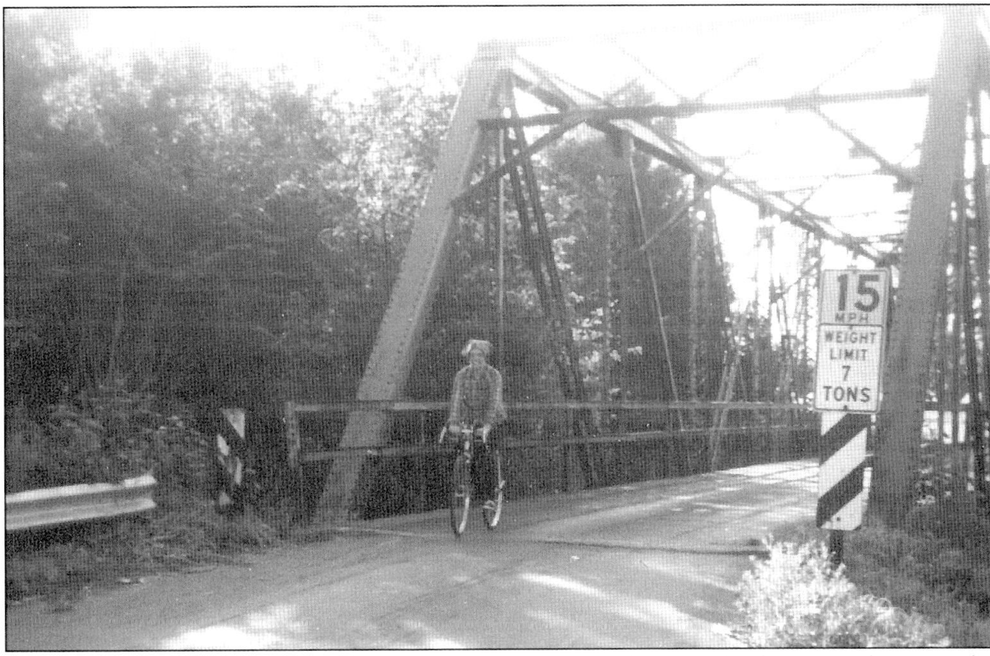

Several bridges crossed Swan Creek as it meandered through the township. In the above 1977 photo Ruth Ederer bicycles across the picturesque Geddes Road Bridge. This Warren truss bridge was built at the turn of the 20th century, and was improved through the years. Although the bridge deck is concrete, it was still a narrow horse and buggy bridge with a load limit forcing cars to take their turn in order to cross.

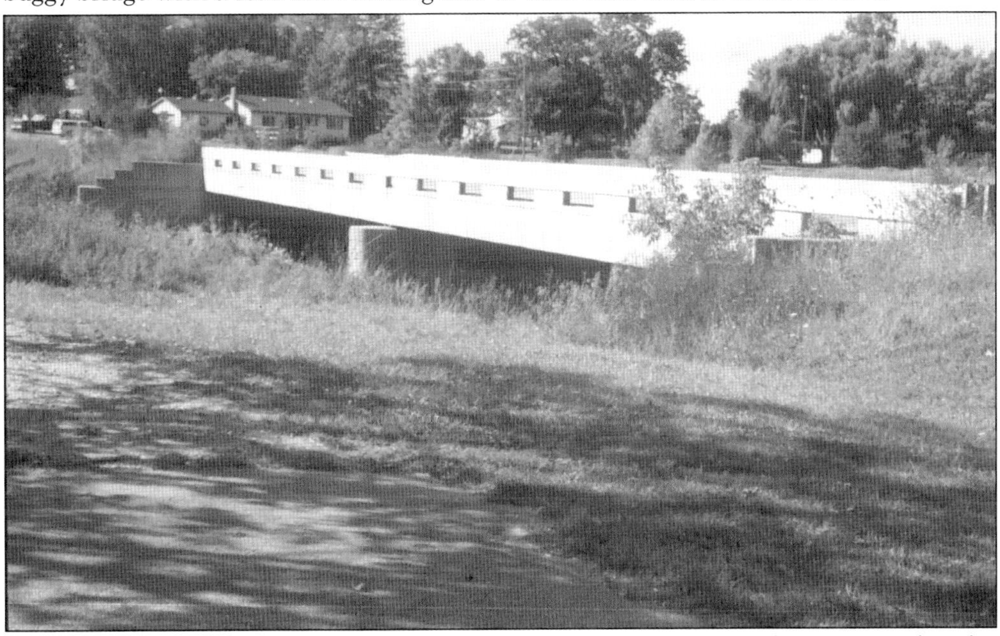

As pictured in this October 1999 photo, the new Geddes Road Bridge carries vehicular traffic faster and easier than ever before. This type of construction is representative of the many small bridges which have been built to replace the horse and buggy bridges which crossed Swan Creek on several roads.

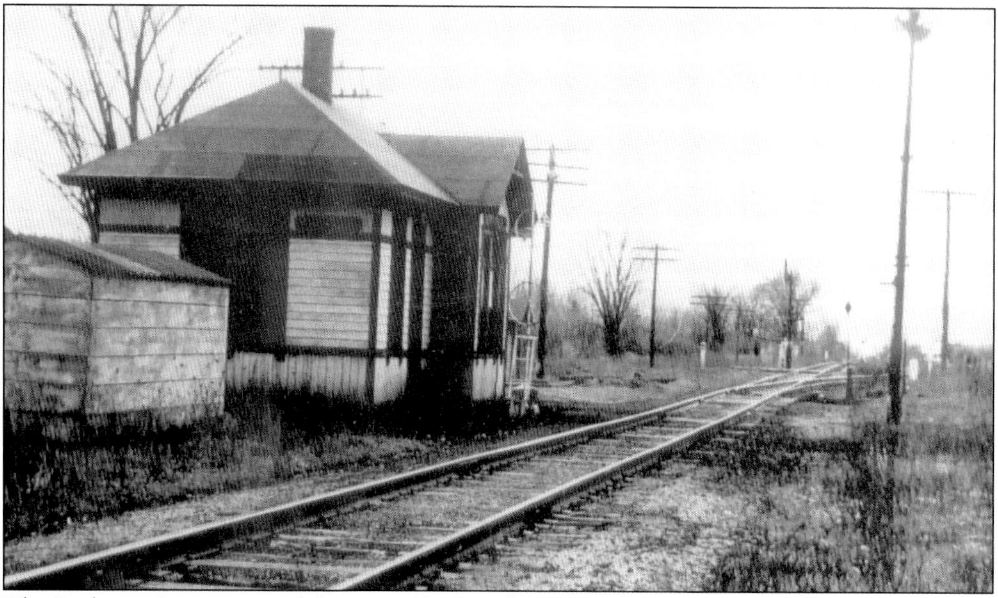

The Jackson, Lansing, and Saginaw Railroad was organized in 1867 and came through James Township's Paine's Junction Station, shown above. Thomas Township residents also used the train. Carl Frye was its station agent for many years. As many as 14 passenger trains came through the station daily, providing fast, easy transportation to and from Saginaw City. Brick and coal were also shipped out on this railroad. The Chesapeake and Ohio uses the track today, but, unfortunately, Paine's Station is gone.

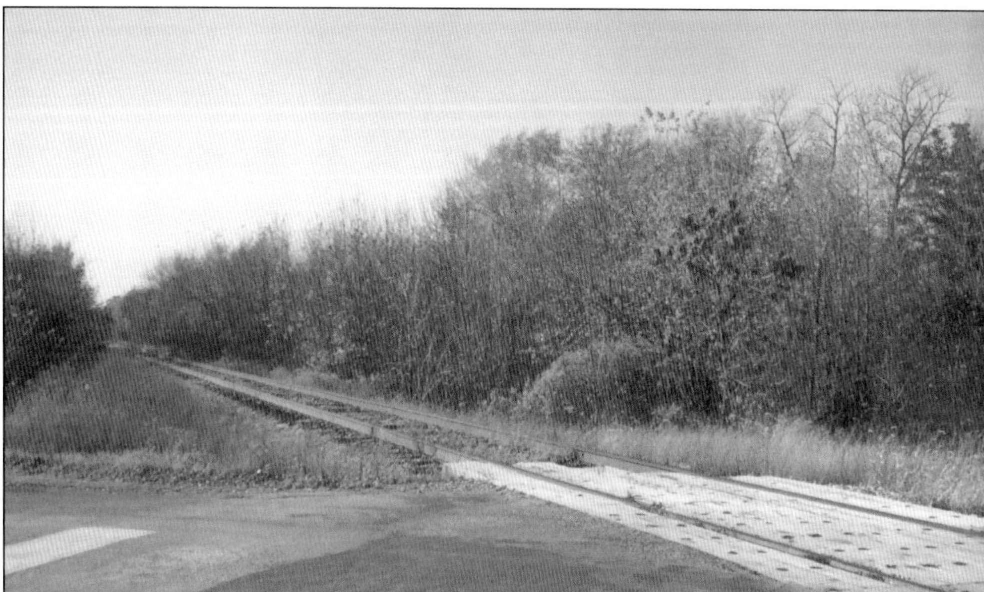

These railroad tracks run next to Schomaker Road and cross the Swan Creek trestle. Trains still pass through Thomas Township today, but they haul only freight. The picturesque tracks extend for miles through wooded and wet terrain. The train whistles are sometimes heard miles away as they announce their arrival. In days gone by, the train whistle would warn a farmer to clear his cattle off the train tracks.

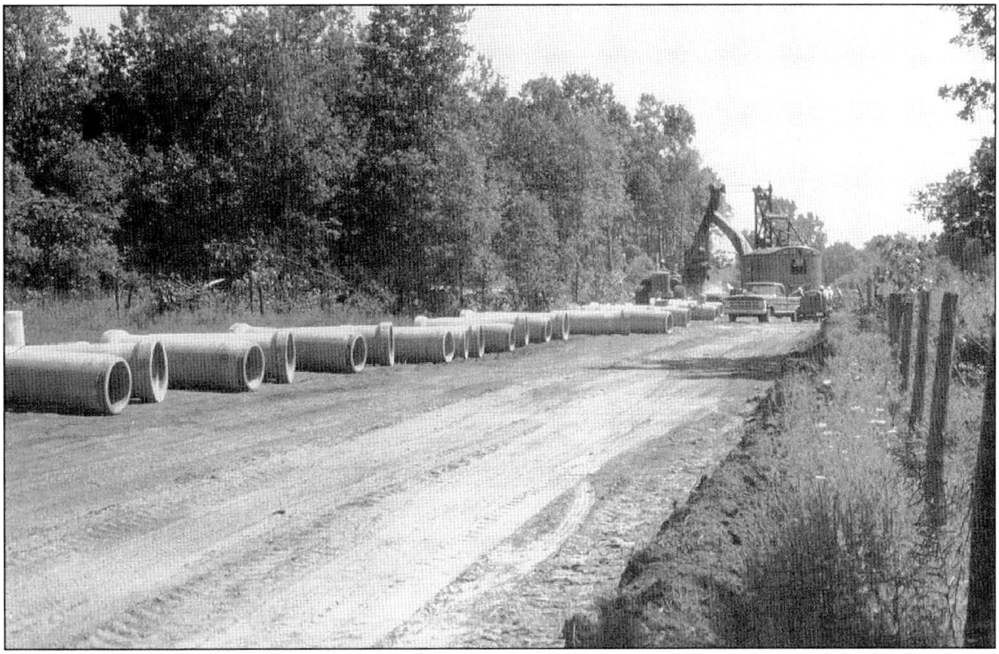

Construction of the sanitary sewer along Robert's Park is underway in this 1970 photo. The temporary road was constructed in order to haul in the 24-inch pipe needed for this section of the project. The new sanitary sewer allowed for the development of new subdivisions and apartments in Thomas Township.

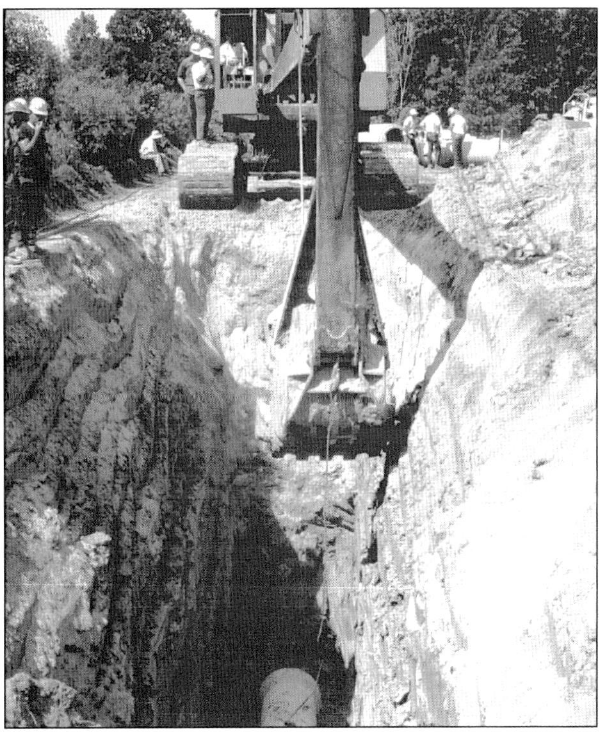

Workers install another section of 24-inch pipe in a 20-foot deep trench for the new sanitary sewer in Thomas Township. This photo is taken in what is now the location of baseball diamond #2 at Robert's Park.

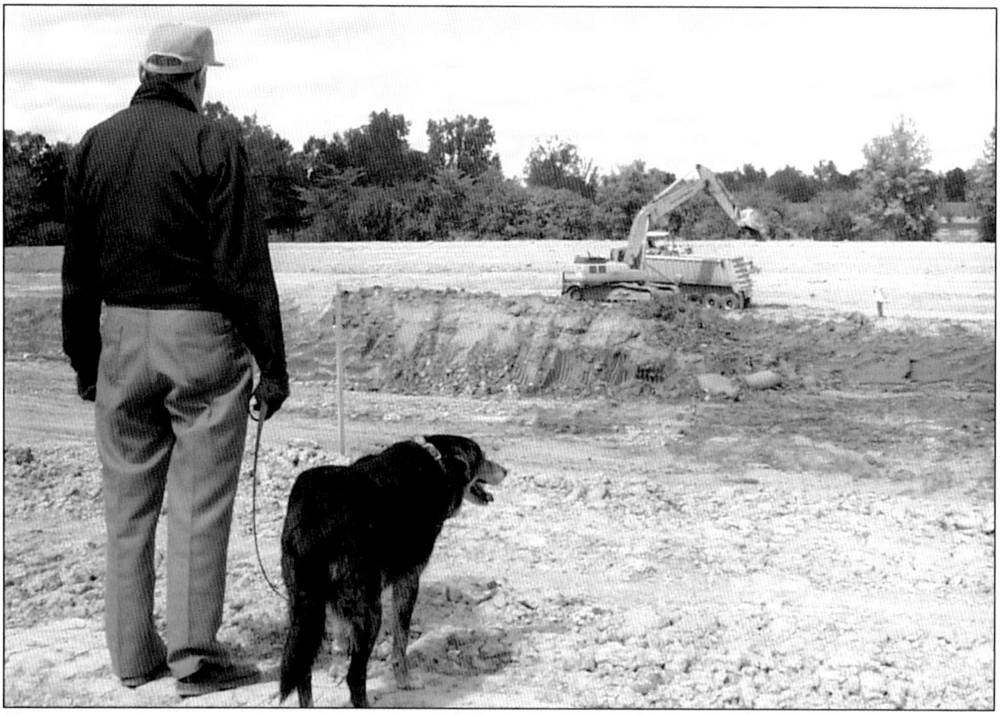

Construction is an ongoing project in Thomas Township. Frank Picardi and his dog Queenie watch as the holding pond is being dug for the Companion Drain Project, started in 1998.

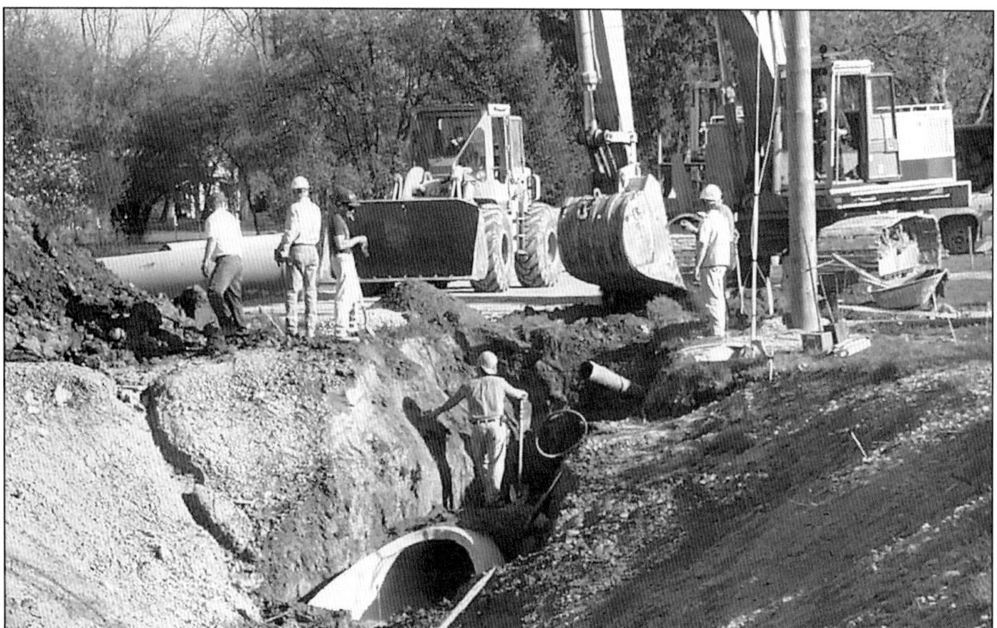

The Companion Drain on Bacon Road is still under construction in the spring of 1999. This drain is designed to alleviate chronic draining problems in the areas bordered by River, Deborah, Miller, and McCliggott Roads.

Five

Mind, Body, and Spirit

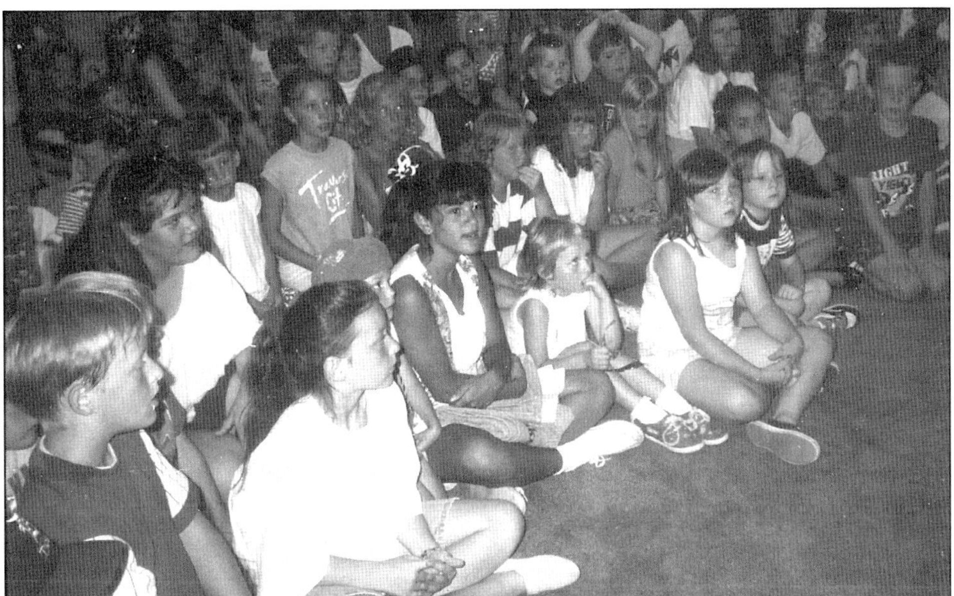

Pictured above is a group of enthusiastic children listening to a story hour held at the library. With subdivisions and increased population came more recreational activities and the construction of a library, parks, and new schools, named after early settlers who established them, beginning in 1856. Local residents continue to be involved in organizing and naming new facilities.

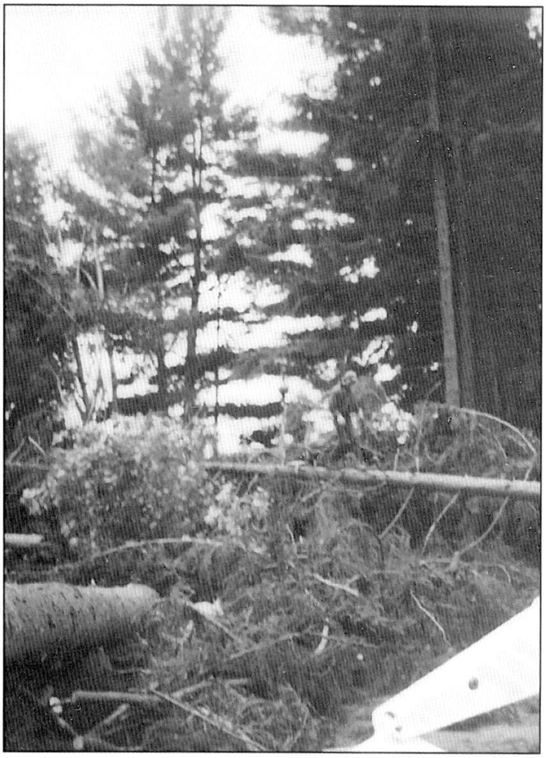

The early morning thunderstorm of May 31,1998, blew down many of the old pine trees that had been in Owen Cemetery for decades. When the six acres on a sandy knoll overlooking the Tittabawassee River was purchased from Thomas Owen in 1875, there were numerous weeds and blackberry bushes but few trees (the trees were planted afterwards.) These uprooted trees were removed with funding received from the Federal Emergency Management Administration.

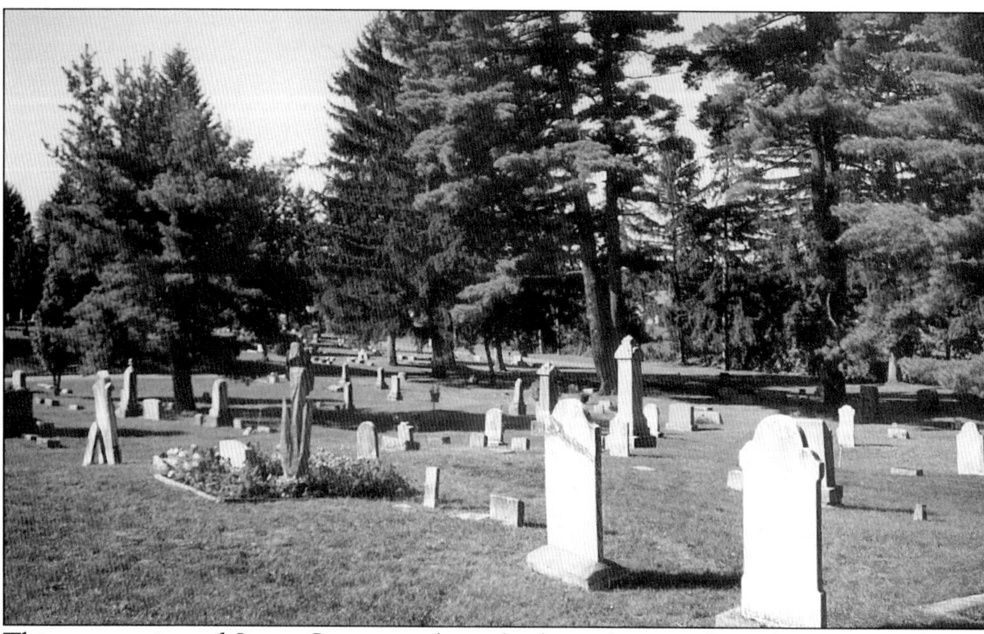

This recent view of Owen Cemetery shows both tombstones from the 1800s and some from the past few decades. In spite of the recent storm damage, stately pines still stand throughout and around the cemetery. A water system has been installed and the roads have been paved. The Township Parks Department cares for the cemetery today.

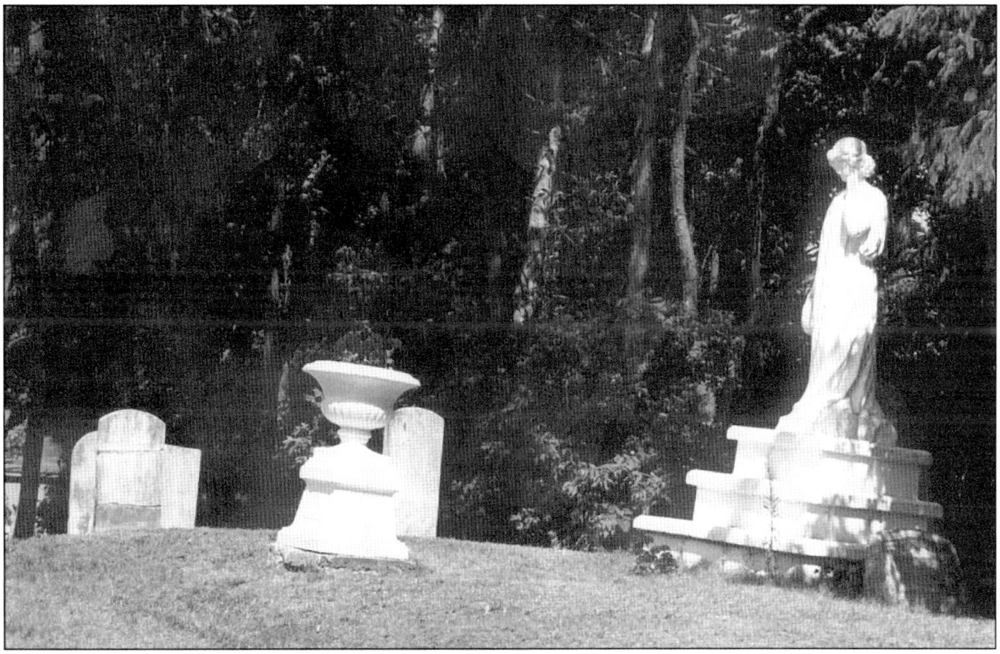

This statue and flower urn were constructed in memory of Thomas Owen who sold six acres of his land for $500 in 1875. This Owen family plot has an inscribed tombstone for Thomas Owen who died on October 23, 1895, at 81 years of age. Another tombstone for Henry T. Owen shows life dates of 1854–1936. The Owen family plot is high on a knoll where the angel statue watches over the beautiful, quiet little cemetery.

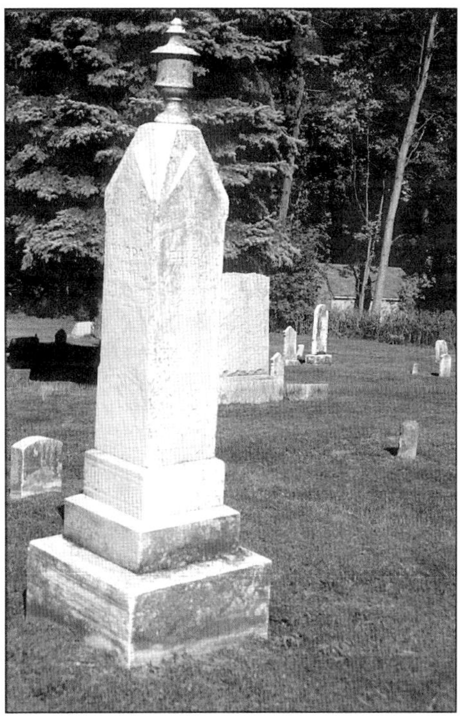

Four Wiltse family graves surround this unique 1800s tombstone. On each side of the tall commanding tombstone is carved names as follows: (a) Eliza, dau of J & H Wiltse, May 15, 1873, Aged 23 years, one month, twelve days; (b) Rhoda, dau of J & H Wiltse, died September 26, 1865, aged five months; (c) Hulda, wife of John Wiltse, May 5, 1880, aged 49 years; and (d) John Wiltse, 1826–1906.

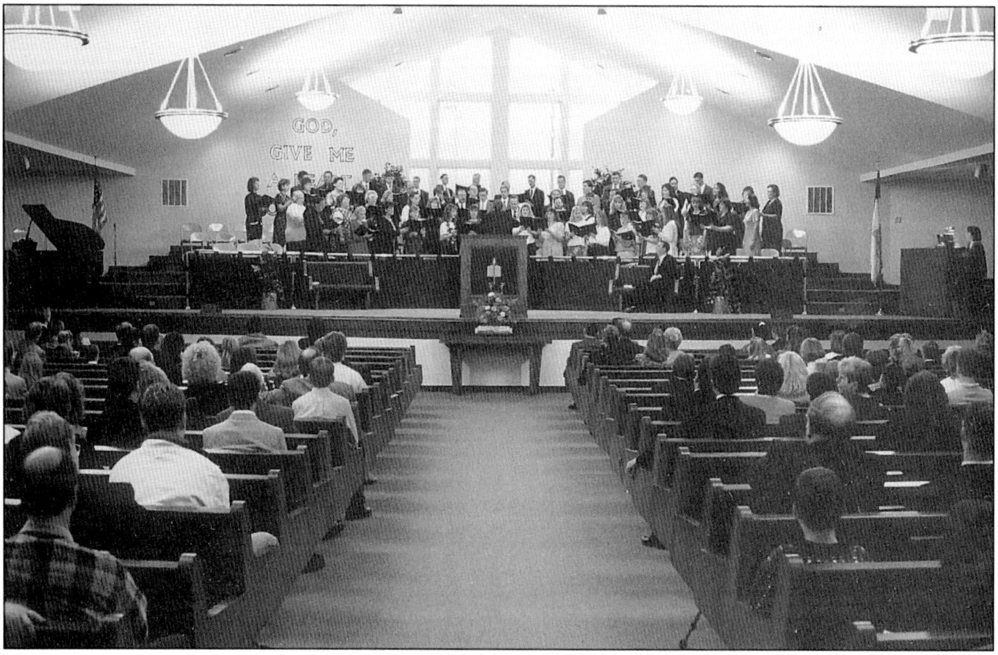

The Community Baptist Church of Shields at 8331 Gratiot Road is celebrating its anniversary with a mission conference in this 1989 photo.

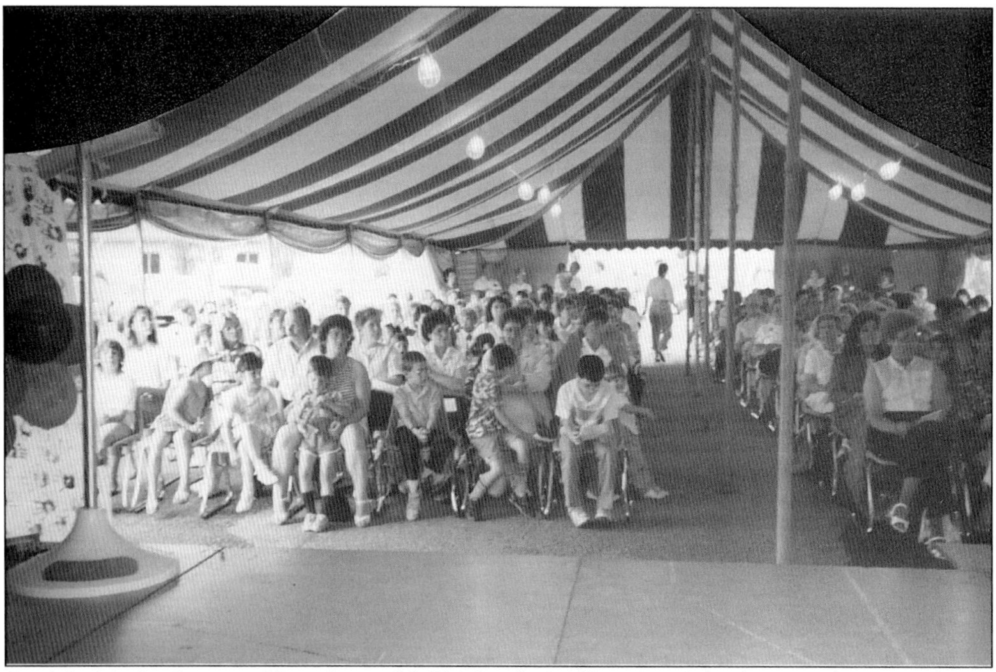

St. Mark's Lutheran Church at 2565 North Miller Road had over 500 people in attendance for its three-day tent gathering in the 1990s.

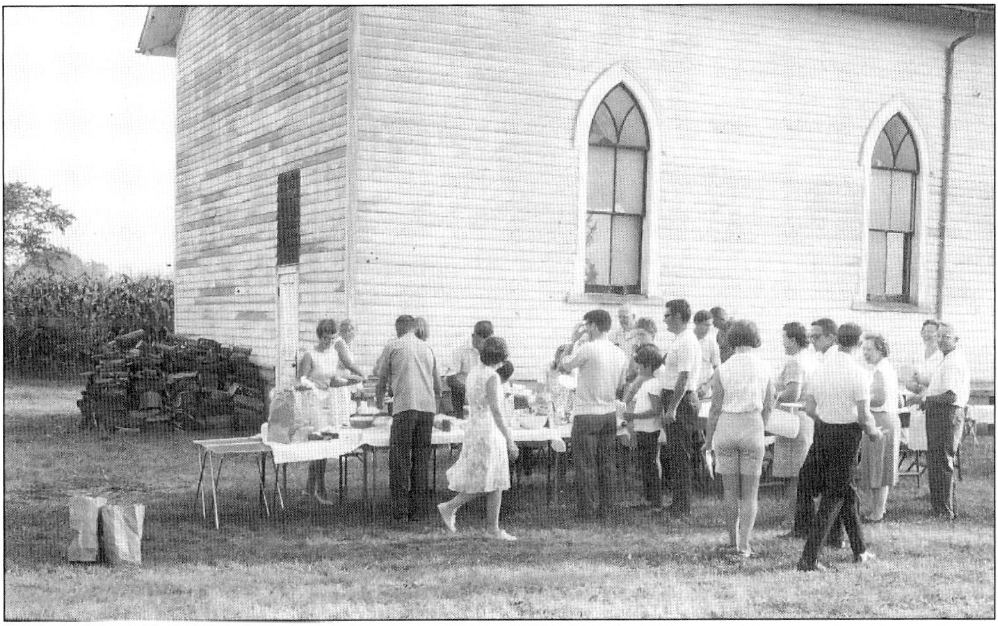

The Hubbard M.E. Church Congregation bought the Forest Grange Hall on Lone Road in 1884, remodeled the two-story building into a one-story structure, and added a steeple. It was used as their church for 45 years. In the 1971 photo above, the Swan Valley United Methodist congregation enjoys a summer picnic outside the Hall.

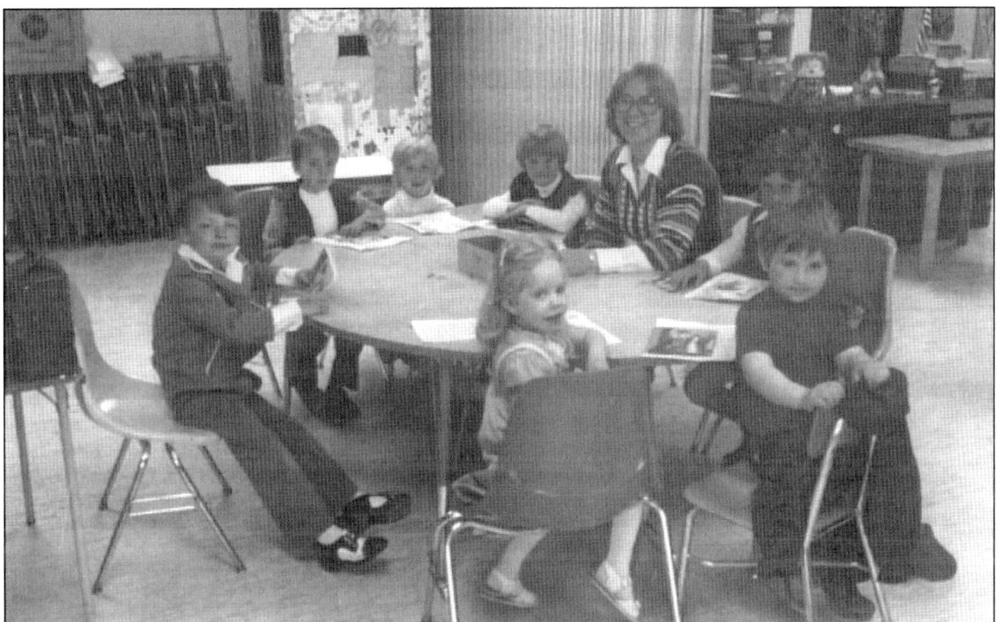

Many Thomas Township residents helped organize and build Christ Lutheran Church on Ederer Road in 1903. Its members come today from Thomas, James, and Swan Creek Townships. In this photo, a Sunday school class is being held in its new school built in the 1970s. Day classes were taught in the two-room parochial school for years before their new educational facility was constructed.

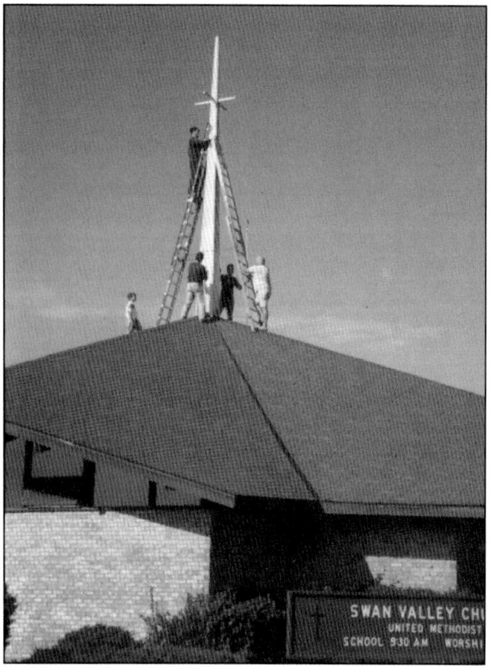

A cross and steeple are being raised on the roof of the Swan Valley United Methodist Church by Troy Wilsey, Jim Wilsey, Sam Crawford, John Byan, and Pastor Peter Crawford in this 1972 photo. Church services were first held in living rooms in 1969, then moved to the Grange Hall on Lone Road. In 1972 this beautiful little church was built on Geddes and Kennely Roads with Reverend Charles Kolb as the minister.

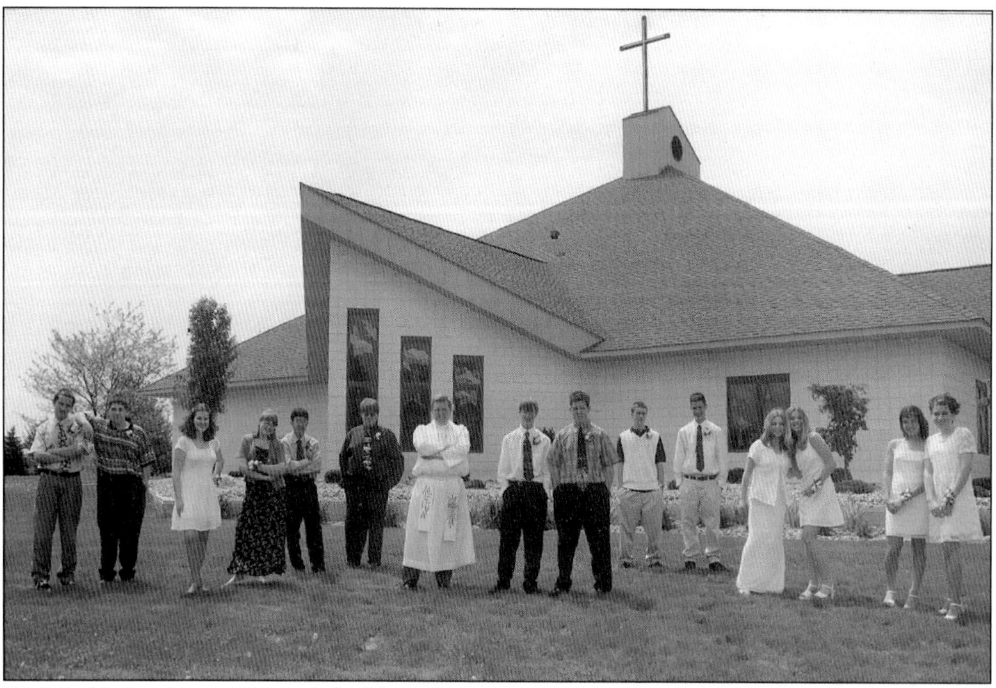

St. Mark's Lutheran Church held its first services on January 20, 1980 at Community State Bank, then moved to Holy Spirit Catholic Church for Sunday services. A ten-acre parcel on River and Miller Roads was purchased in May of the same year. A multi-purpose building was constructed and Missouri Synod Lutheran services were held here until the church was later built. A confirmation class poses with Reverend Daniel L. Krause in front of their newly constructed church.

The congregation gathers around Christ Lutheran Church on Ederer Road on August 14, 1904, when the church was dedicated as a Michigan Synod church. It later became affiliated with the Wisconsin Evangelical Lutheran Synod. This wooden-frame church is representative of the churches built in the 1800s and early 1900s in the township. Although remodeled in 1959, it was demolished for its new church dedicated on May 7, 1967.

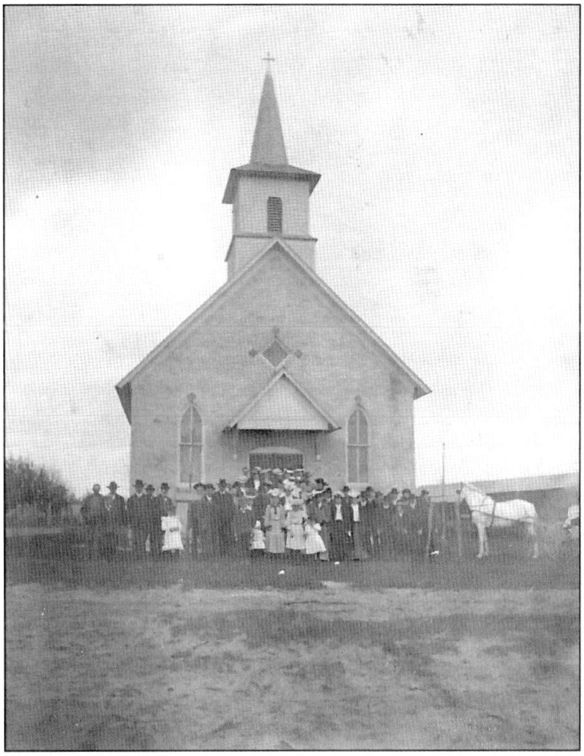

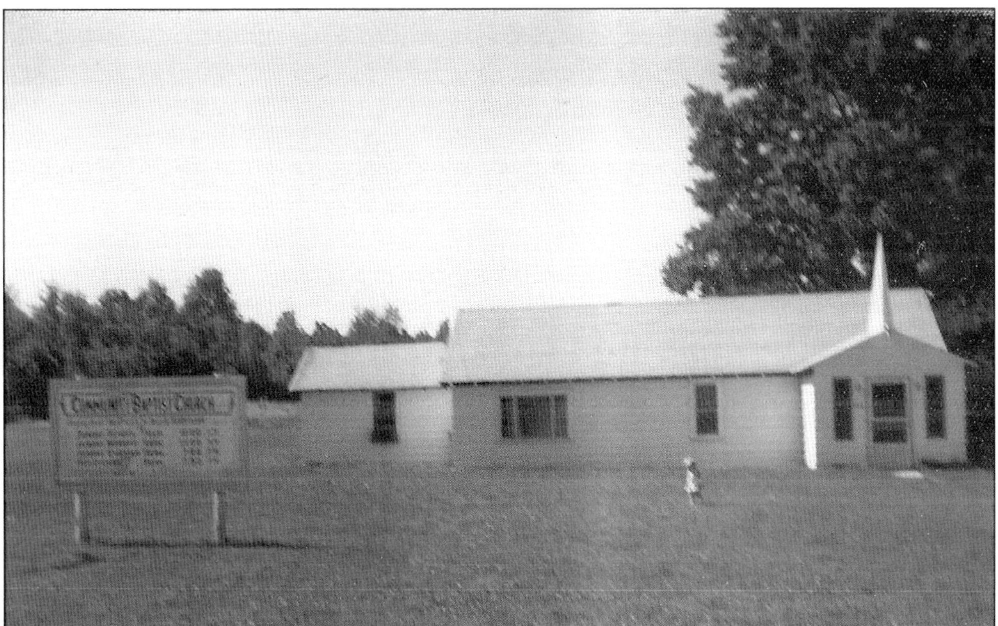

The Community Baptist Church of Shields originally met in a house on Trinklein Road in 1959. Two years later, the church was built on this site at 8331 Gratiot Road. The original church shown above has been replaced with a larger, more modern facility.

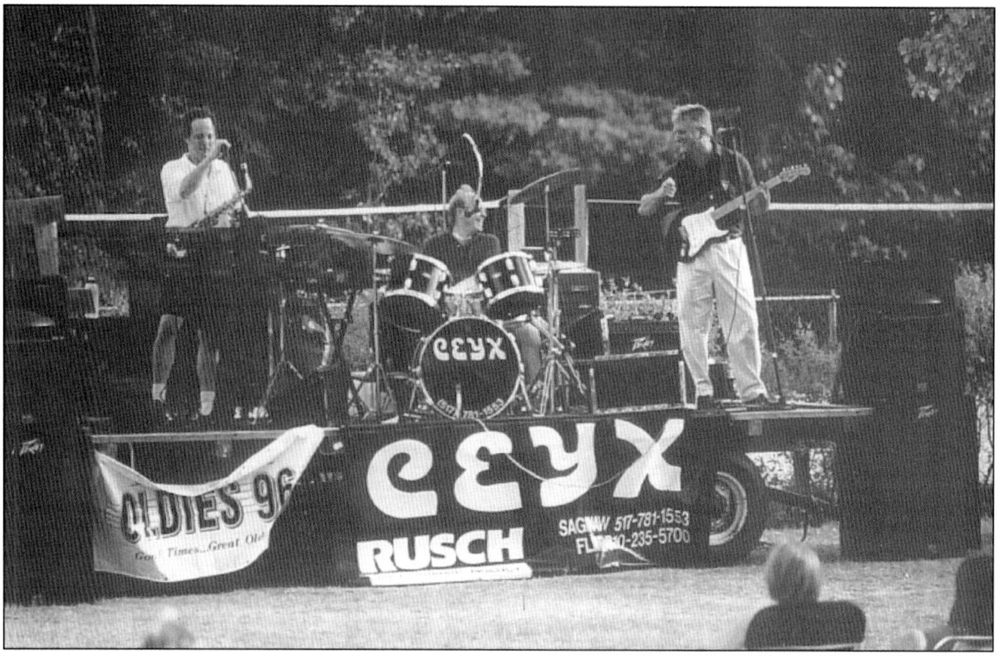

The Roethke family purchased 160 acres on Gratiot and Leddy Roads in 1891. In 1973 Margaret C. Roethke deeded 72 acres of this land in memory of her son, Carl L. Roethke, to the township for use as a park. The township purchased another three acres from her. Many activities for all ages are held here at Roethke Park. In the above photo the Rusch CEYX Band plays to a large crowd in an outdoor July evening concert. In the photo below the Swan Valley Swingers, who meet monthly, are enjoying their noon meal at the park's depot building.

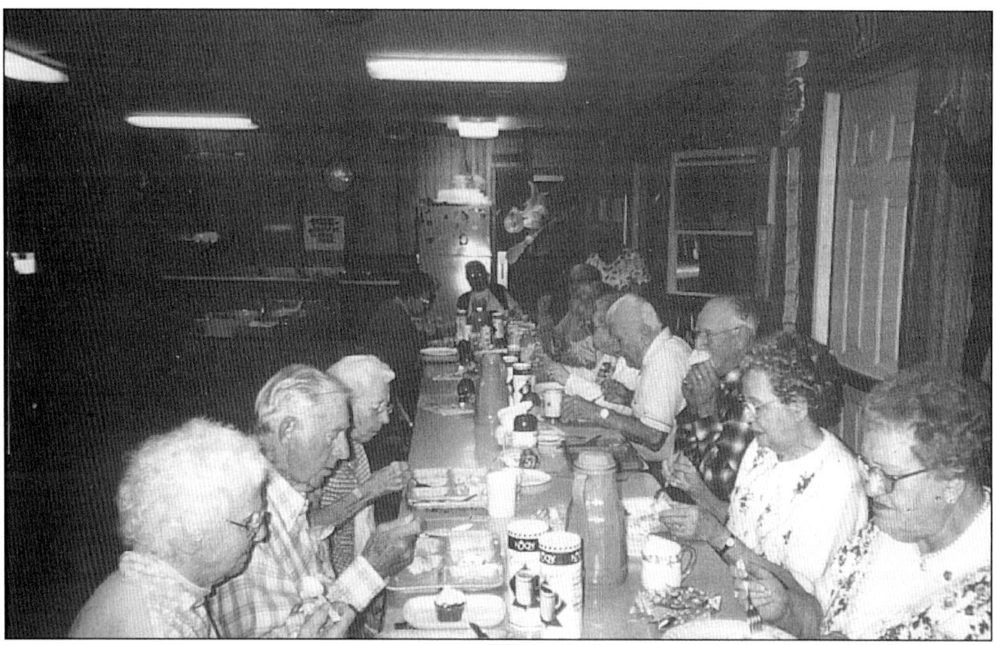

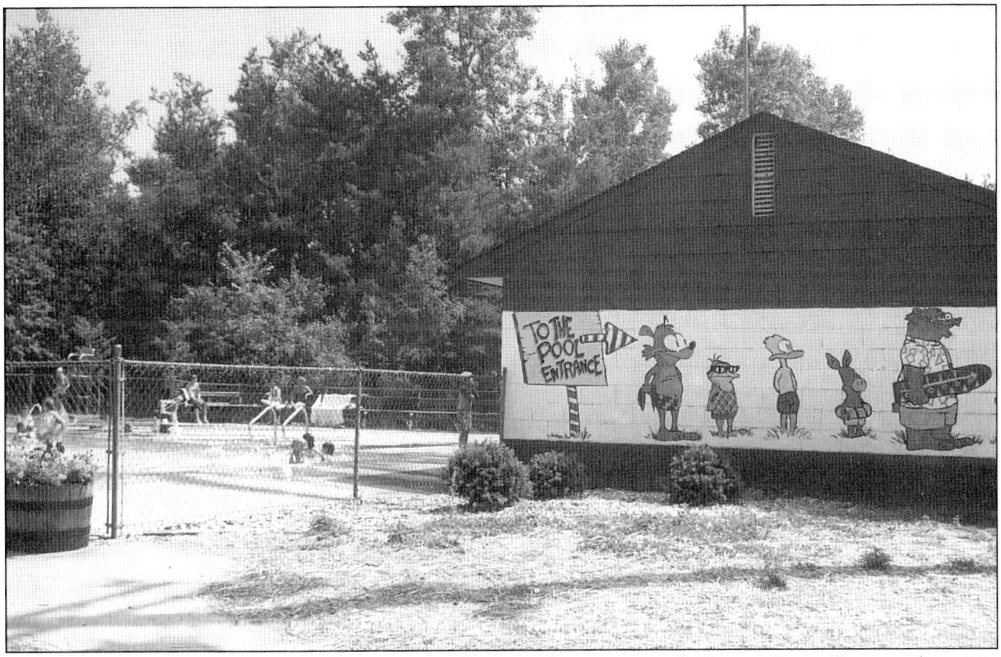

The swimming pool at Roethke Park, shown above, was dedicated on September 10, 1967, and named in honor of Stephen J. Colby. The "L" shaped pool has both deep and shallow ends. Many families spend a delightful afternoon in the pool.

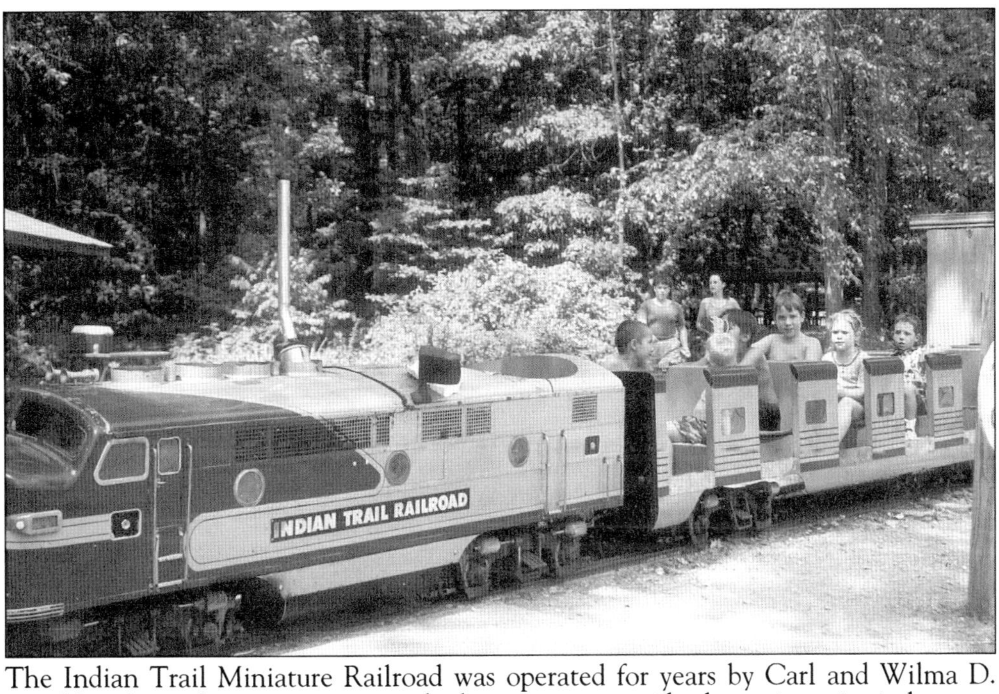

The Indian Trail Miniature Railroad was operated for years by Carl and Wilma D. Roethke. A good time is guaranteed when passengers ride the train as it circles over a mile of track through the wooded park. The Haunted Train Ride, sponsored by the Shields Kiwanis Club, is an especially fun event every Halloween.

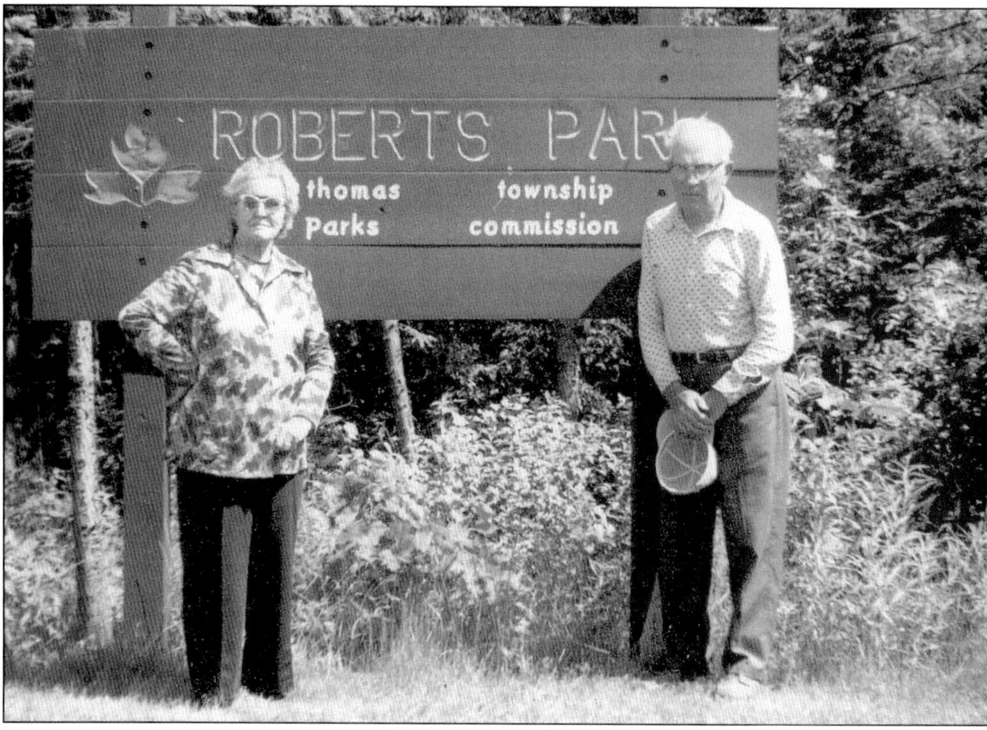

Eleanor and Fay Roberts stand in front of the ten-acre park which bears their name. For years they had farmed this land, raising gladiolus. The Bacon Road land was purchased and a park was constructed by the Shields Men's Club, then deeded over to Thomas Township. Since its dedication on June 2, 1974, the park has provided countless activities on its ball diamonds, swings, slides, and at an indoor shelter building.

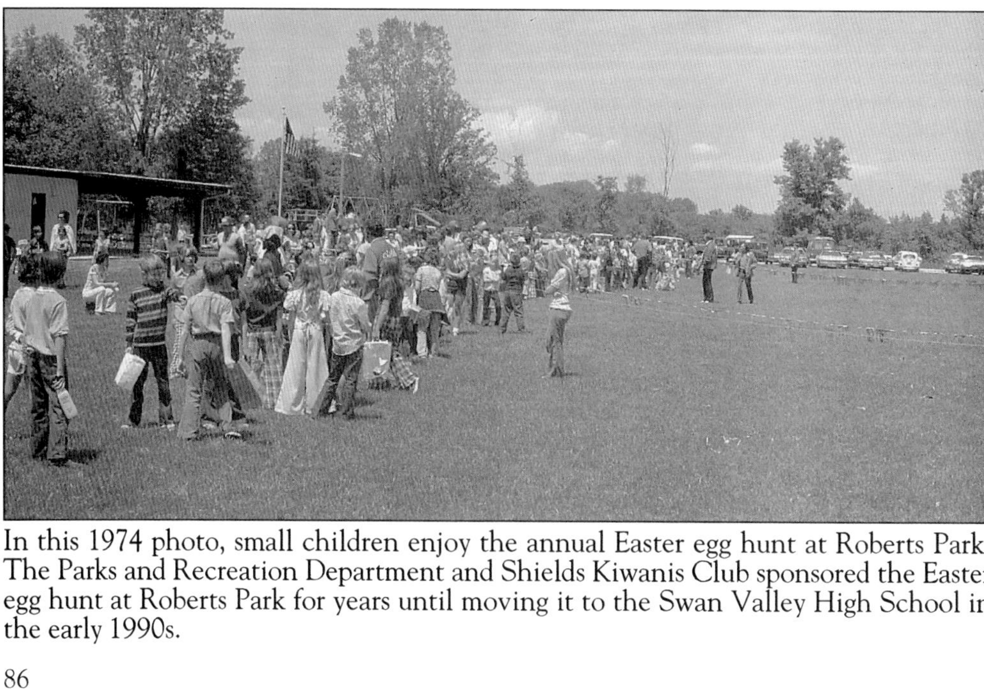

In this 1974 photo, small children enjoy the annual Easter egg hunt at Roberts Park. The Parks and Recreation Department and Shields Kiwanis Club sponsored the Easter egg hunt at Roberts Park for years until moving it to the Swan Valley High School in the early 1990s.

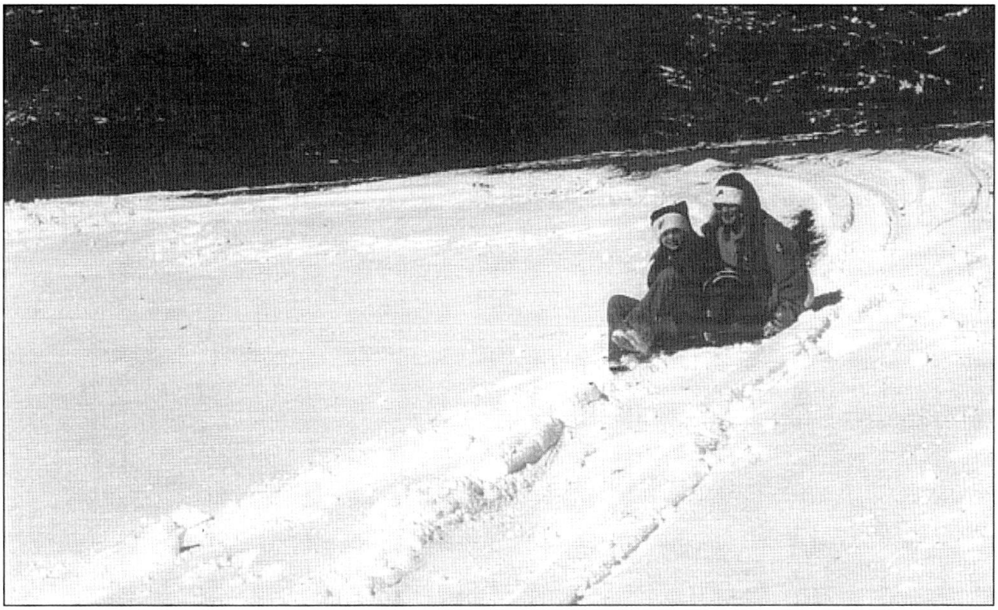

Sledding has been a popular winter time activity at South River Road's Day Park. The sledding hill was constructed from excess soil excavated for the Companion Drain Project. Football is played in the park during the summer and fall months.

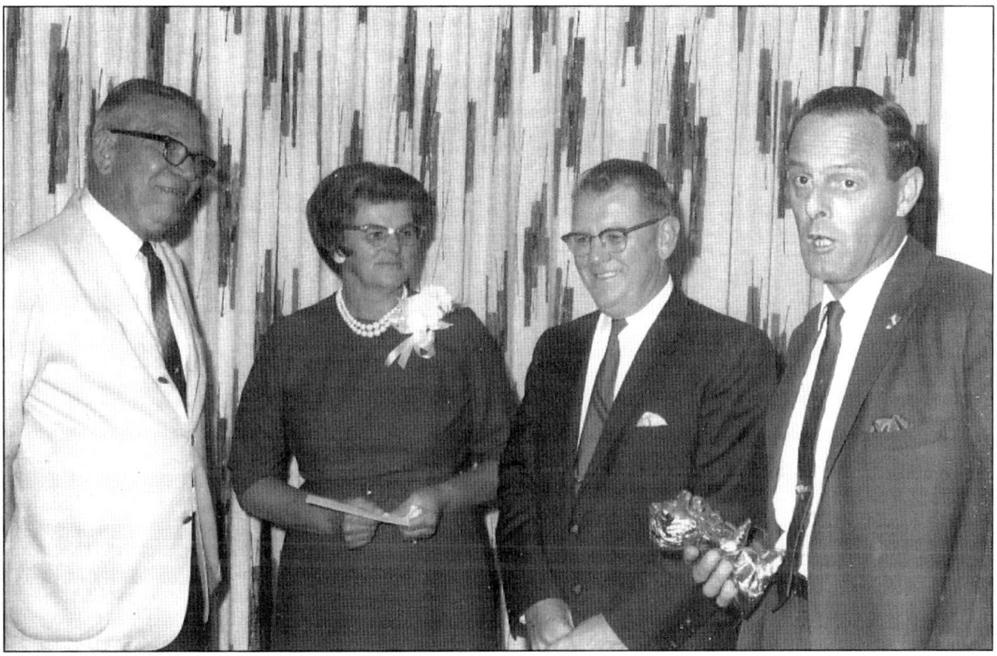

Marion Ederer, a lifelong James Township resident, was the lucky person who thought up the name "Swan Valley School District" for the new consolidated school system for Thomas, James, and Swan Creek Townships. In this September 28, 1966 photo she is being presented with a $25 U.S. Savings Bond by C. M. Lauckner (left), President of the Shields Lion Club, and Virgil L. Sanford, President of the School Board.

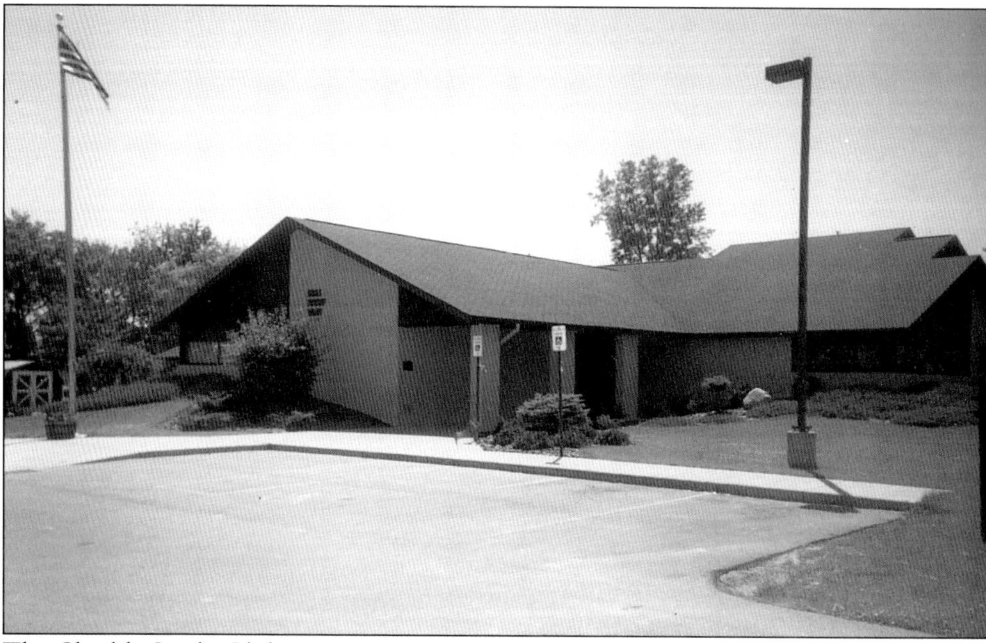

The Shields Study Club sponsored a township library in 1962. The first library room was opened on July 15, 1964, in the Fire Department Building with 600 books. With subsequent donations and a millage, the library opened in May 1989, in this modern large facility on Shields Drive.

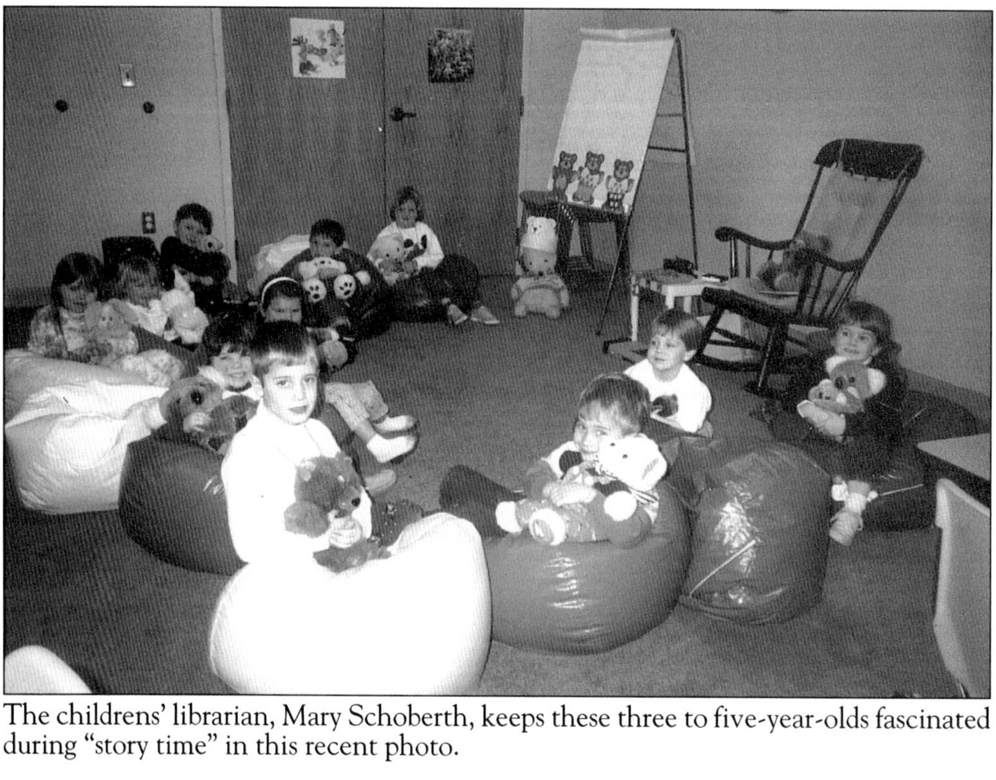

The childrens' librarian, Mary Schoberth, keeps these three to five-year-olds fascinated during "story time" in this recent photo.

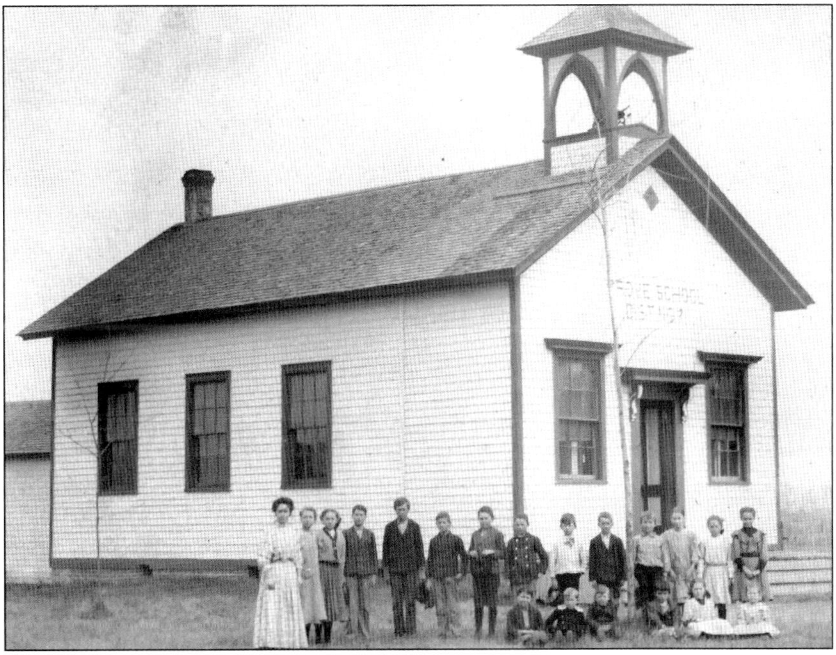

Grove School No. 4 was one of six township schools when it was built in 1873 in a grove of oak, birch, and maple trees on Gratiot Road where Meijer's store is presently located. This 1908 photo of Grove School is representative of the township schools in the 1800s and early 1900s. These one-room wooden frame school houses had a bell tower, an outdoor water pump, and outhouse.

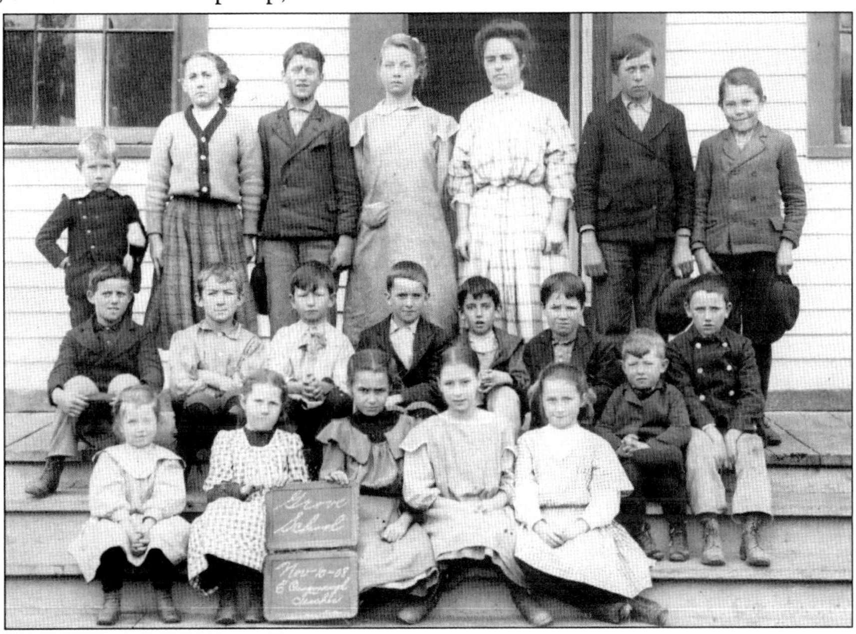

The teacher and the entire school pose outside the building in these two 1908 photos. In this photo, Walter Kluck is second from right in the top row with the teacher next to him (all others are unidentified). This building was used until 1925 when it burned down and a brick Standard School was constructed.

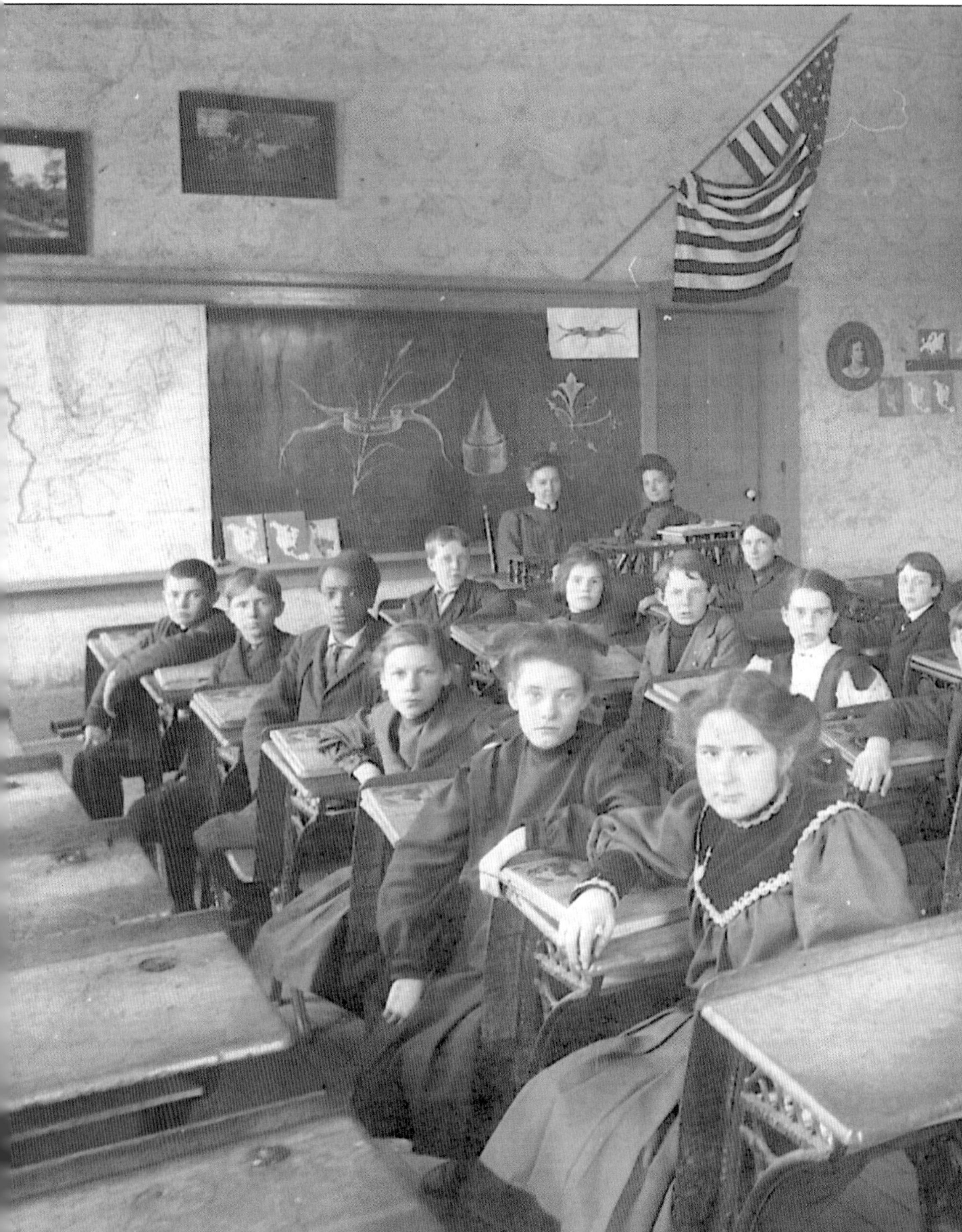

A classroom is seen in this view of Grove School taken in the late 1890s. The children were obviously dressed in their Sunday best waiting for the photographer that day.

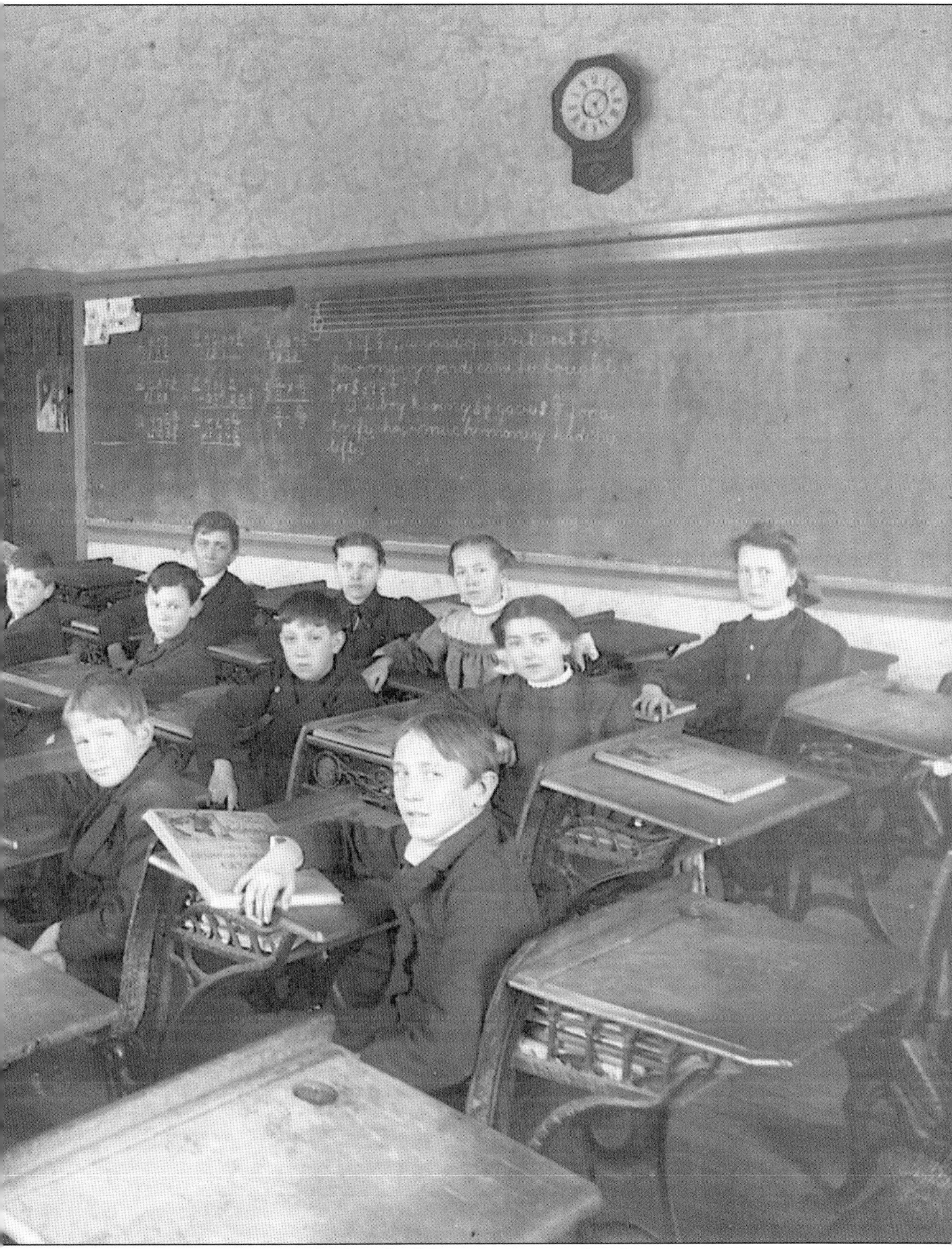

Two teachers are sitting at the head of this one-room school.

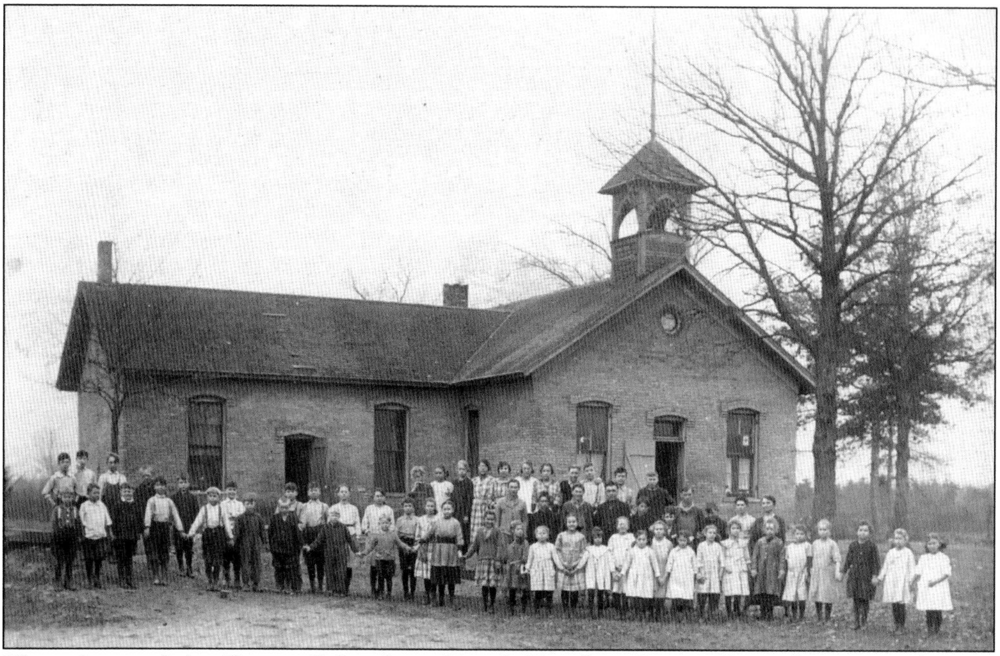

This photo of the Paines School on Dutch Road in James Township was taken in 1920. Many children from the Shields area attended the Paines School. In 1927, when overcrowding became a problem, a new school district at Gratiot Heights was created. Children in the general Shields area were split between Grove School, Paines, and Gratiot Heights. This schoolhouse was a brick Standard School which met all the new state requirements.

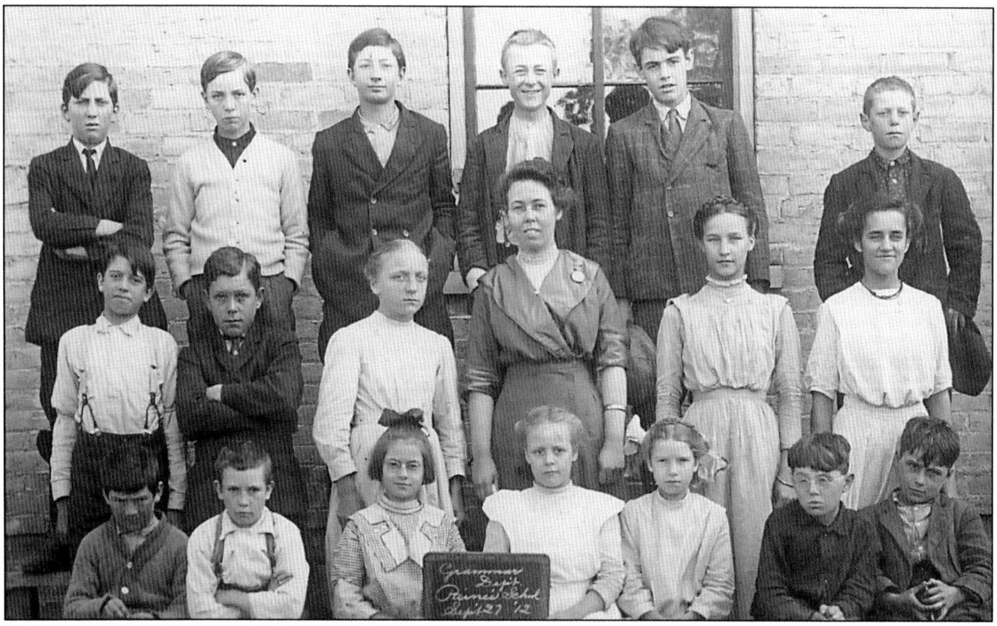

This 1912 photo of the teacher and students at Paines School show Teacher Maude and the unidentified children attending at this time. Paines School was a two-room school.

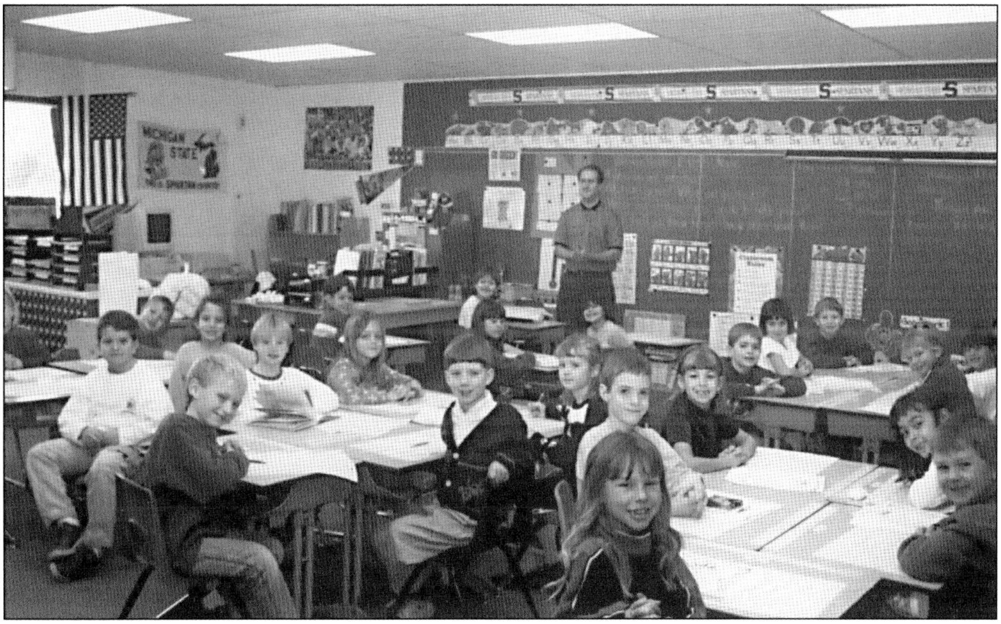

Chris Wenzel teaches his eager first graders at Havens Elementary School during the 1998–1999 school year. Children sitting around the front tables are, from left to right, Christian Knutson, Matthew Wenzel, Lauren Simon, Matt Reardon, Chelsi Greketis, Erin Muter, Joshua Cass, Michael Mammel, Katie Jo Dwenger, Courtney Draus, Raymond Remmert, Kelsey Krzyzaniak, Joey Sackrider, and Sara Nestell. Robert B. Havens Elementary School was opened in September 1971 on Van Wormer Road.

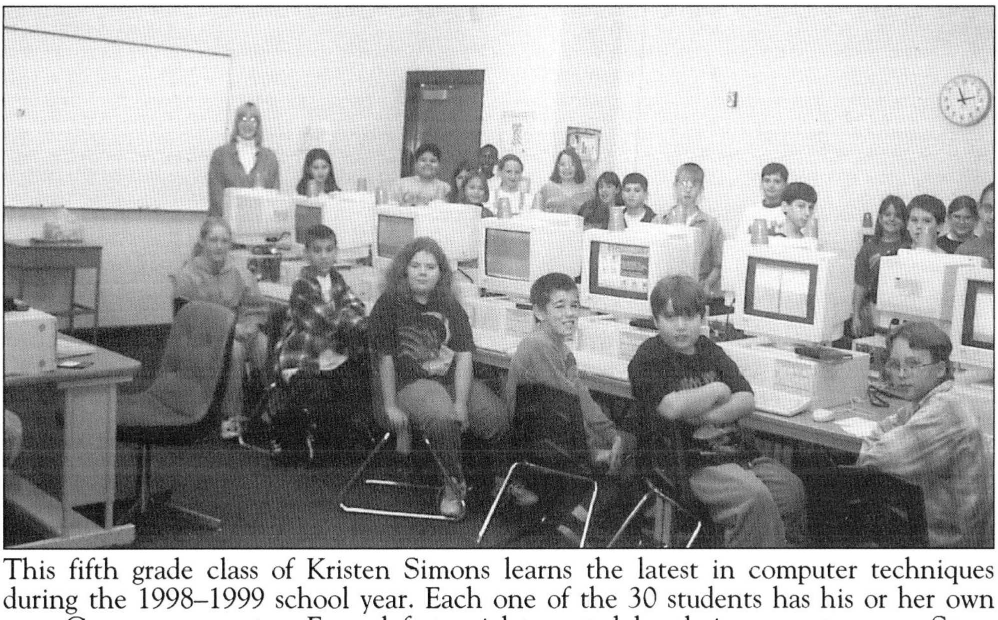

This fifth grade class of Kristen Simons learns the latest in computer techniques during the 1998–1999 school year. Each one of the 30 students has his or her own new Compaq computer. From left to right, seated by their computers, are Stacy Anderson, Kyle Barocko, Diane Winkler, Timothy Williams, John Van Haaren, and Matthew Valvano.

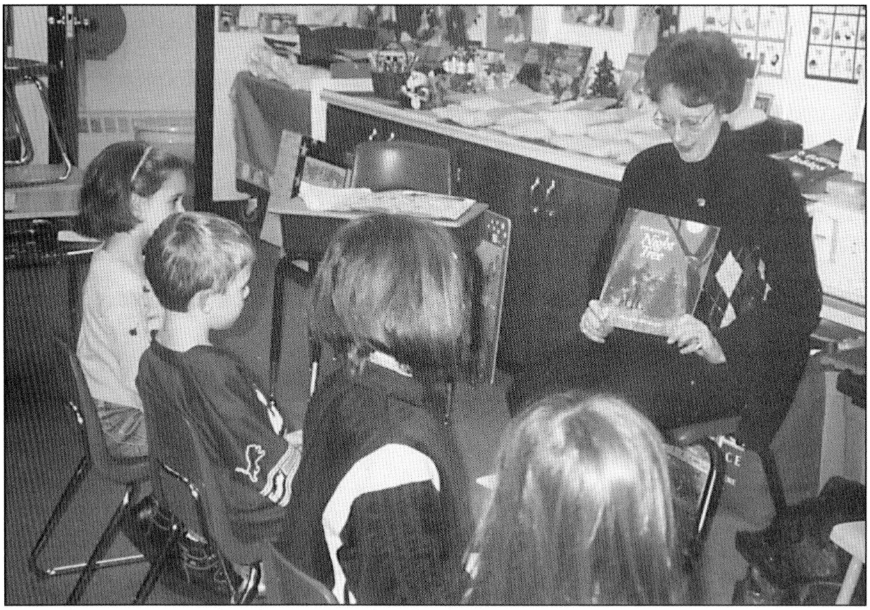

Parents and community leaders often lend a helping hand at the schools. School board member Linda Rudzinski is reading a story to Havens students on "Read Me A Story" night in December, 1999. Local residents volunteer their time on this special evening reading stories to young children while their parents finish their Christmas shopping.

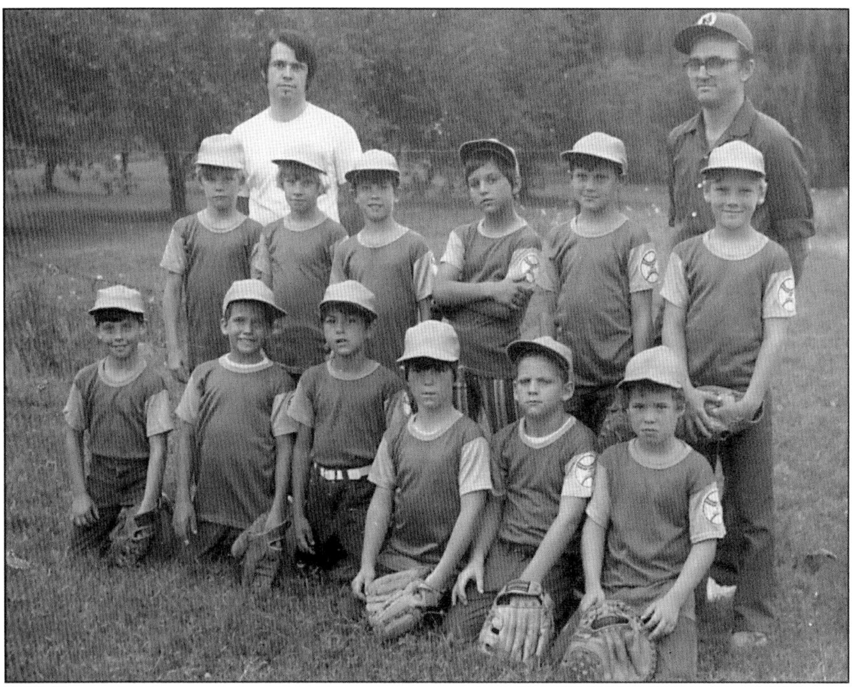

Coach Doug Donovan is shown with his Swan Valley Little League team in this mid-1970s photo. The softball team plays from April through June after school, evenings, and Saturdays on school grounds. Children from all elementary grades are eligible to participate. Parents volunteer their time working with the children.

Six

Gone, But Not Forgottten

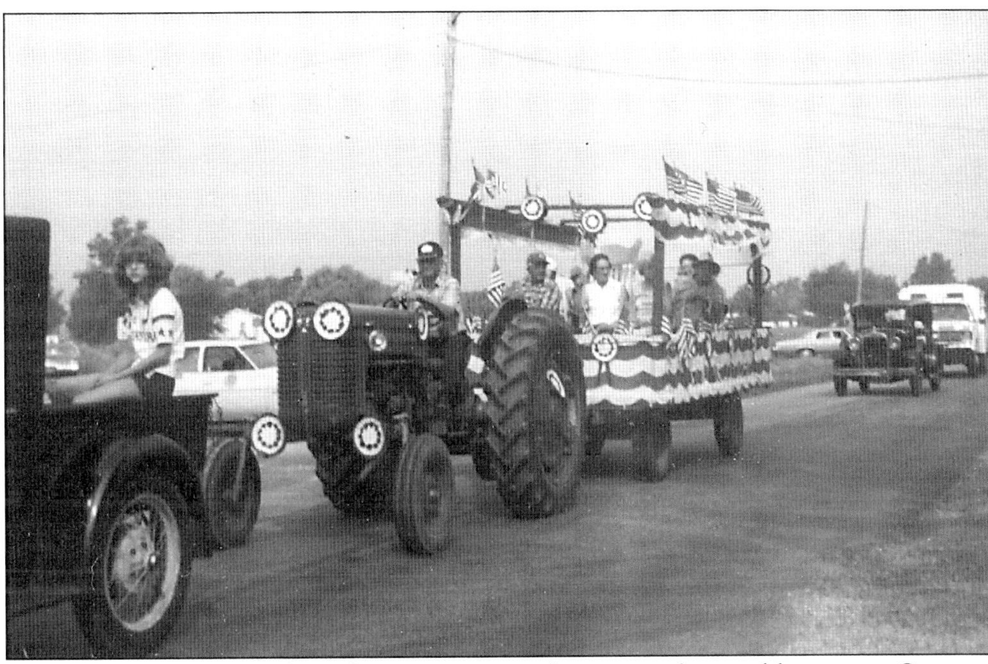

Thomas Township residents have experienced many unforgettable events. Some of them, such as the Flood of 1986, bring bad memories to mind. Others, such as the annual Shields Festival and the Swan Valley Homecoming, renew pleasant recollections of those times when everyone worked together to make a most memorable event. Paul Ederer is driving his decorated tractor and hay wagon with James Township's Gents and Jennies in the 1977 Shields Parade in the photo shown.

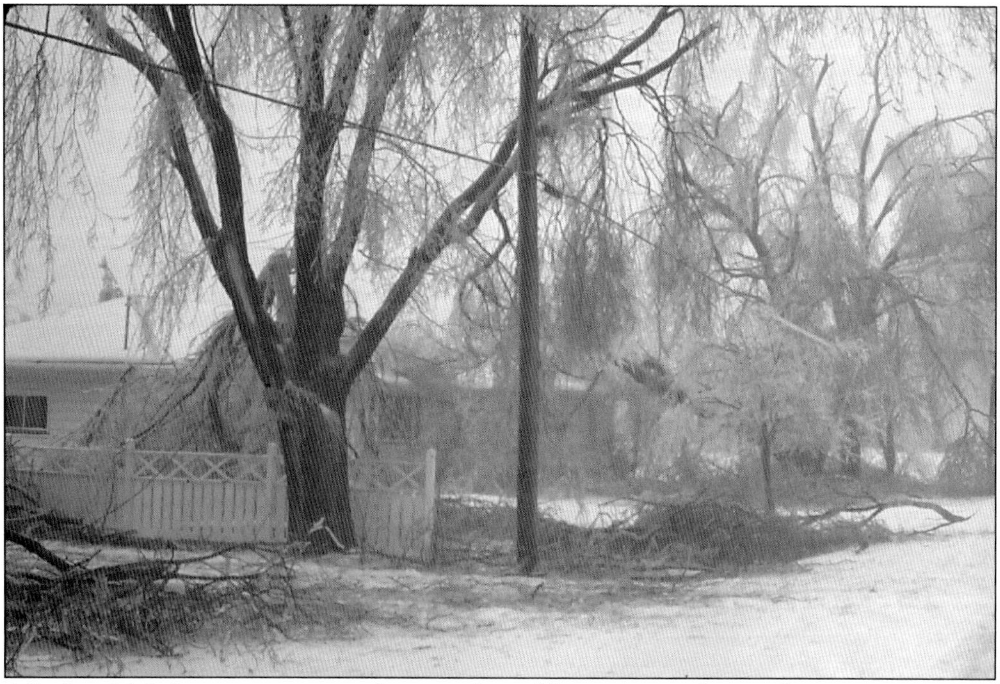

All of mid-Michigan experienced two inches of freezing rain during this winter storm of March 1 and 2, 1976. Tree limbs or large shade-trees were lost from many yards, power lines were downed all over, schools closed for five days, and some people lost power for over a week. Consumer Energy trucks from other states came to Michigan to help restore power and clean up fallen trees. The photos shown here were taken on Bacon Road during this ice storm.

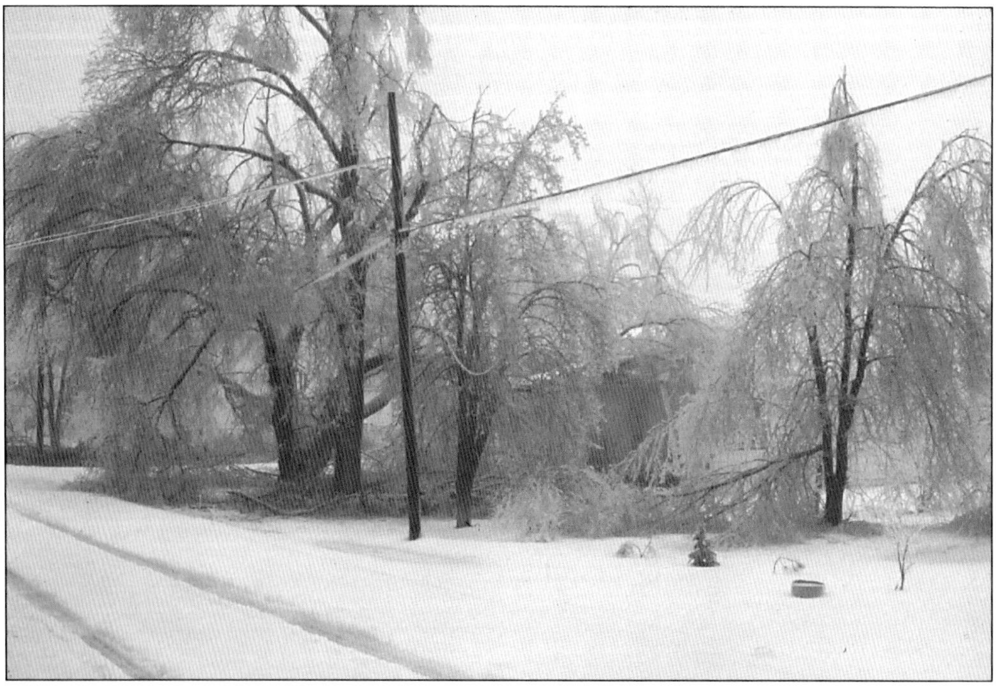

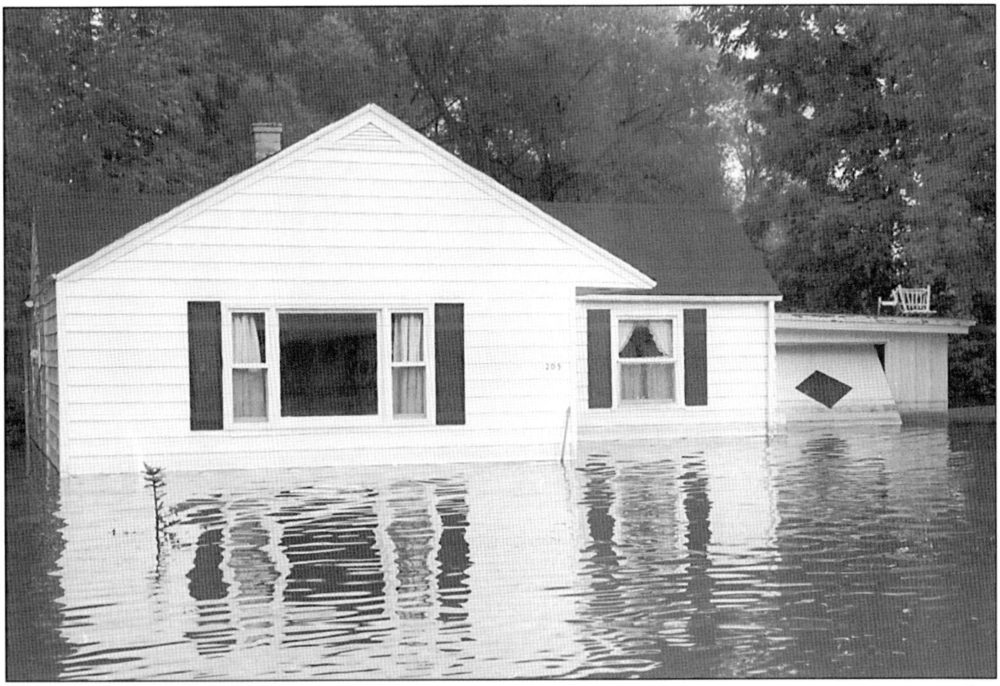

The Great Flood of 1986 began September 10 with two days of pouring rain. The flood waters kept rising higher and higher until Saturday, September 13 before they began to recede. The photo above was taken on September 14 at 205 Adams Road. Residents were forced out of their homes. Paddling by rowboat down River Road and other roads, as shown in the photo below, was the only method of transportation available for days.

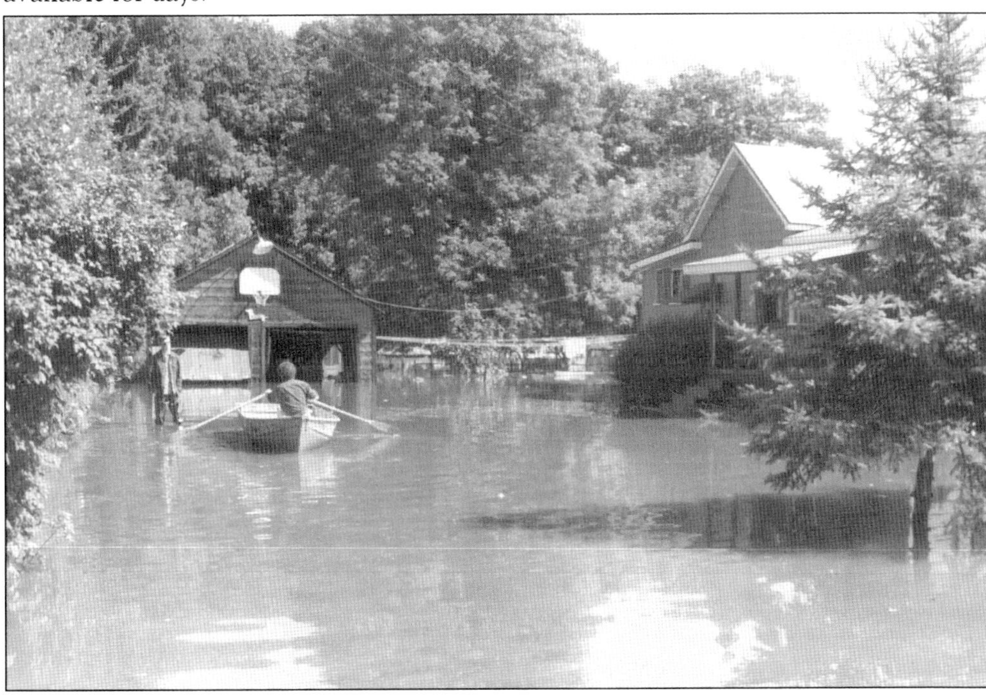

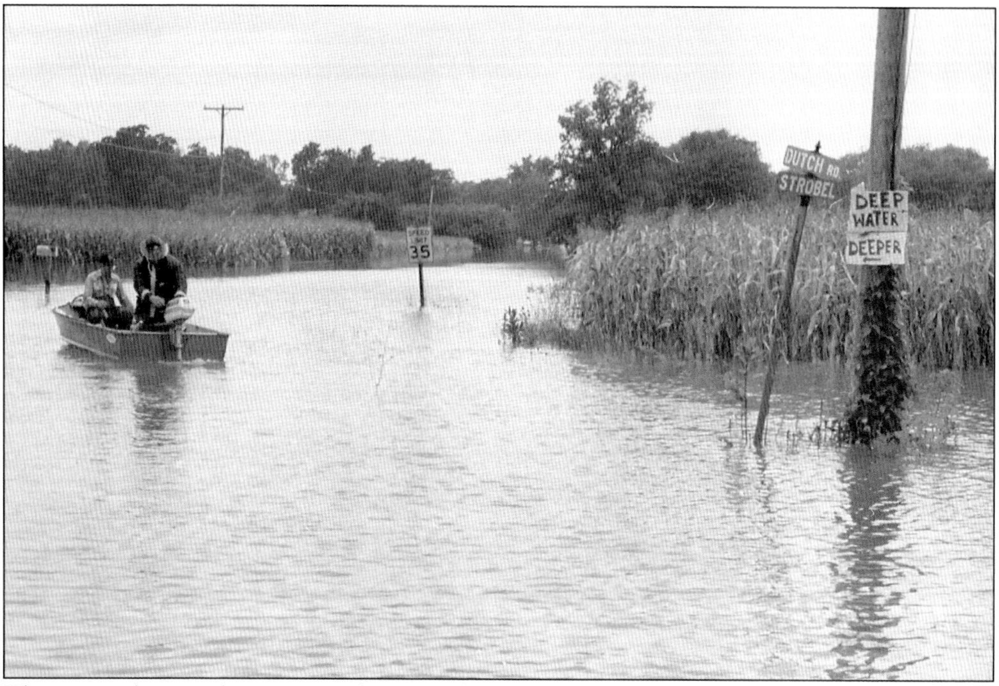

The view shown above was taken on the morning of September 14 at Stroebel and Dutch Roads. Thousands of acres of farm fields were submerged under several feet of water— the water just kept getting deeper. The James Township Fire Department is attempting to rescue a dog from a stranded pickup truck on Dutch Road. The flood waters covered every available inch of ground, even several miles from the river, as shown in the photo below.

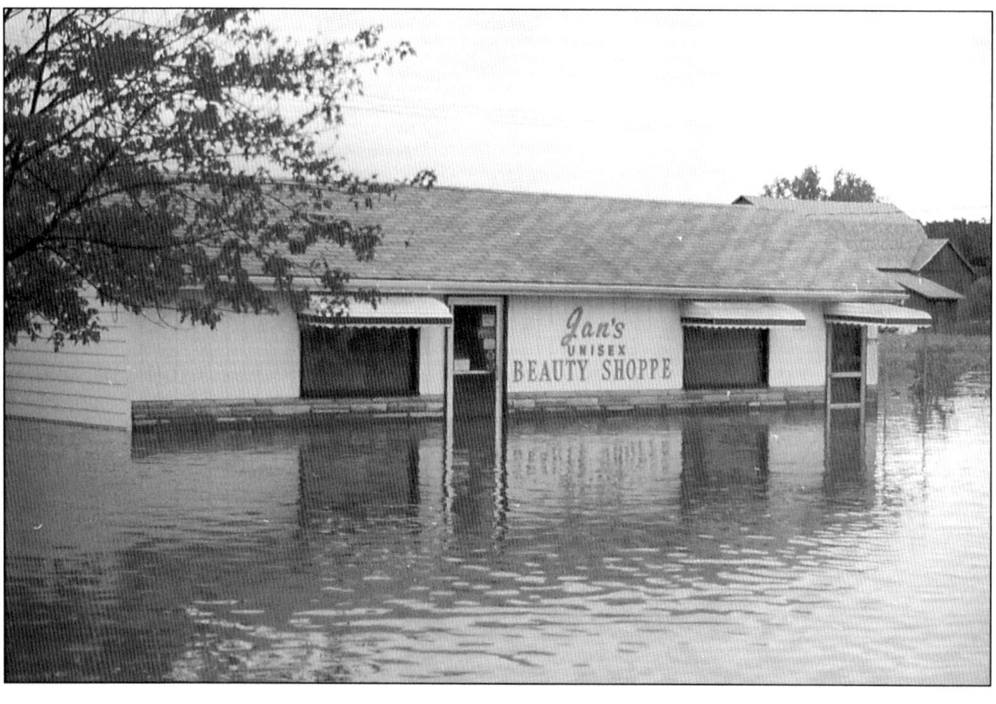

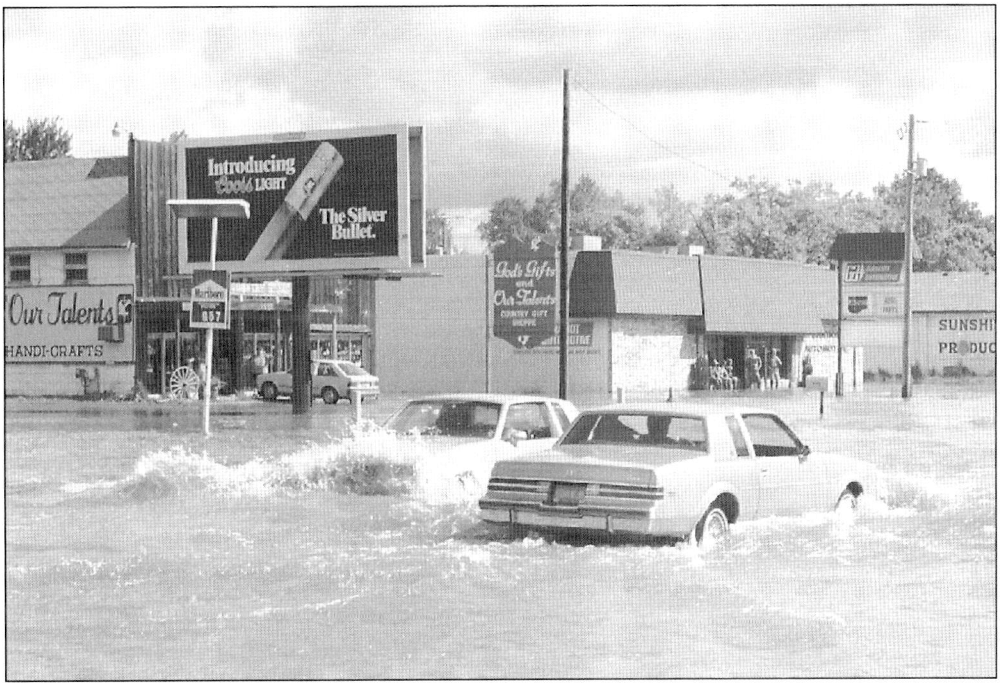

The above photo was taken on September 13 at the Gratiot and River Road intersection. Vehicles were taking chances of stalling in the high water, but there was no other route available as high water had closed all roads and bridges over the Tittabawassee River south of M-20 in Midland. The image below is another view of the high water spilling over onto sidewalks and businesses.

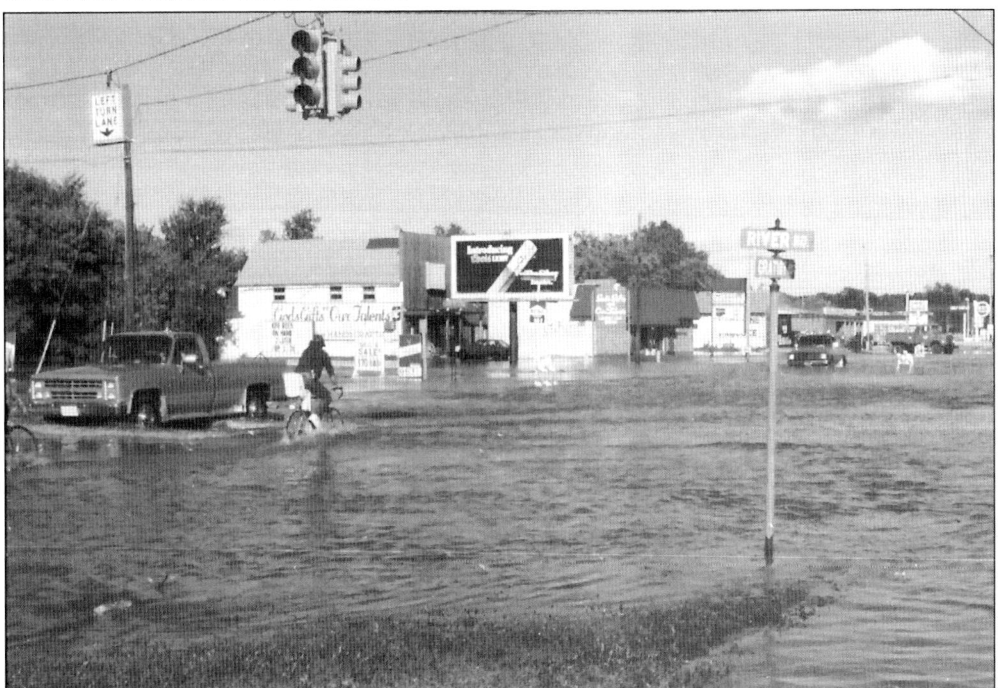

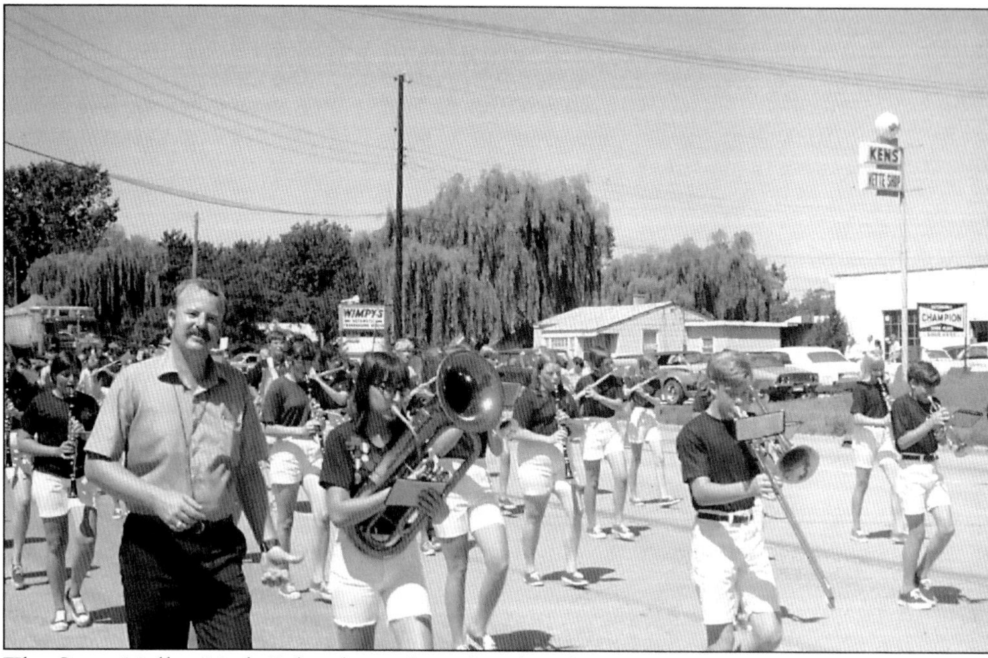

The Swan Valley High School marching band is always a main attraction at the Shields Festival Parade. Band director Gary Silvernail is leading his high school band in this 1970 Homecoming Parade.

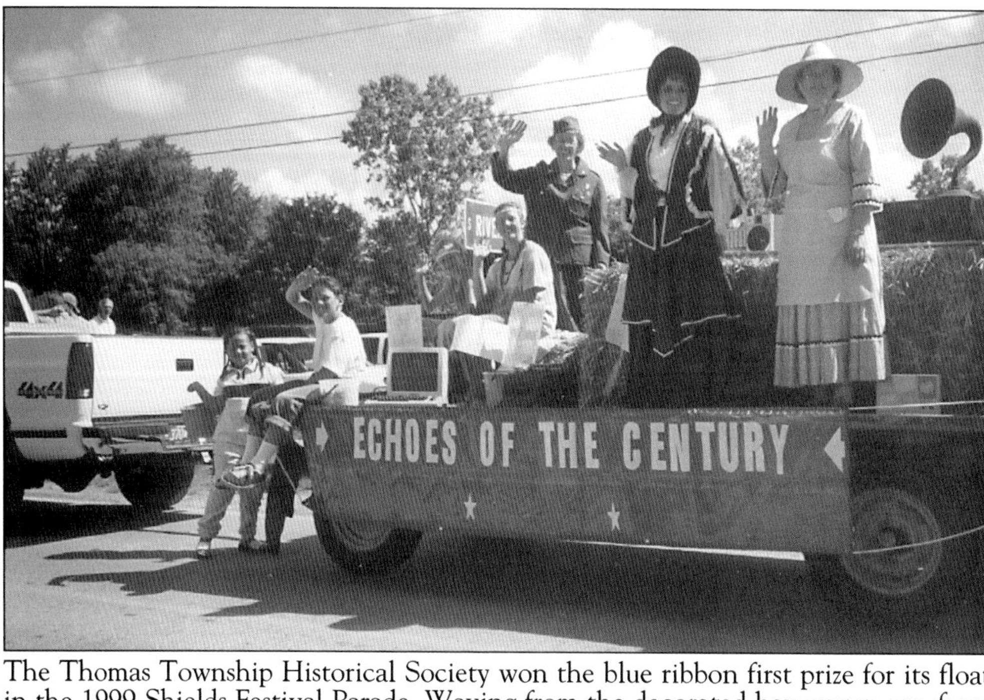

The Thomas Township Historical Society won the blue ribbon first prize for its float in the 1999 Shields Festival Parade. Waving from the decorated hay wagon are, from left to right, Jessica Bingham, Steven Oatten, Christopher Oatten, Stephanie Oatten, Marcia Strong, Stephanie Beyersdorf, and Roselynn Ederer. Each costume represents a different era during the past century.

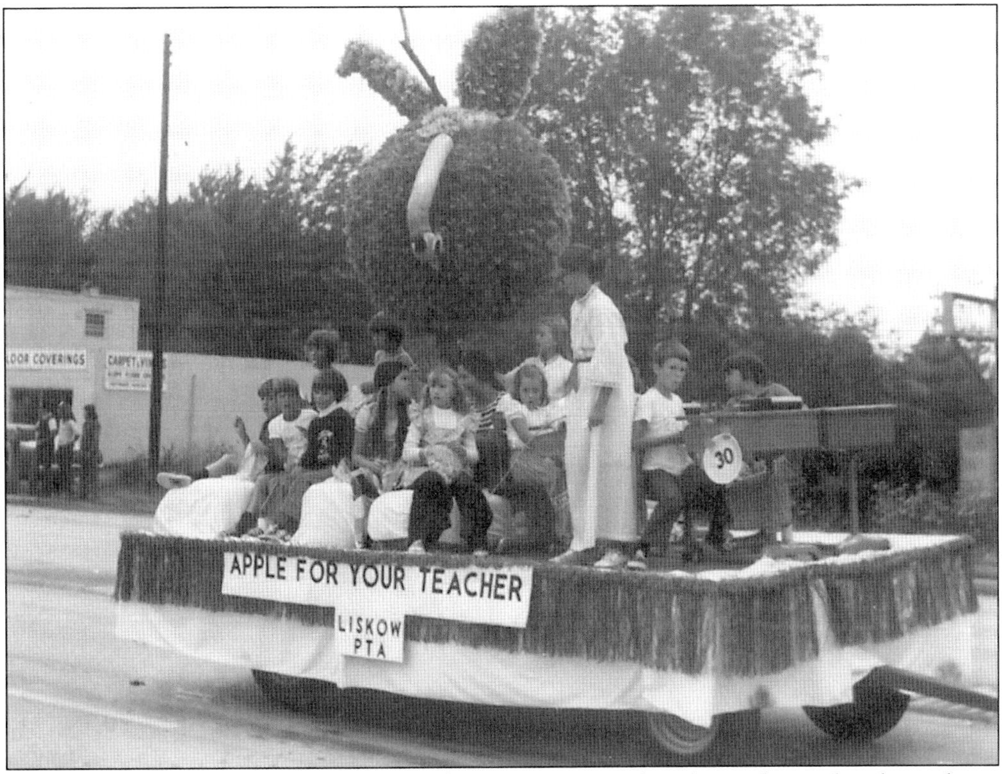

Many people, schools, and businesses have participated in festival parades throughout the years. In the above photo from the 1970s, the Liskow School PTA sponsored a float with Liskow school children. Some employees and their families participated in the float sponsored by Meijer's in the 1999 Parade.

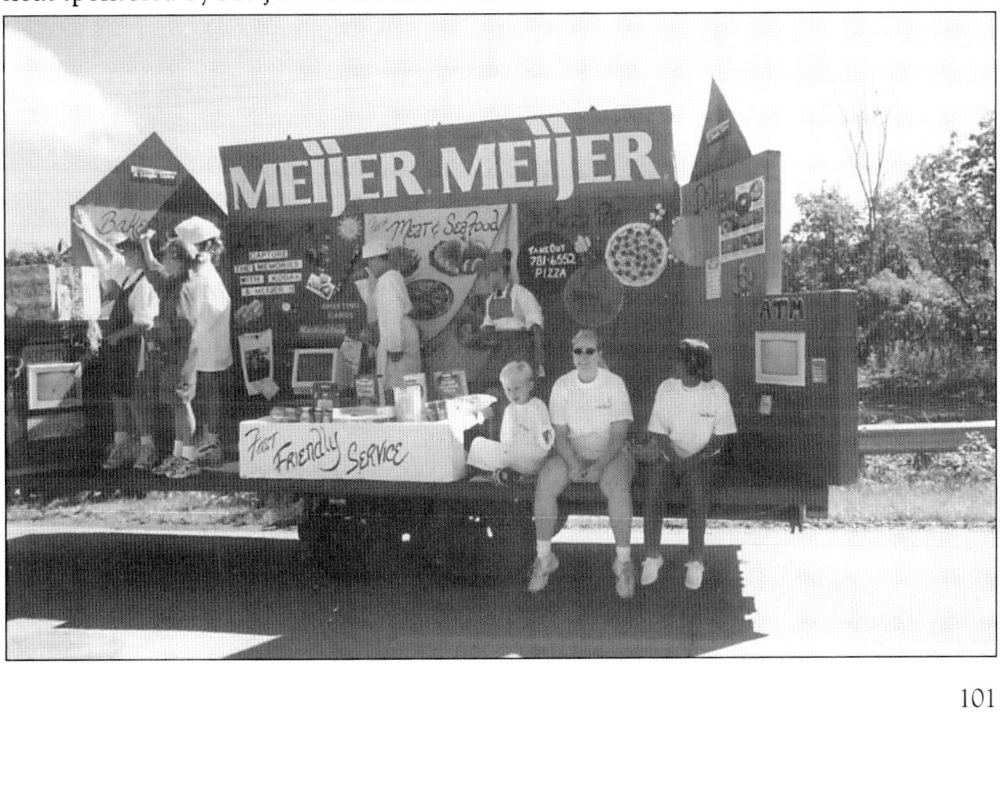

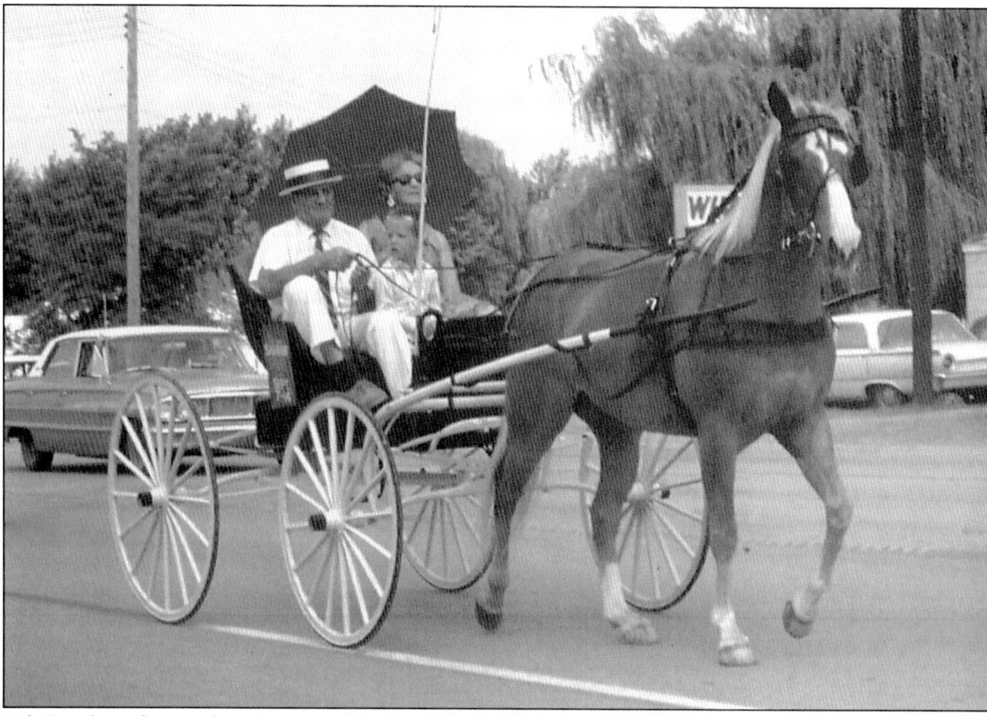

Ed Snider always hitched up his horse and buggy and had an enjoyable time in the Shields Parade. Ed and Ida Snider and their grandson are shown in this 1988 parade with Buddy pulling the buggy, sponsoring the Lions Club Leader Dog for the Blind.

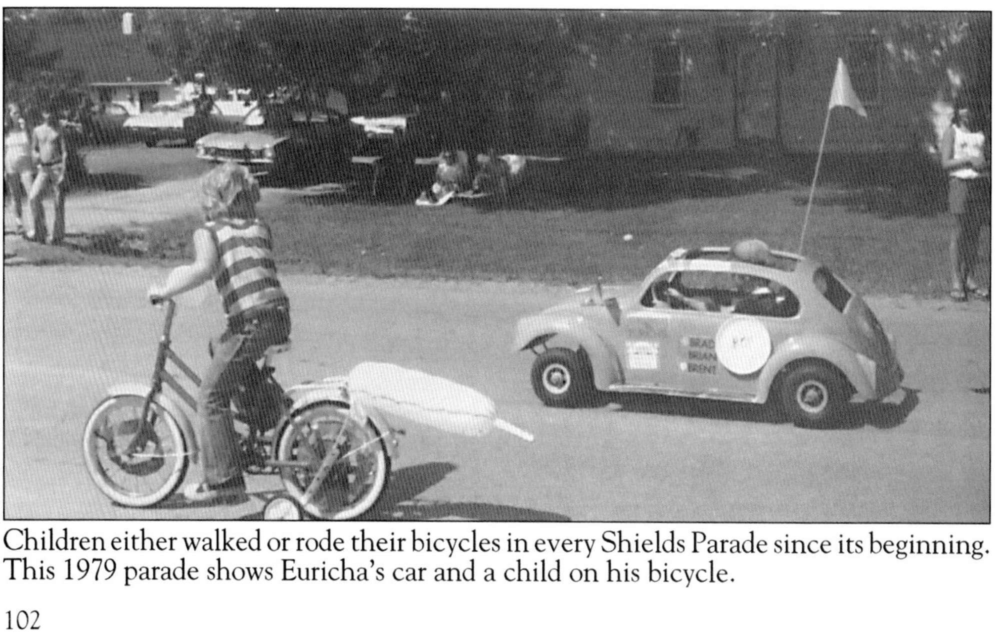

Children either walked or rode their bicycles in every Shields Parade since its beginning. This 1979 parade shows Euricha's car and a child on his bicycle.

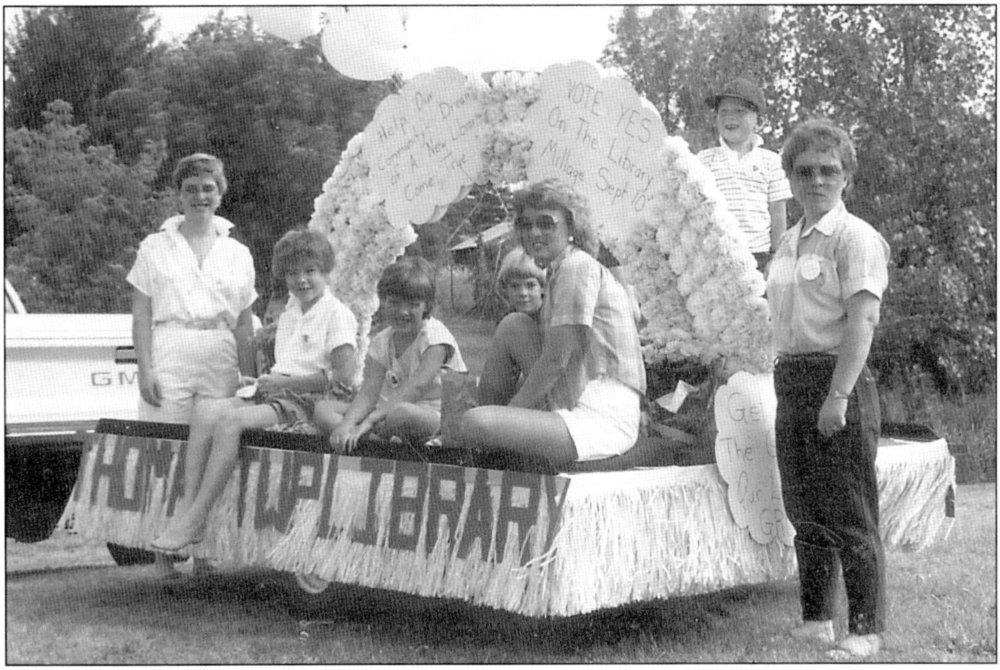

This group spent many hours building this library millage campaign float, used in an early 1980s parade. Pictured, from left to right, are Sherri Cottrell Greene (standing), Michelle Cottrell, Elizabeth Wolinski, Jeff Cottrell, Sally Coleman, an unidentified boy, and Betty Coleman (standing). In the photo below, Michelle Cottrell poses with her winning slogan for the library millage campaign.

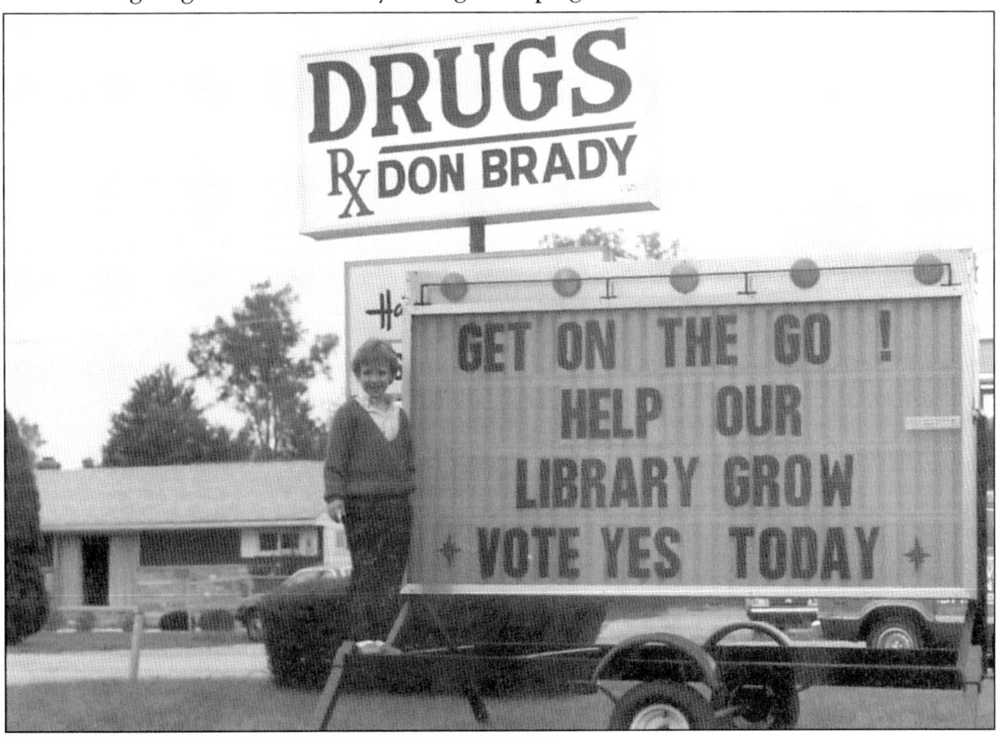

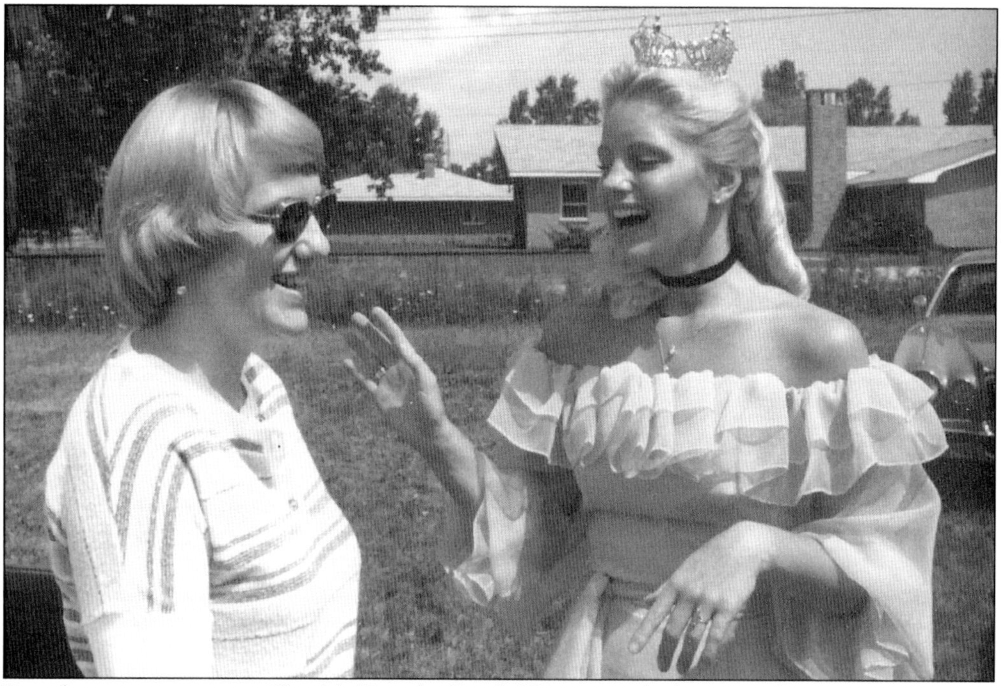

Royalty reigns at every Shields Parade. Ruth Wagner is helping Bethany Wright, Miss Michigan 1979, get ready for her ride in this parade.

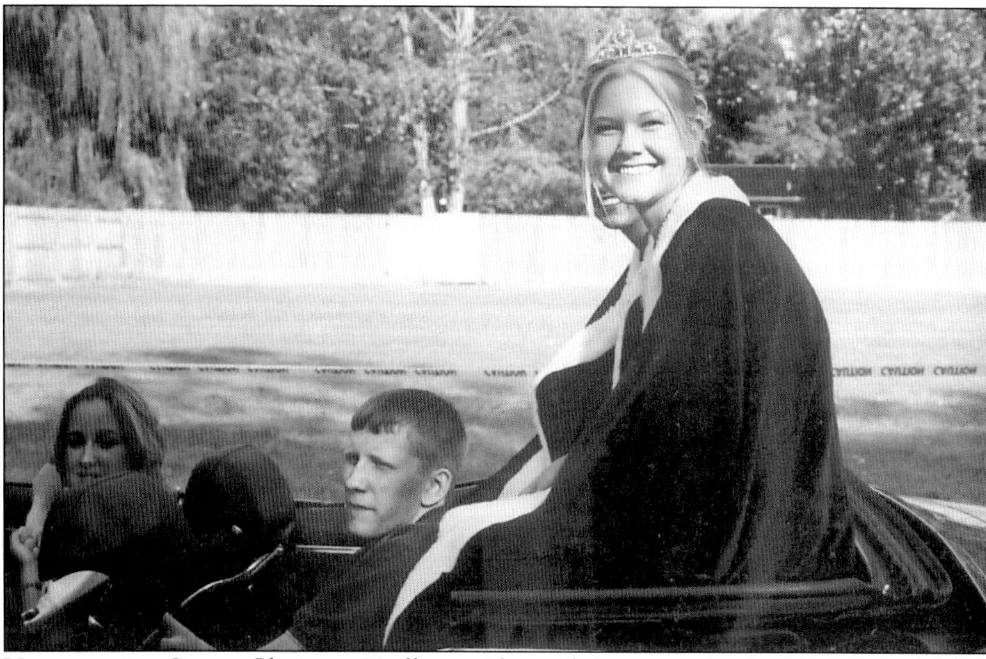

Homecoming Queen Christine Hoffman rides with her court in the 1998 Swan Valley High School Homecoming Parade. This Friday parade occurs in September or October on homecoming night just prior to the big football game. The parade originates in the parking lot at St. Mark's Lutheran Church, travels up North Miller Road to O'Hern Road and the high school.

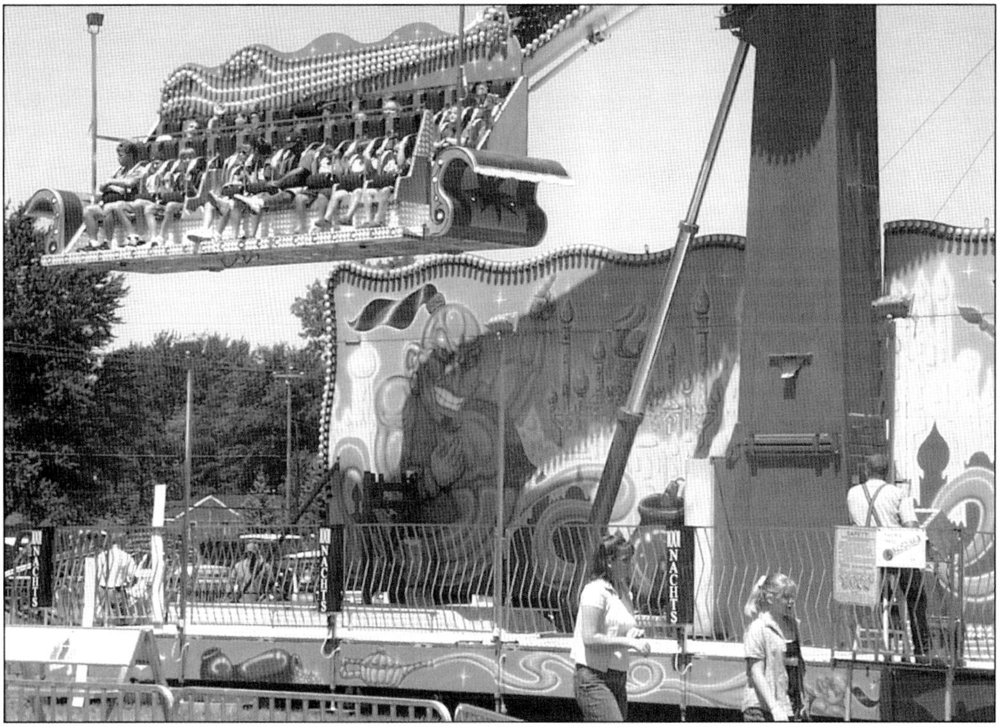

McDonagh's Amusements have set up several thrilling rides in the Shields Men's Club Park during the Shields Homecoming Festival for the past 41 years. These rides are enjoyed by adults and children of all ages. In the above photo, "The Magic Carpet" takes several people up and away for an exciting ride. In the bottom photo, Matthew Oatten is enjoying his escapade on "The Dragon." Both photos were taken during the 1999 festival.

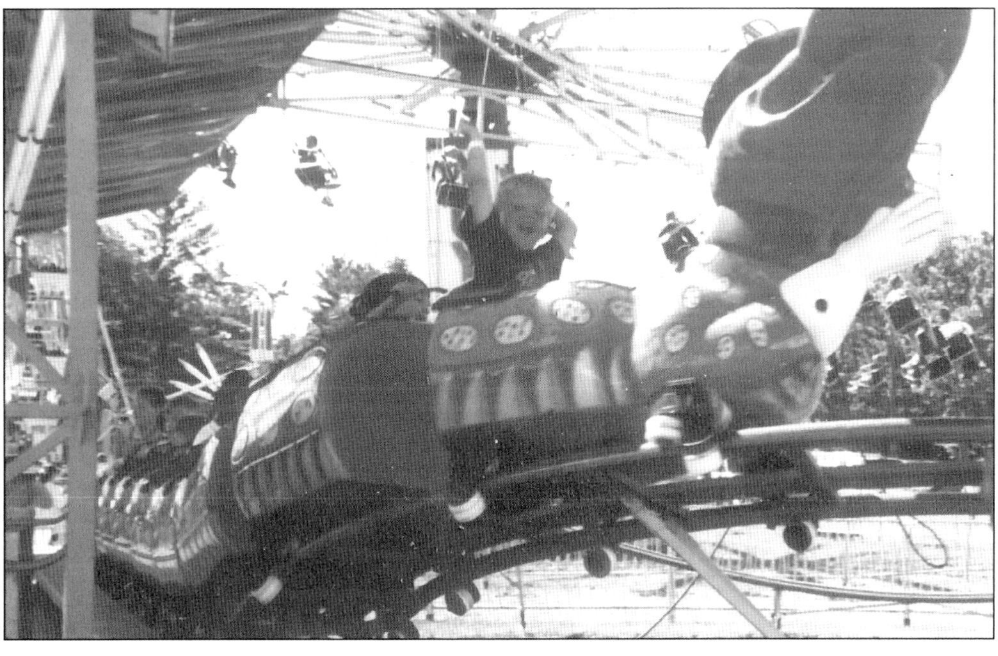

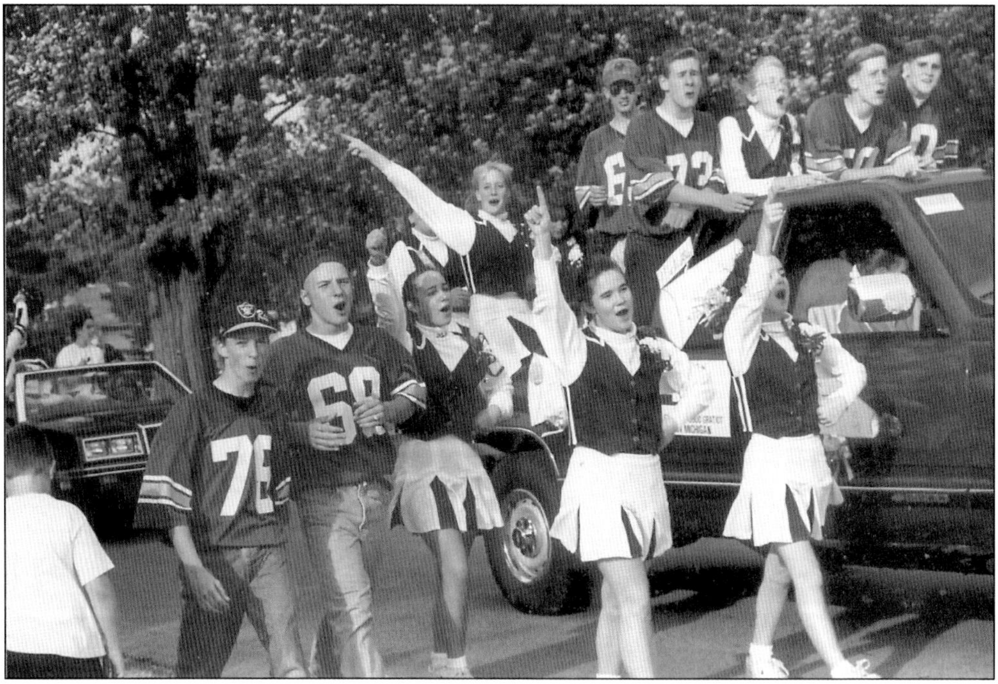

A parade is never complete without cheerleaders and pompon squads. The class of 1998 is seen in the 1994 Homecoming Parade just prior to the football game. From left to right: Mark Gosen, Jeff Cottrell, Katie Jacobi, Michele Brown, Tiffany Harless, and Lindsey Markle. The Swan Valley Pompon Squad is shown in the 1999 Homecoming Parade below.

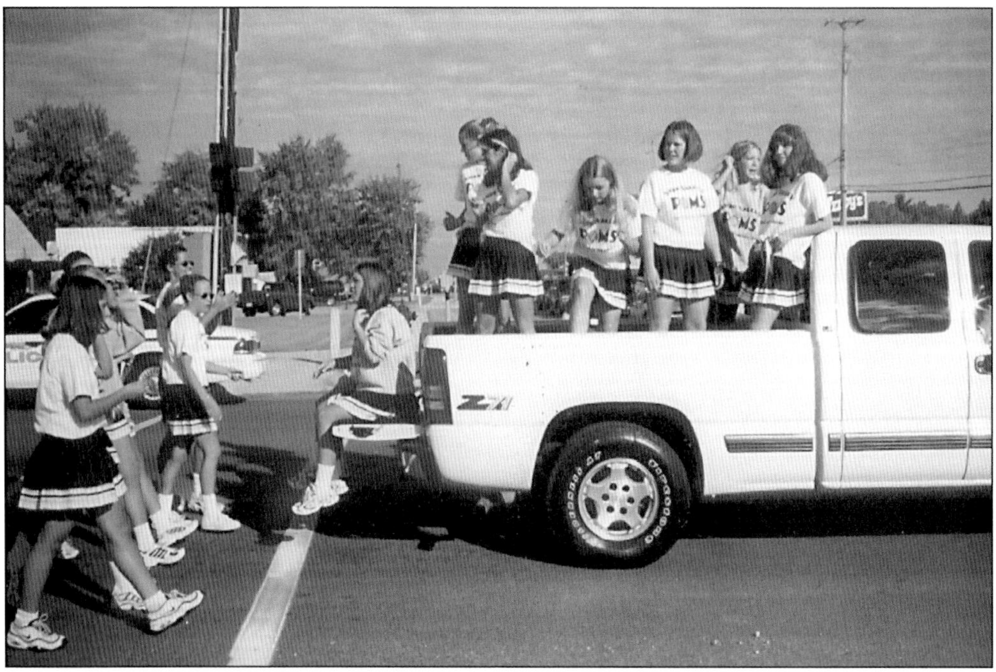

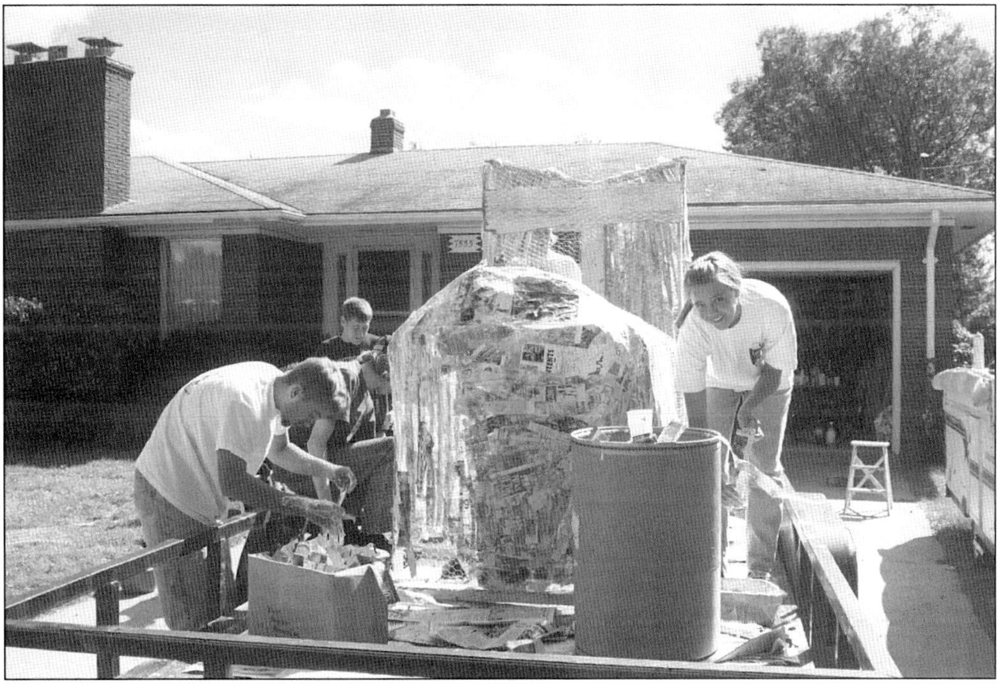

Many hours and weeks of volunteer time are needed to build the beautiful floats for any parade. The Swan Valley High School Class of 1998 is shown building their 1996 float in the above photo. The bottom photo shows the proud students riding on their finished float in the parade. Kara Greene is riding in the lower right corner. All others are unidentified.

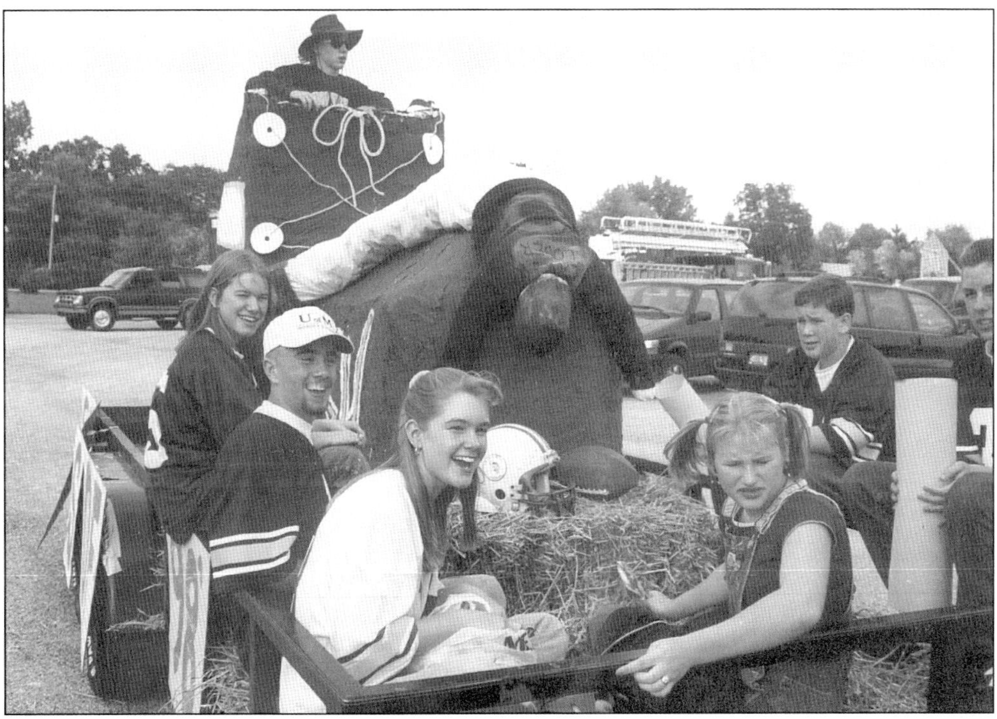

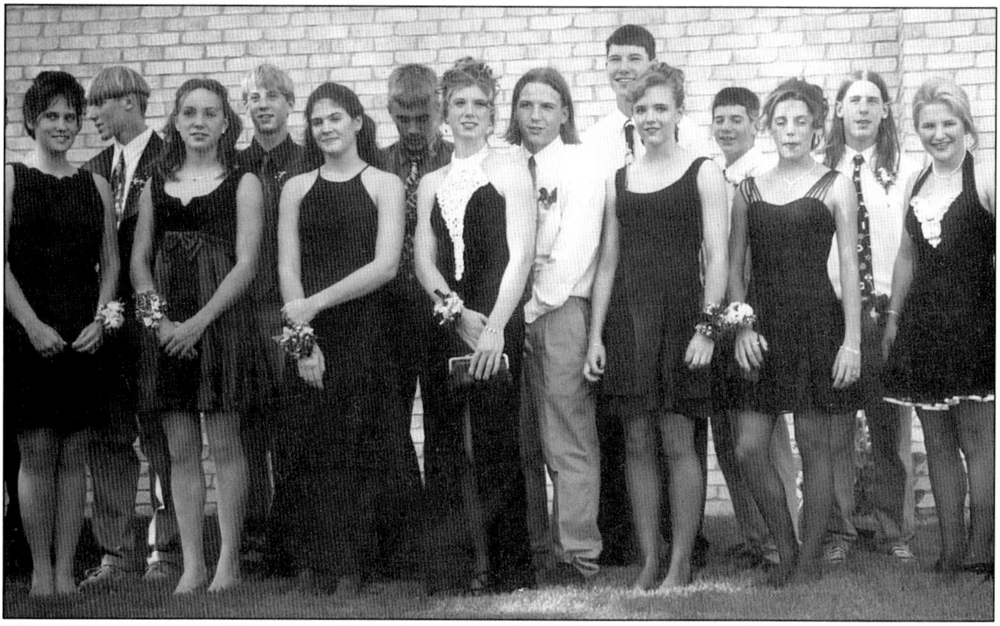

The Homecoming Dance takes place on Saturday evening after the big game on Friday night. A group of friends from Swan Valley High School have posed for a photo session before their dance in this 1996 photo. Kara Greene is on the far right. All others are unidentified.

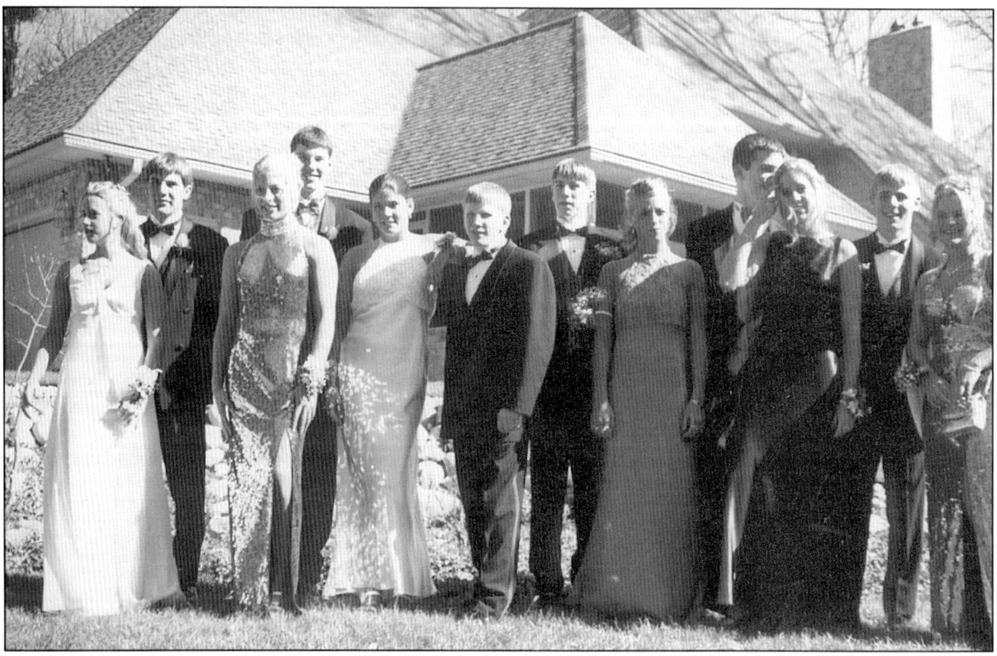

Each year the Swan Valley junior class sponsors the prom for the seniors on a Saturday night in late spring. This semi-formal event is one that many juniors and seniors look forward to each year. A group of friends have gathered for a photo session on the night of their big prom in 1998.

Seven

The Township At Work

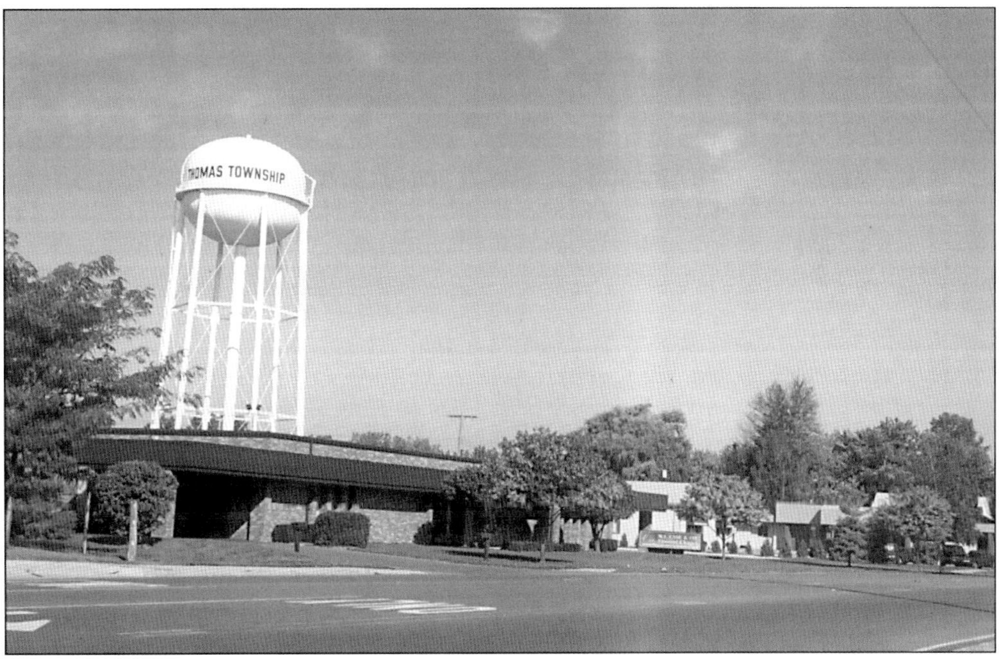

As the township developed and expanded, water, sewer, fire, and police protection were needed. The township contracted with neighboring townships for both fire and police protection until it organized its own departments. All departments have expanded as the township has grown. The township's large water reservoir towers over the North Miller Road neighborhood behind the government complex of buildings, as shown in the photo above.

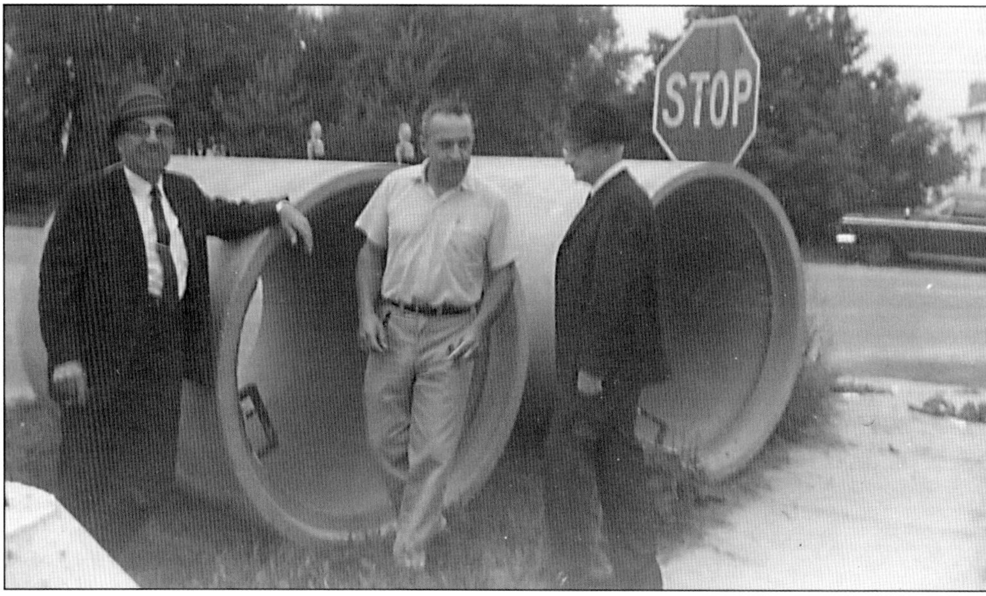

Saginaw County Drain Commissioner Herbert Dietrich, Thomas Township Water Superintendent Buck Wiltse, and Cliff Spicer of Spicer Engineering are shown in this 1971 photo as they confer about installing the new sanitary sewer lines at the Stroebel and South River Road intersection.

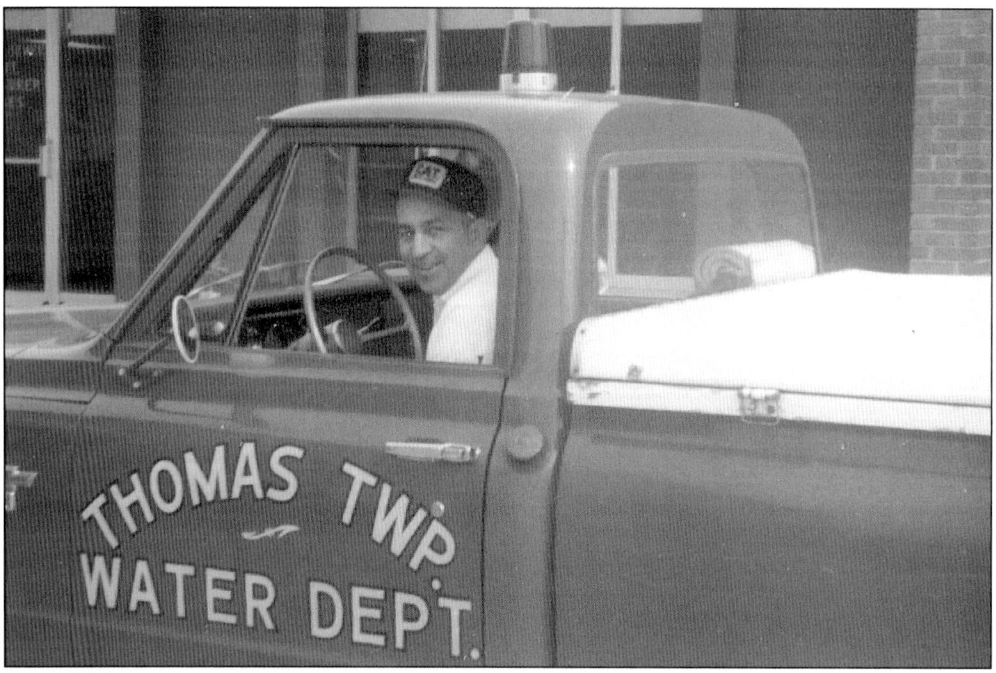

Buck Wiltse *was* the Water Department when he began in 1959. He worked for both the township and for himself, installing water lines, calling on customers, and sending water bills. The Township Water Department developed and became a full-time position requiring several employees as the township developed. Buck is shown in this 1964 photo in front of the township garage.

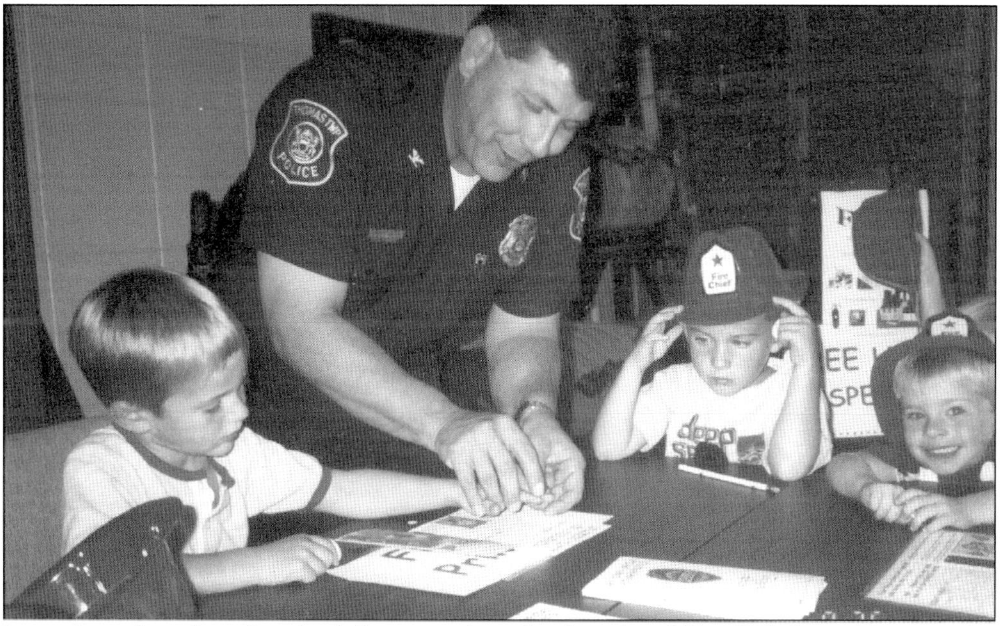

Larry Sicard was hired as the full-time police chief on April 17, 1975. Steve Kocsis is the township's full-time police chief now. He is shown in this 1999 photo finger printing three children, from left to right, Jordan, Dillon, and Logan Honsinger.

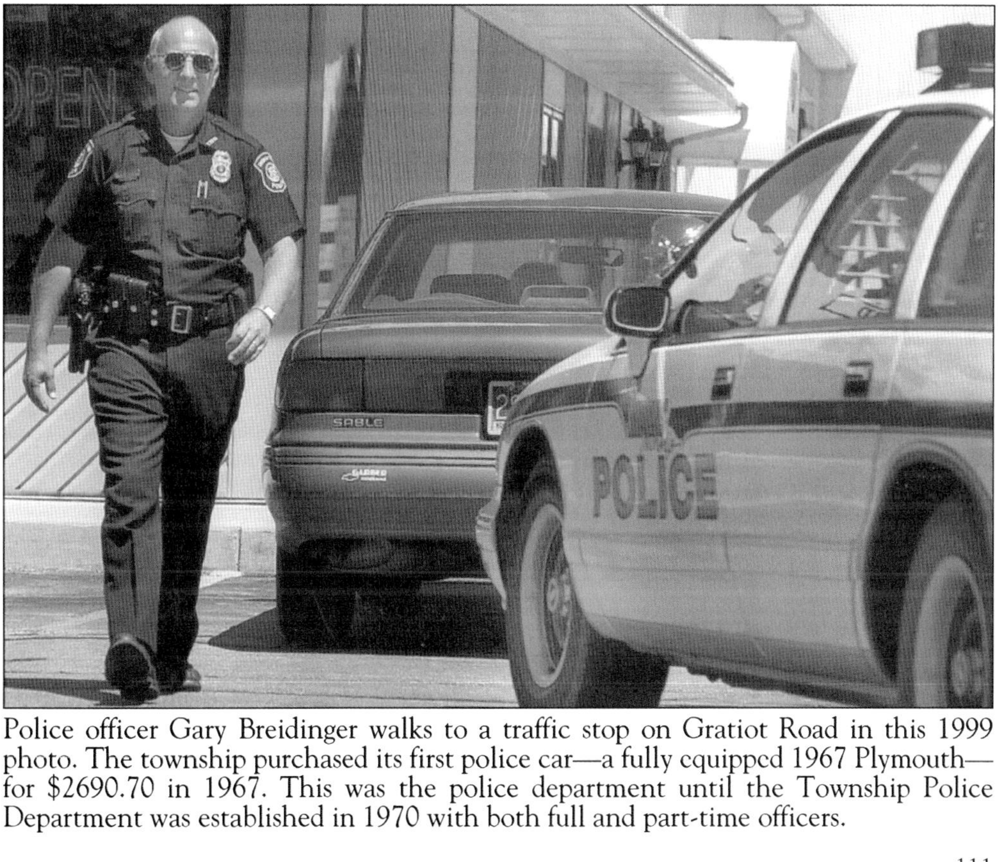

Police officer Gary Breidinger walks to a traffic stop on Gratiot Road in this 1999 photo. The township purchased its first police car—a fully equipped 1967 Plymouth—for $2690.70 in 1967. This was the police department until the Township Police Department was established in 1970 with both full and part-time officers.

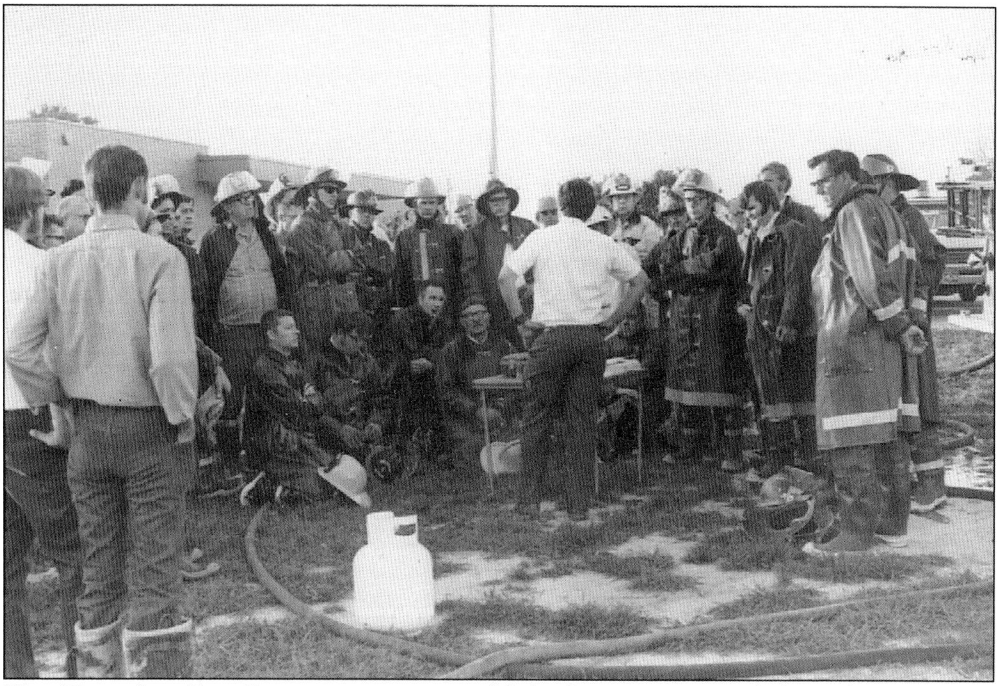

The Township Fire Department was established in 1963. Until then the township depended on fire equipment from neighboring townships to help in the event of a fire. The fire department has been staffed with volunteer firemen, shown here in a training session in this 1972 photo.

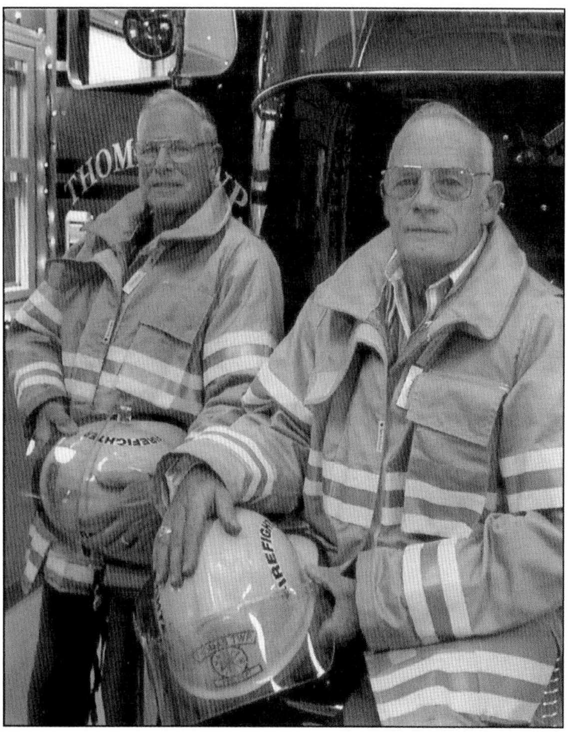

Autoworkers George A. Schmidt and Edward R. Kragenbrink helped organize the township's fire department in 1963. They were the first volunteers and worked 36 years as volunteers putting out fires and rescuing people from their flooded homes. The department expanded from two trucks to seven vehicles today.

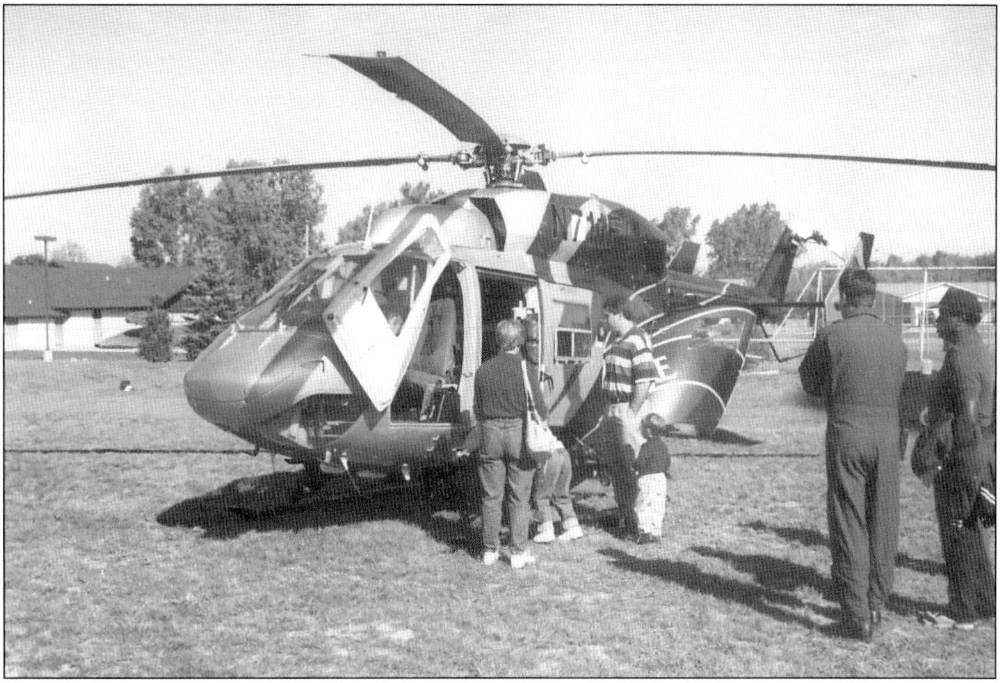

This Medi-Flight helicopter from St. Mary's Hospital landed in Thomas Township during the firemen's open-house in October 1999. Scott and Cameron Bryant are looking over the helicopter. The helicopter has transported many Michigan accident victims to area hospitals for immediate medical attention.

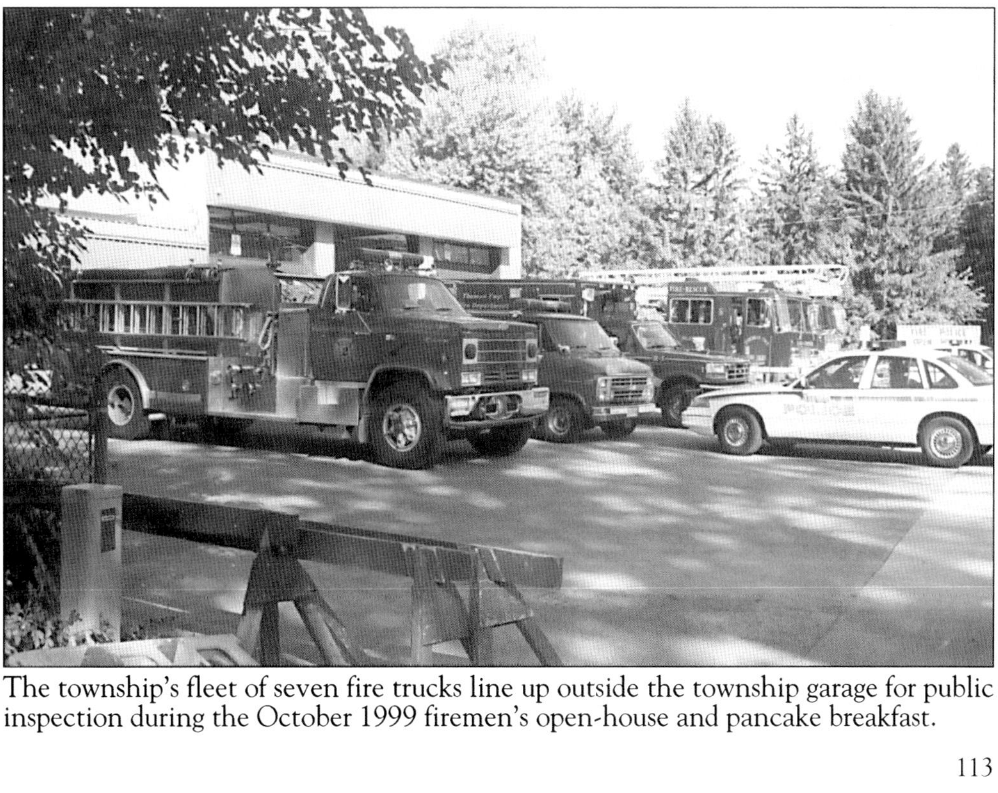

The township's fleet of seven fire trucks line up outside the township garage for public inspection during the October 1999 firemen's open-house and pancake breakfast.

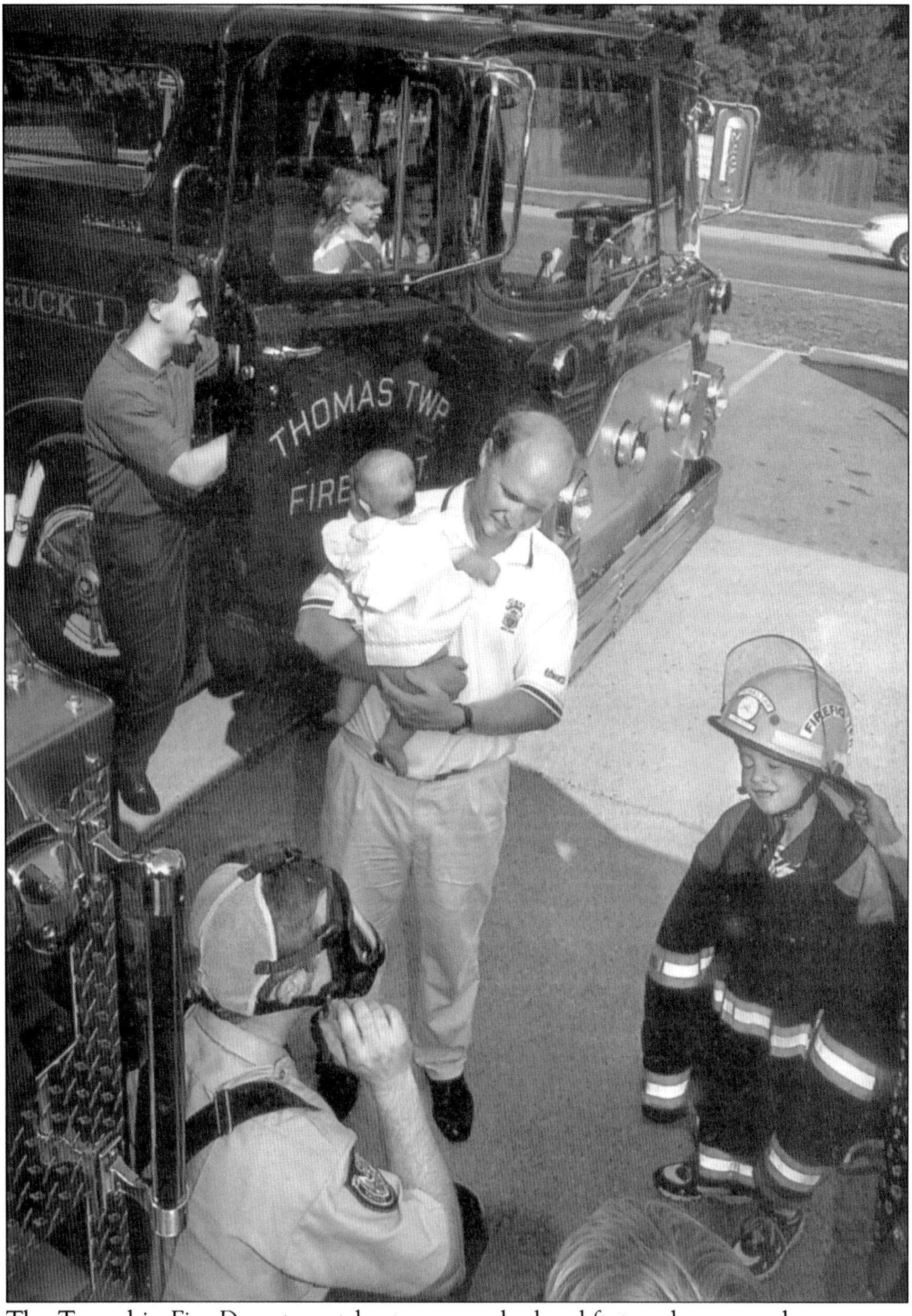

The Township Fire Department hosts a pancake breakfast and an open-house every October during Fire Prevention Week. Citizens can tour the facilities and become aware of the duties and services offered by the department. This photo was taken during the October 1998 open-house.

Eight

Past and Present Residents

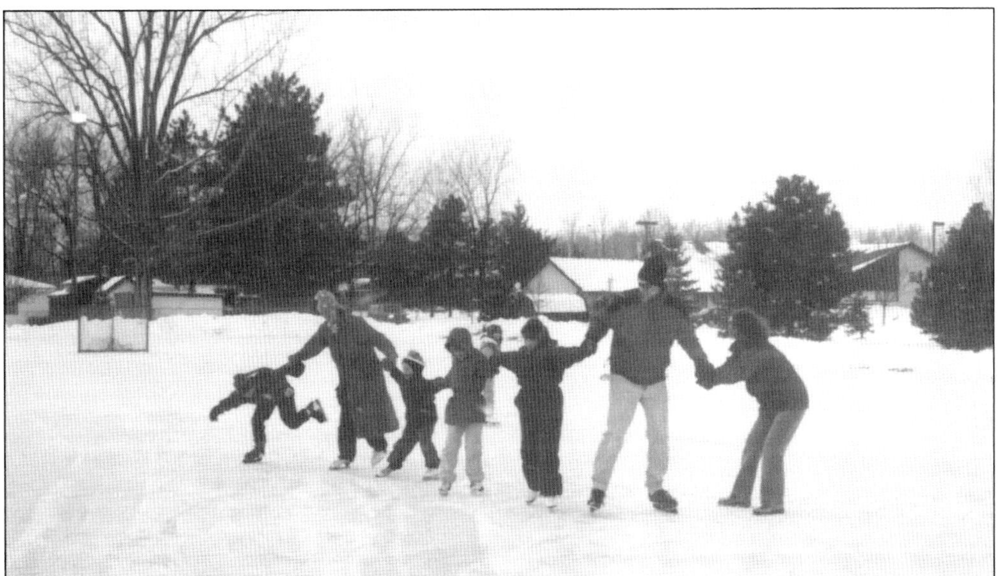

Since the 1850s, Thomas Township residents have spent time in enjoyable pastimes, volunteered many hours to make the township a better place, and enjoyed the friendship of other local residents. The family shown above is having a good time on the township skating rink in the Community Park in this February 2000 photo. Pictured, from left to right, are Michael, Melany, Madeline, and Catherine Novack; Megen, Jason, and Chris Raedy.

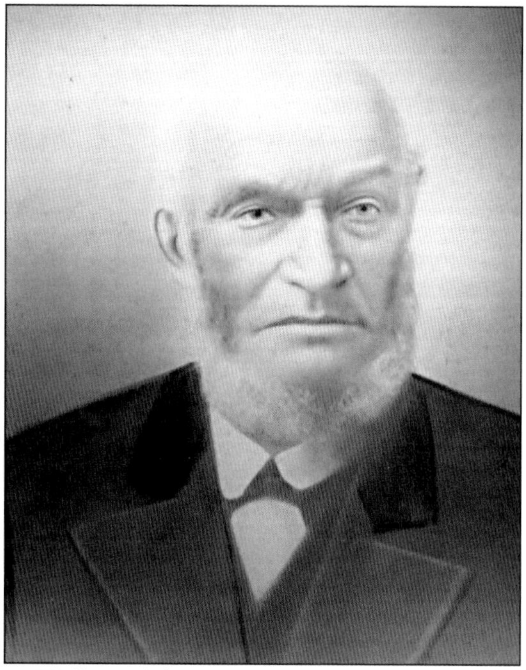

The Shields brothers—William (above) and Arthur (below)—were born in 1826 and 1830, respectively, in Ireland. Both immigrated to Montreal, Canada, and then came to Michigan, settling in Thomastown in 1842. The bachelor brothers settled on 120 acres in Section 3. Eventually, the southeastern part of the township came to be called the Shields area while the remaining part was called Liskow area. John Liskow came from Prussia in 1851, settling on 80 acres in Section 23. There were no roads at this time so it was essential to give directions according to a settler's homestead. William died in 1894 and Arthur in 1905. Both are buried in Owen Cemetery.

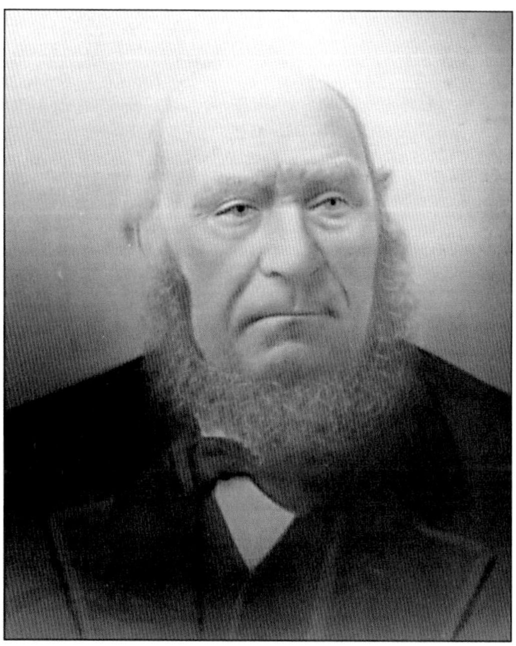

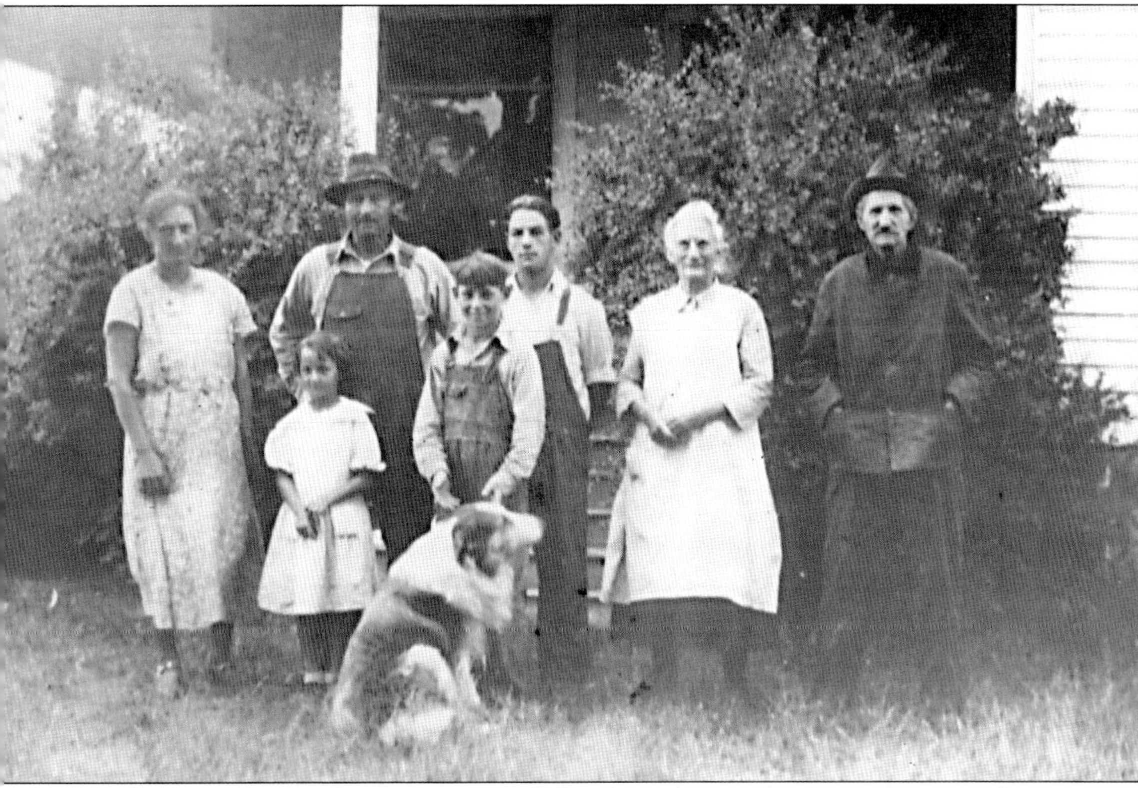

This three-generation family portrait of the Leuenberger family in front of their centennial farm-house was taken in 1936. Frederick Krenz worked in the logging business and walked from Saginaw City to Thomas Township in 1880. He purchased his 60 acre farm on Summerfeldt Road in 1884 and built a log house and barn. Fred and Mary built their house in 1895 and gradually rebuilt their farm buildings. In 1913 Lawrence Leuenberger and his bride Frieda Krenz bought the farm. Together they continued their full-time farming operation with dairy cows, chickens, and cash crops. Their three children—Lester, Marian, and Harvey—helped on the farm. Their collie dog Mike helped with the dairy cows, rounding up the herd for evening milking chores. Harvey, active in Farm Bureau and township activities, continues to own and operate the centennial farm today. Pictured, from left to right, are Frieda Krenz Leuenberger, Marian Leuenberger (child), Lawrence Leuenberger, Harvey Leuenberger (child), Lester Leuenberger, Mary Krenz, and Frederick Krenz.

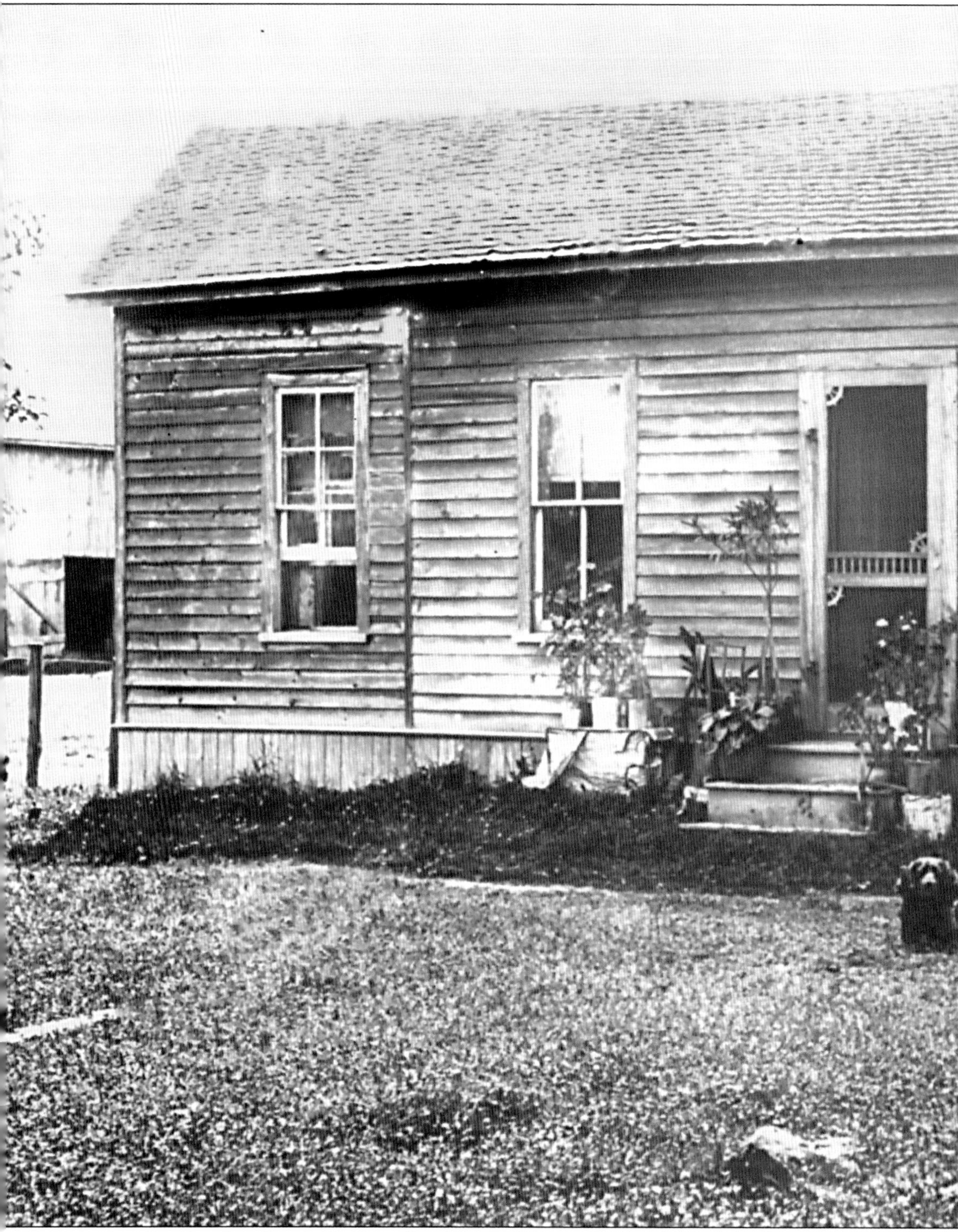

The Dinning family pose in their front yard at their 830 South Graham Road homestead in 1895. Their 80-acre farm was bordered by Graham and Gratiot Roads and Williams Creek. They milked a dairy herd, had an orchard, and a large garden. Son John is on

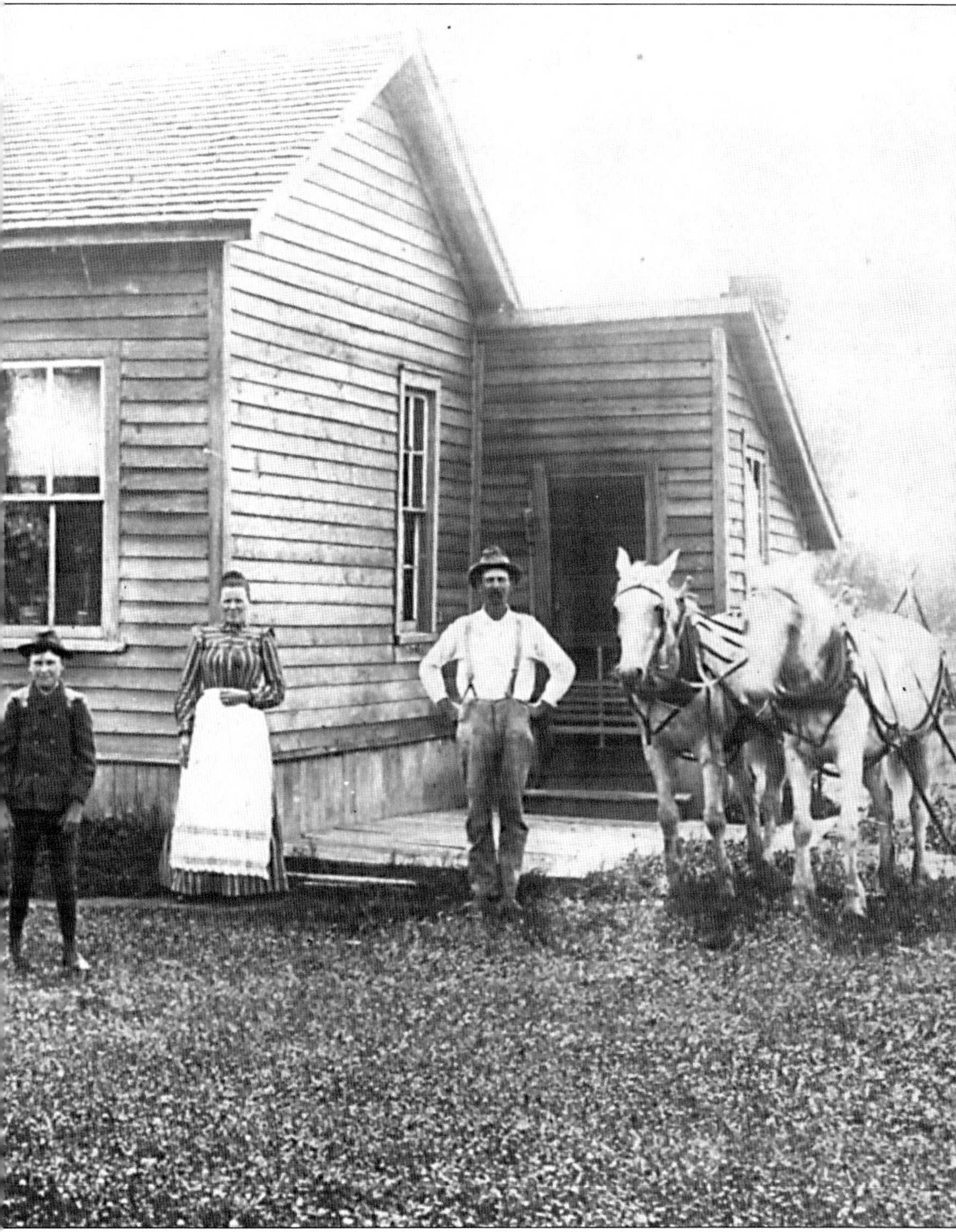

the left side. Rebecca's Rutledge family farmed nearby on Schomaker Road. George is standing next to his team of horses.

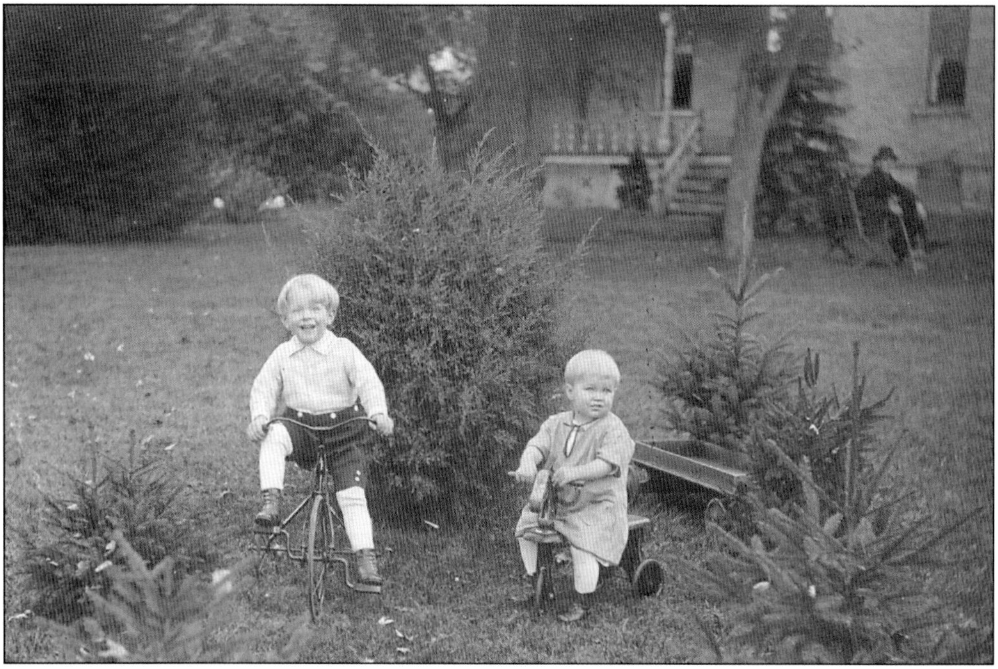

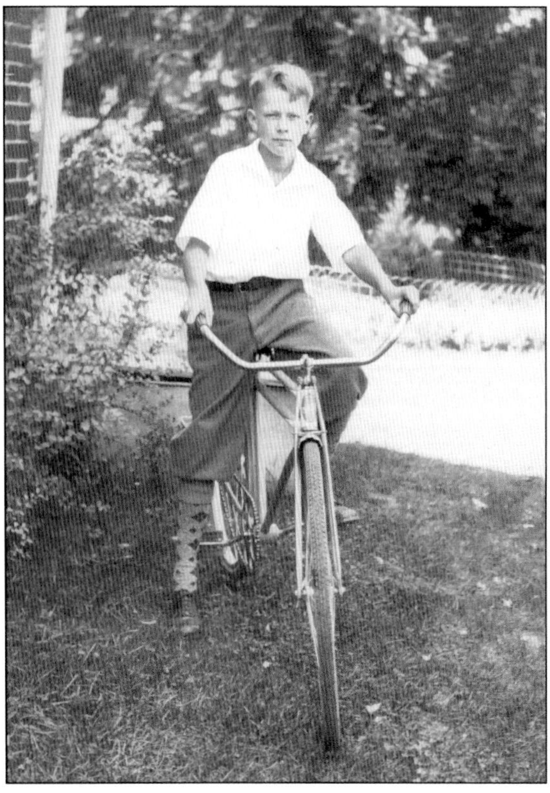

Children can never start too young riding a bicycle. Shown above are Edward and Eleanor Kluck, riding their tricycles on their parents' farm in March 1924. They are the children of Walter and Frieda Kluck. Twelve-year old Edward poses with his bicycle in this October 1933 photo shown to the left.

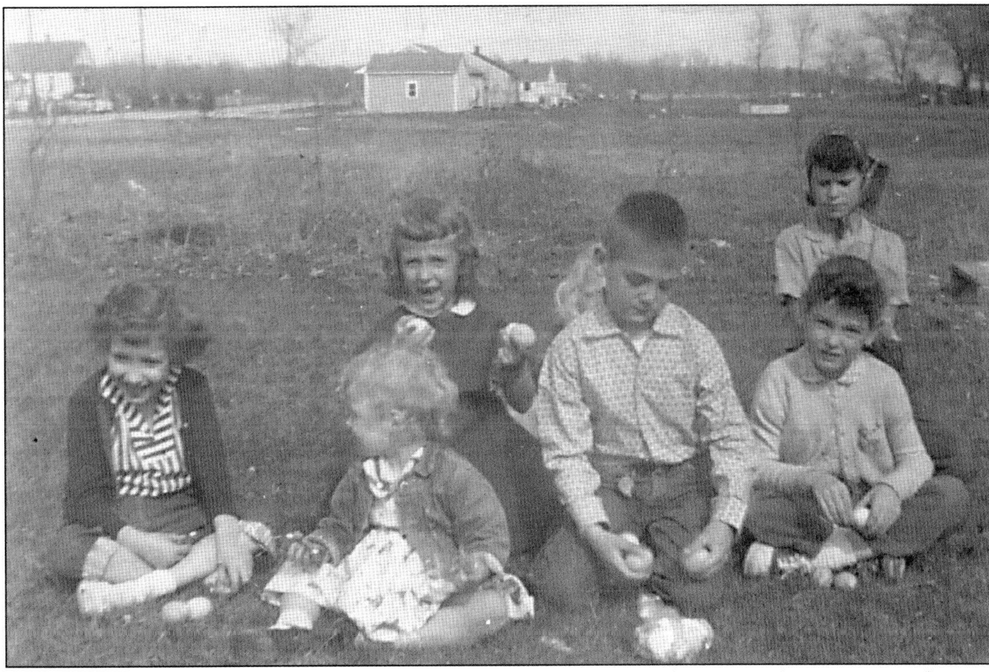

Buck and Neola Wiltse conducted an Easter egg hunt in their North River Road back yard for over 30 years for their own children, grandchildren, nieces, nephews, and neighborhood children. The above photo, taken in 1957, shows an undeveloped Shields Drive in the background. The children, from left to right, are Vickie Masucci, Brenda Wiltse (in back), Sherri Wiltse (in front), Craig Griese, Pam Eddy (in back), and Becky Griese.

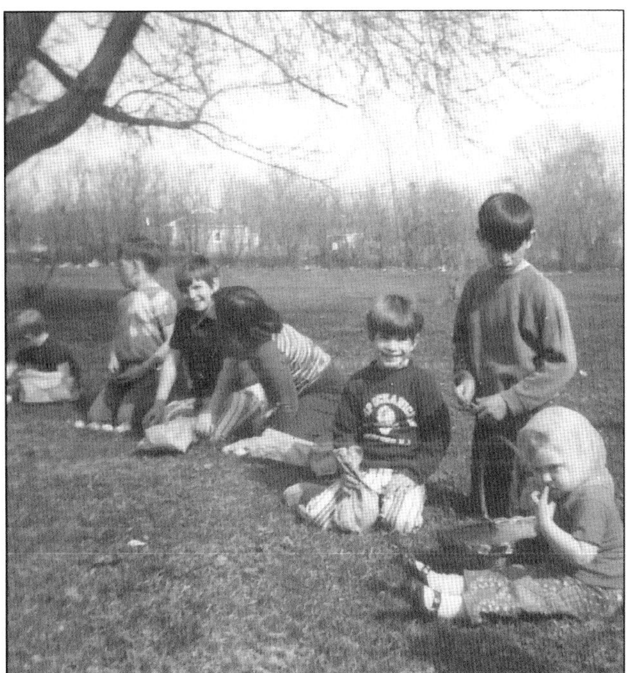

The tradition continues in the 1971 photo shown at the right, taken in the same spot as the photo above.

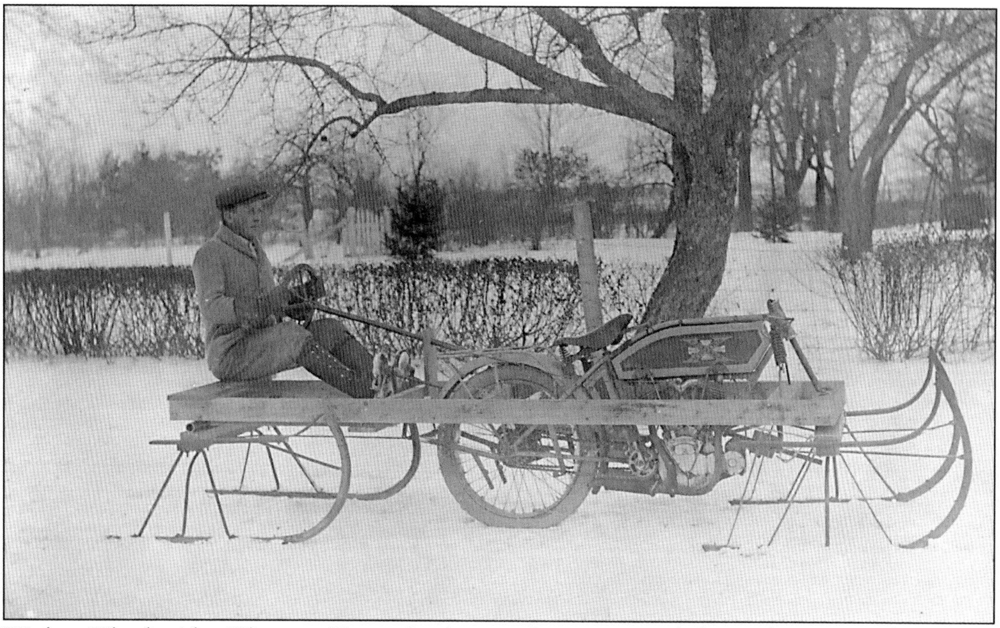

Walter Kluck rides Thomas Township's very first snowmobile in this 1919 photo. He concocted it using his old motorcycle and a bobsled. He had fun traveling over the snow banks with his merry snowmobile.

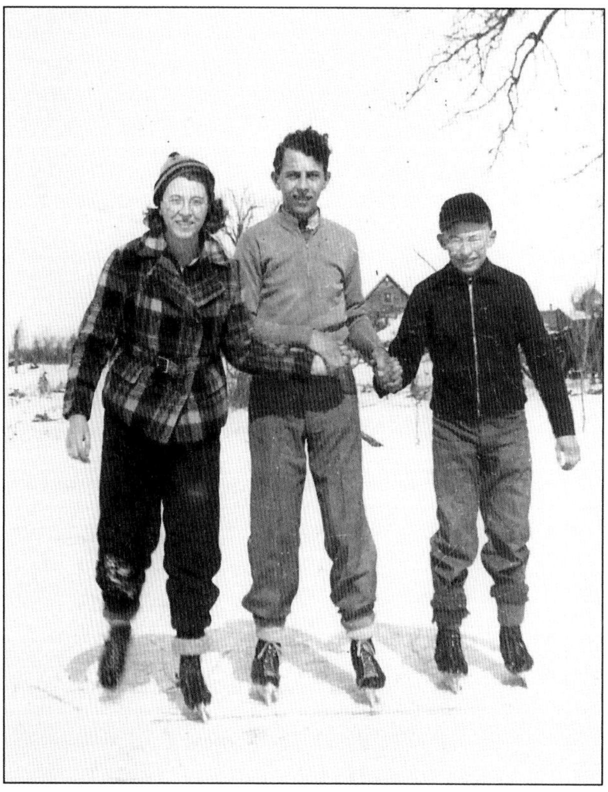

Ice skating is a favorite winter activity, and the Roberts family found ice skating especially delightful on the pond that forms in the fields every year behind their Bacon Road house. Shown in this mid-1930s photo are Shirley, Paul, and Ralph Roberts.

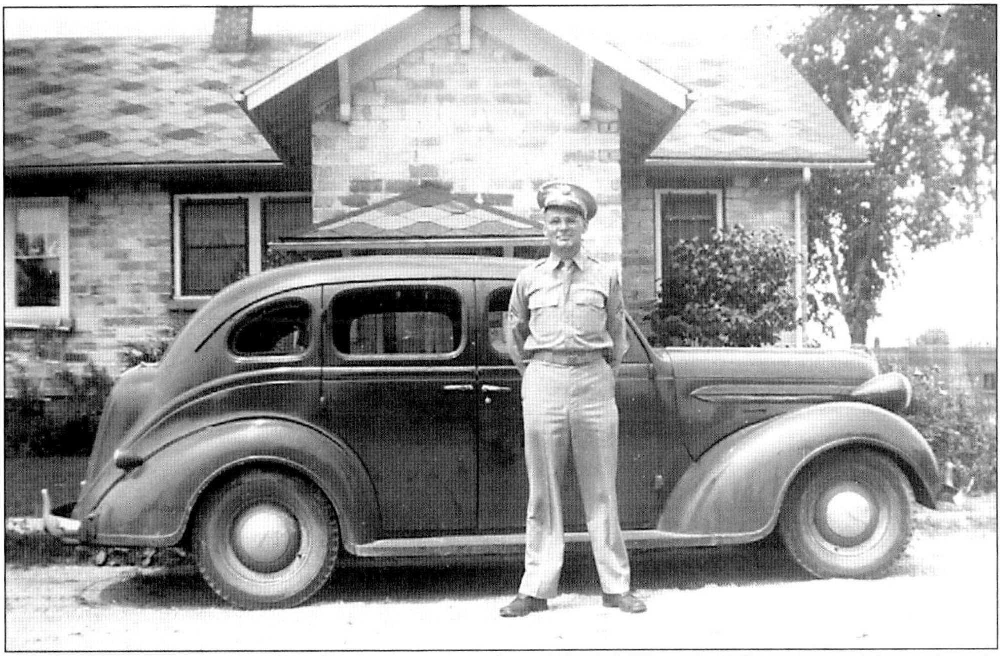

Several Thomas Township residents served in World War II. When Donald Frederick was home on leave, he visited his uncle, Art Fretter, on South River Road in this June 12, 1943 photo.

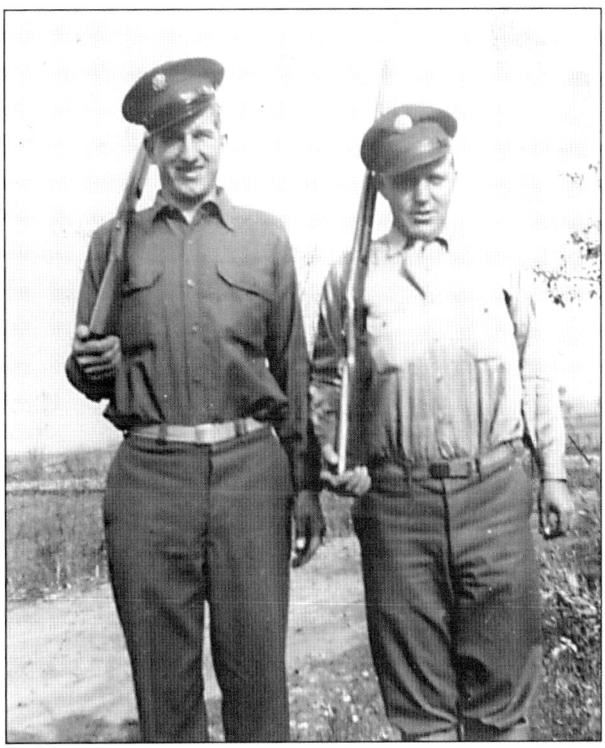

Corporal Clarence Schultz, on the left, and Sergeant Edward Borm, on the right, were called home to help their ill uncle, Richard Borm, with his farming operation in this 1940s photo. Cpl. Schultz refused to take orders from Sgt. Borm on how to do the work since he had enough of the sergeants in the Army. But somehow, the crops were harvested.

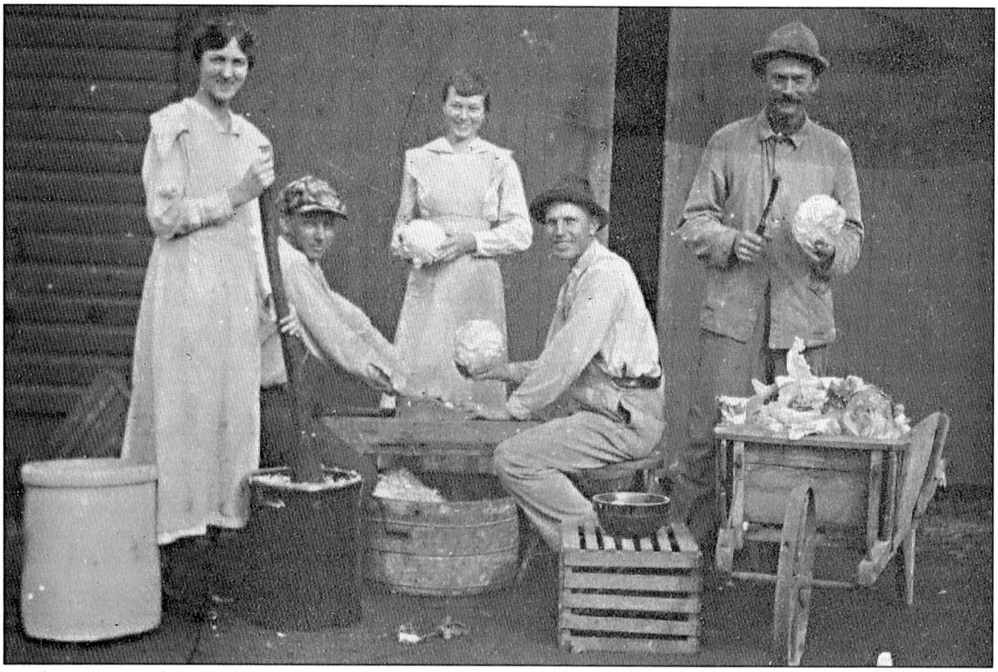

Making sauerkraut has been a fall tradition for many German township residents for decades. Pictured is the Zorn family, from left to right, Nora, Martin, Frieda, unidentified, and George, working together to get the kraut cut, shredded, and stomped in record time in this 1919 photo. Making sauerkraut today is still done the same way as shown above.

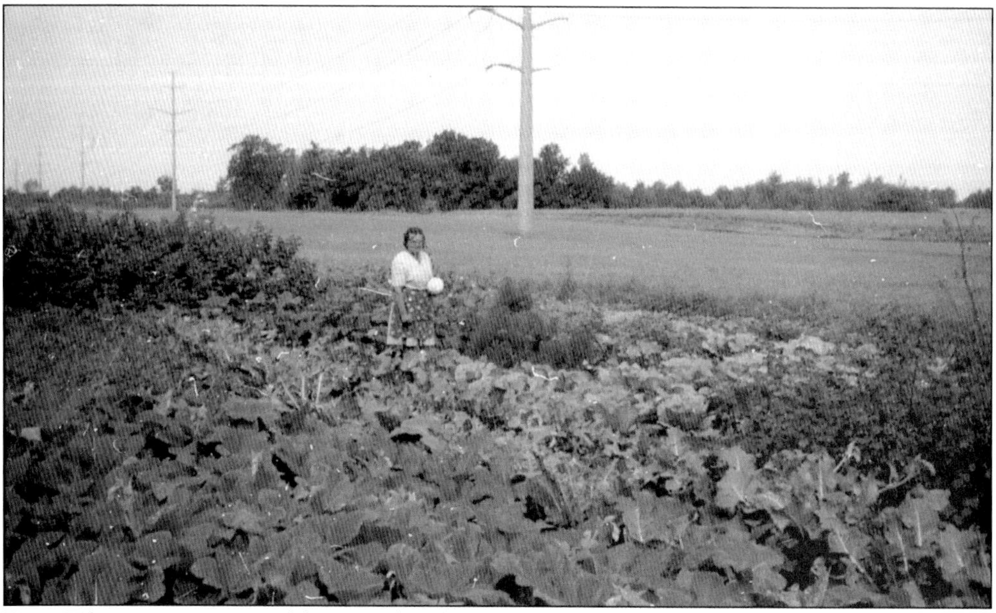

Erna Ederer is cutting cabbage in her large garden. The cabbage patch grows next to the soybean field, the squash vines, and the raspberry bushes in this 1977 photo. Many township residents have gardens in their backyards, and raise a variety of vegetables for their own use or for sale.

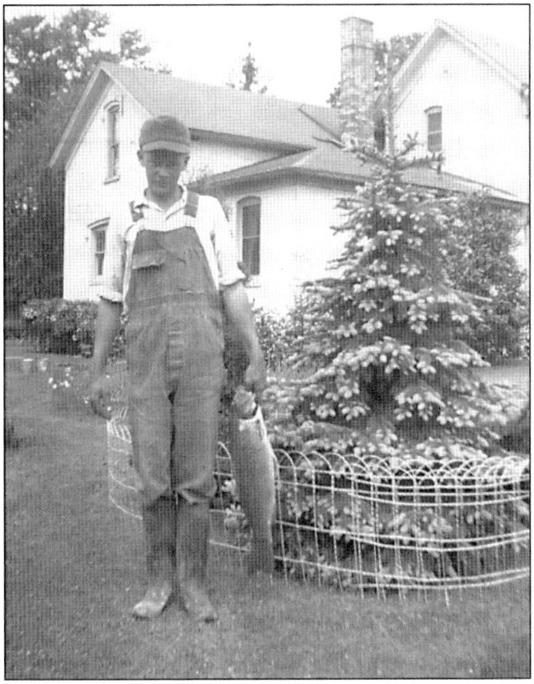

Fishing has always been good in Thomas Township, and is enjoyed by many. Both the Tittabawassee River and Swan Creek are nearby. Who can tell the biggest fish story? Edward Kluck has caught a big one in this 1930s photo above. Walter Kluck has caught an even bigger one in this 1920s photo below.

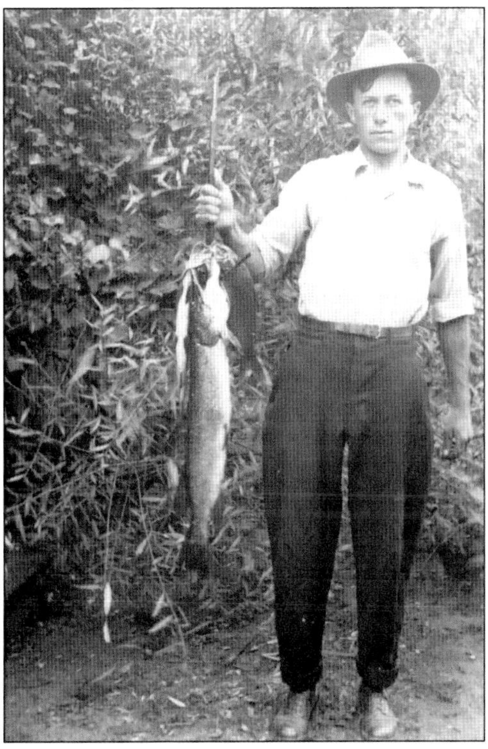

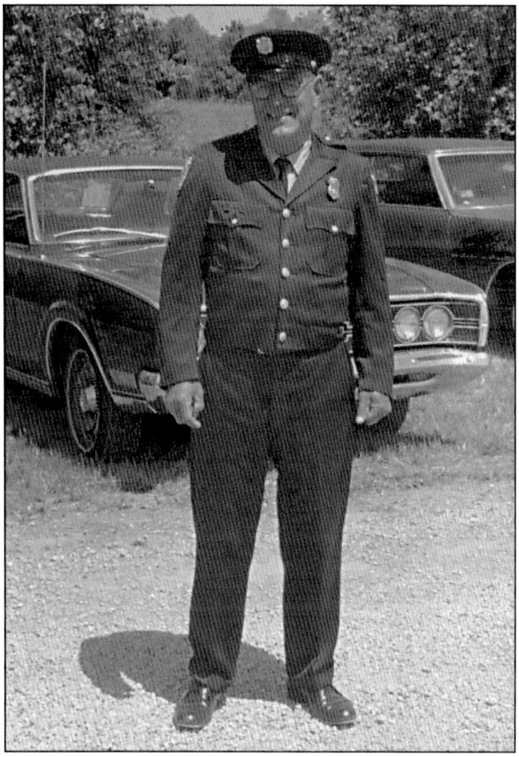

Township farmer Richard Borm Sr. drove Swan Valley school buses and also worked as a volunteer in the Fire Department. He is shown in uniform in this 1970s photo when he helped out with the Easter egg hunt at Roberts Park.

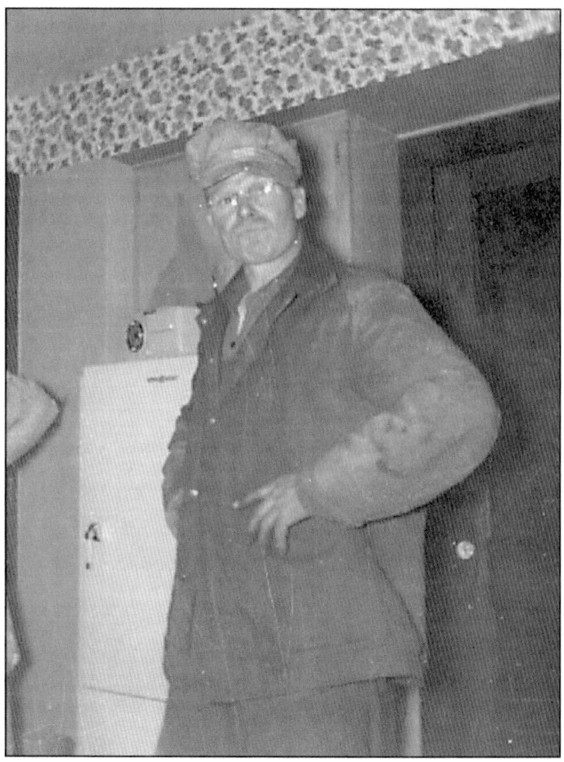

Art Fretter was indispensable to many people. He repaired cars, farm machinery, and Swan Valley school buses in his back yard garage. There was very little formality in his business, and one never left without having a long, friendly conversation with Art.

Cub Scouts under cubmaster Dan Haft eagerly await the next small wooden car in the Pinewood Derby race at Shields Elementary School in 1966. This was an annual event of the Cub Scouts.

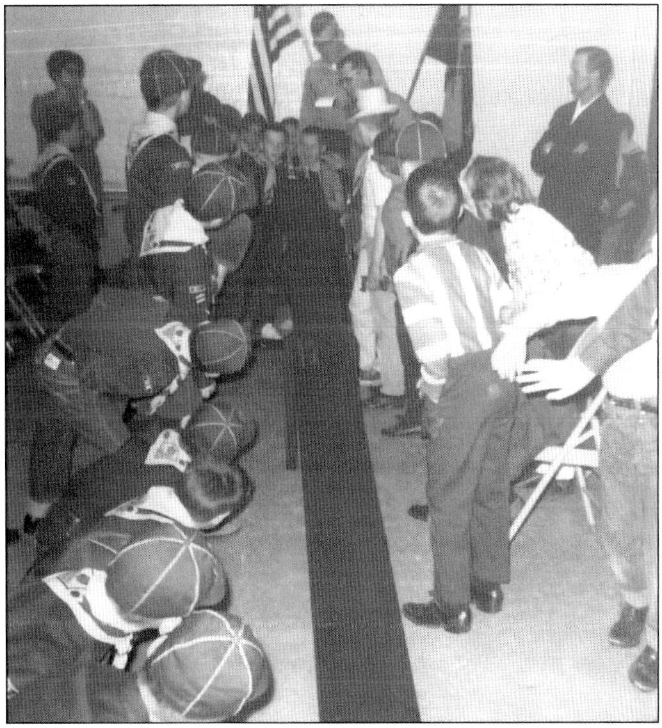

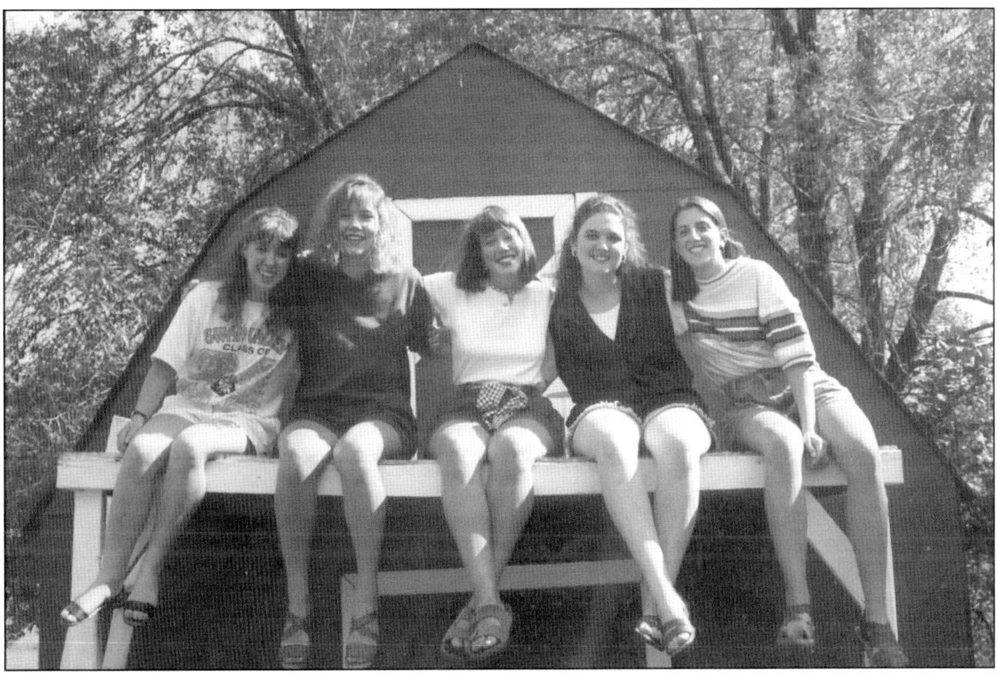

Friends from the Swan Valley Class of 1994 gather together for Michelle's back yard graduation party. Pictured, from left to right, are Michelle Cottrell, Elizabeth Wolinski, Audrey Adams, Kelly Diebel, and Kristine Grillo. Their friendship has lasted long after their school days which brought them together.

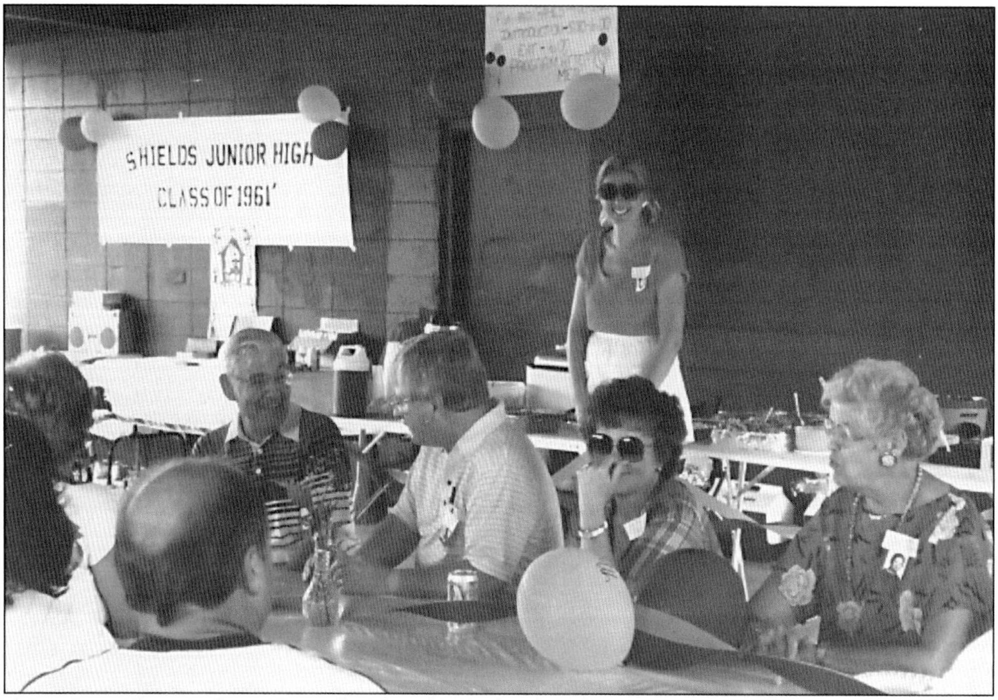

A park is the perfect place for family and school reunions. The class of 1961 from Shields Junior High had an enjoyable time at their 25th reunion in 1986 at Roberts Park as shown here. Superintendent Alvin Thom chats with Grant Smith while Mrs. Smith and former teacher Julie London look on. Valerie Jersevic is standing.

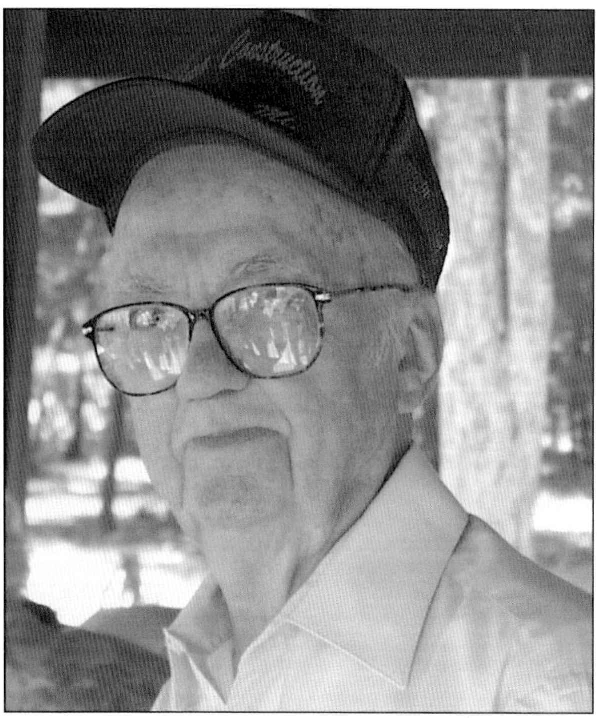

Jim Halm is pictured in this 1998 annual reunion of the Gratiot Heights School at Roethke Park. He was the first teacher at "the little building" and later drove the first school bus, taking high school students to Saginaw schools. Later on, he became the county 4-H extension agent. July and August are homecoming months for past and present Shields residents who look forward to seeing their old friends at the Shields Festival and school and family reunions.